RECLAIMING ACCOUNTABILITY IN TEACHER EDUCATION

RECLAIMING ACCOUNTABILITY IN TEACHER EDUCATION

MARILYN COCHRAN-SMITH
MOLLY CUMMINGS CARNEY
ELIZABETH STRINGER KEEFE
STEPHANI BURTON
WEN-CHIA CHANG
M. BEATRIZ FERNÁNDEZ
ANDREW F. MILLER
JUAN GABRIEL SÁNCHEZ
MEGINA BAKER

TEACHERS COLLEGE PRESS
TEACHERS COLLEGE | COLUMBIA UNIVERSITY
NEW YORK AND LONDON

Published by Teachers College Press, 1234 Amsterdam Avenue, New York, NY 10027

Copyright © 2018 by Teachers College, Columbia University

Library of Congress Cataloging-in-Publication Data is available at loc.gov

ISBN 978-0-8077-5931-8 (paper)
ISBN 978-0-8077-5932-5 (hardcover)
ISBN 978-0-8077-7710-7 (ebook)

Printed on acid-free paper
Manufactured in the United States of America

25 24 23 22 21 20 19 18   8 7 6 5 4 3 2 1

To teacher educators—
in the United States and around the world—
who are committed to the democratic project

Contents

Acknowledgments

This book grew out of our work as Project TEER (Teacher Education and Education Reform), a group of teacher education practitioners, researchers, and scholars. We were grounded in different disciplines, and we were interested in teacher education at different school levels and in different specialty areas. When we first came together at the invitation of Marilyn Cochran-Smith, some of us already had many years of experience as teachers and teacher educators, while some were newer to the profession. But we were united by a commitment to justice and equity for all the students who are served in the nation's schools and by our growing concerns about the direction "ed reform" was taking in the United States and the impact it was having on teacher education. We worked together for four years to track teacher education reform and the major accountability initiatives that were shaping the field. We spent countless hours in animated, sometimes heated, discussion, raising questions, pushing one another to follow points to their logical conclusions, and building on one another's ideas. Along the way, we came to know one another's strengths, passions, and idiosyncrasies as thinkers, writers, and educators, and we all learned an enormous amount about writing, rewriting, and rethinking. This book is the product of our joint work and the ideas that emerged and took shape from our long and sometimes rambling discussions about the power and the limits of teaching and teacher education, the meaning of democracy, and what the future holds for teacher education practice and policy.

We want to thank our colleagues at the National Education Policy Center (NEPC), the American Education Research Association (AERA), the New England Education Research Organization (NEERO), and the Massachusetts Association of Colleges for Teacher Education (MACTE), who made it clear from the beginning that this work was important and worth pursuing.

We especially acknowledge the people who helped bring this book to fruition. In particular, we thank the doctoral students and staff who worked together in Campion Hall, Room 113—Moira Raftery, who kept everybody on track and in good spirits; Rebecca Stern, who helped launch and organize the project; Marisa Olivo, who worked tirelessly on references and manuscript details; and Reid Jewett Smith, who read each chapter with a thoughtful outsider's view. We also thank Isabel Cole, Kelsey Hyland, and Jacob Kelleher, Undergraduate Research Fellows at Boston College, who helped with research and references.

Finally, each of us would like to thank our families and friends, who were patient and supportive as the work for this book intensified and encroached on our time for them. We are grateful that they believed in us and in the importance—now more than ever—of a book that makes the case for a democratic approach to teacher education accountability.

Part I

TEACHER EDUCATION IN THE ERA OF ACCOUNTABILITY

CHAPTER 1

Accountability in Uncertain Times

This book is about teacher education accountability. It exposes the general lack of evidence behind major U.S. accountability initiatives, and it documents the negative impacts they are having on the work of teacher education. Despite its failings, however, we don't conclude that accountability is the wrong direction for teacher education. And we don't simply point out what we think is wrong with current accountability approaches. Rather, we embrace teacher education accountability as a lever for reconstructing its targets, purposes, and consequences in keeping with the larger democratic project. We take the stance that *accountability should serve democracy* and that teaching and teacher education are indispensable in a democratic society. This is particularly so in the acutely polarized society the United States has become, wherein people are animated by deeply dissimilar perspectives, aspirations, and values, some of which revolve around intolerance—even hatred—of conflicting viewpoints and those who hold them.

The central argument we make in this book is that all of us who are involved or invested in the larger teacher preparation enterprise should reclaim accountability for the democratic project by taking a new approach, which we label *democratic accountability in teacher education*. By "democratic accountability," we do not simply mean accountability with more participation by the stakeholders involved, although that is part of what we call for. Rather, as we explain below, we mean accountability grounded in both *strong democracy* (Barber, 1984) and *strong equity* (Cochran-Smith, Stern, et al., 2016). We elaborate these concepts below and in later chapters. For now, we note only that we do not mean democracy whose primary purpose is to protect private interests and preserve the freedom of the market. Instead, we want a stronger democracy that promotes civic participation, seeks the common good, and actively challenges the systems that perpetuate inequity. Throughout the book, we make the case that even though we need democratic accountability now more than ever, the major accountability initiatives and policies currently in place in teacher education do virtually nothing to address democratic values and goals.

As the authors of this book, we are a group of teacher education scholars and practitioners who have worked together over the last four years as members of Project TEER (Teacher Education and Education Reform) to track teacher education's accountability policies and mechanisms within the larger context of "ed reform." Our proposed new approach to teacher education accountability grows out of this work.

RECLAIMING ACCOUNTABILITY

For many in the rapidly expanding community of people involved or invested in the preparation of teachers over the last two decades, the term "accountability" has almost always been coupled with modifiers such as "tighter," "tougher," "more stringent," or "with more teeth." For people with this viewpoint, accountability has been almost a magic word that conjures up images of fixing teacher preparation once and for all through the uniform implementation of reliable and rigorous systems of outcomes assessment and public reporting. For other people in the teacher education community, however, accountability has decidedly not been a magic word. In fact, it's more like a dirty word that implies a deep mistrust of teacher educators and reflects profound misunderstandings about the relationship between preparation and practice, the impact of local schools and communities, and the complexity of teaching and learning. For people with the latter viewpoint, it is clear that more accountability of the kind we have now will *not* fix teacher education. Worse, it will likely exacerbate the deprofessionalization of teaching, perpetuate social and educational inequities, and undermine the democratic project. Competing stances on teacher education accountability reflect widely divergent ideas about what it means to teach, what it means to help others learn to teach, and what the relationships of teacher preparation, teaching practice, student learning, and social change are (and ought to be) in a democratic society. This book addresses questions about the current dominant approach to accountability in teacher education, how it came to be central to teacher education reform in the United States, its impact on the work of teaching and teacher education, and its failure to take up issues related to strong equity and democratic education.

This book also explores what it would mean for the teacher education community to *reclaim accountability*—to learn from critiques and promising practices to try to get accountability right for the next generation and in support of democracy. We use the word "reclaim" here very deliberately. Many dictionary definitions of the word focus on the idea of retrieving or getting something back that was previously lost or denied (e.g., reclaiming one's right to the throne) or temporarily separated from the owner (e.g., reclaiming one's luggage), or they highlight the idea of bringing a resource that was previously unusable into usable condition through cultivation or treatment (e.g., reclaiming swampland or water). In addition to these meanings, the *Merriam-Webster* definition of "reclaiming" (2017) also includes the idea of rescuing something from an undesirable state or reforming something from wrong or improper conduct. Our use of the term "reclaiming" to talk about accountability is closest to this latter sense. We explicitly want to rescue teacher education accountability *from* its current immersion in market ideology and the human capital paradigm. These zero in on teacher quality narrowly defined, based on the assumption that boosting teacher education quality will not only boost the quality of schools, but also the nation's place in the competitive global economy. We want to rescue teacher education accountability *for* democratic education, which not only prepares students for participation in democratic deliberation but also identifies and works to eradicate the structures and systems that reproduce inequity.

This book works from two interrelated premises about accountability. The first is that accountability is not a new phenomenon in education generally or in teacher education specifically. Rather, the current emphasis represents an intensification of attention to accountability prompted by post–World War II economic, social, and political changes, which were part of a larger sea change in educational accountability writ large—from accountability for inputs, resources, and processes to a more "dramatic" kind of accountability (Cuban, 2004) focused on results, effects, and outcomes. The second premise is that teacher education accountability is inherently neither good nor bad—neither a magic word nor a dirty word—but rather depends on the larger agendas to which it is attached and the underlying assumptions it makes about who is to be held accountable for what, to whom, under what conditions, with what consequences, and for what purposes.

ACCOUNTABILITY AND DEMOCRATIC EDUCATION

Working from these premises, this book makes three central arguments. First, we argue that teacher education's "era of standards" (Roth, 1996), which was itself a significant historical change in the field during the 1980s and 1990s, evolved during the late 1990s and early 2000s into the "era of accountability (and standards)," with the primary emphasis squarely on accountability. We show that in the United States, new teacher education accountability mechanisms, often prompted by a perceived "crisis" of mediocrity or of lack of public confidence, were layered on top of older accountability mechanisms. At the same time, new education reformers, advocacy groups, and entrepreneurs entered the teacher education arena, bringing new accountability demands and expectations. As is the case in public-sector accountability in Western democracies (Romzek, 2000), we argue that the current teacher education accountability landscape is complex and even confusing. It's characterized by multiple co-existing accountability expectations, rising uncertainty about the consequences of accountability, competing claims to authority, and conflicting expectations for professional work. To make sense of and critique this messy landscape, we offer a new eight-dimensional framework that helps sort out differing accountability goals and targets, competing ideas about what's wrong with teacher education and what it would take to fix it, differing theories of change about the mechanisms that support reform, and new (and old) regulatory, professional, and advocacy actors.

The second argument this book makes is that despite differences and contestations, most of the major initiatives designed to improve teacher preparation lead with the idea that the key to reform is heightened accountability through close scrutiny and public evaluation of institutions, programs, and teacher candidates. Using our multidimensional accountability framework, we deconstruct and critique four of the most highly publicized and politicized U.S. teacher education accountability initiatives. The proponents of these initiatives claim that they will dramatically boost the quality of teacher preparation. However, we show that there is little evidence to support the claims supporters make about existing initiatives and policies. We argue that despite the lack of evidence, these initiatives, which collectively constitute what we call the dominant accountability paradigm, are reshaping teacher education's goals and expectations in subtractive ways by redefining how teacher educators and teacher candidates understand their work, emphasizing a singular and narrow kind of test-based accountability, and reducing the spaces in teacher education for discussion, action, and advocacy related to equity, social justice, and democratic education.

This book expends a fair amount of ink exposing the general lack of evidence behind major U.S. accountability initiatives and documenting the negative impacts they are having on teacher education. Despite this, we do not argue that it is necessary to abandon accountability altogether in teacher education or to champion radical localism. Instead, the third argument this book makes is that a different approach, *democratic accountability in teacher education*, is needed. Democratic accountability has several core ideas, which we take up and work through in detail in the final part of this book. First, as we noted above, we suggest that democratic accountability must be built on "strong democracy" (Barber, 1984) and "strong equity" (Cochran-Smith, Stern, et al., 2016). Strong democracy includes a viable approach to civic participation, public goods, and a self-governing community wherein people with different interests have a way to negotiate their disagreements in terms of their mutuality. Strong equity means that accountability systems must include representation of all stakeholders, and that built into accountability systems there must be recognition of the societal and educational systems and structures that reproduce inequality. Democratic accountability acknowledges both that teachers and teacher educators alone cannot eradicate inequity simply by teaching better, and that policymakers cannot eradicate school and societal inequity simply by increasing access to good teachers.

The next core idea of democratic accountability is that teacher education ought to be accountable for preparing teachers who have the capacity and the will to work with others to enact democratic education, specifically deliberative and critical democratic education that is inclusive and characterized by reasoned consideration of conflicting viewpoints and perspectives. Finally, democratic accountability requires the democratization of power relationships and knowledge sources, which means that accountability expectations are jointly determined by relevant stakeholders, including school-based educators, families, and communities who are regarded as co-equal participants in the larger enterprise of teacher education.

To develop these core ideas—strong democracy coupled with strong equity, deliberative and critical democratic education, and democratized power relationships—we draw from political philosophy, democratic theory, the scholarship of educational accountability, and many years of experience in teacher education research, practice, and policy. We consider what it would mean if teacher education were held accountable in ways consistent with the democratic project. What would state or national accreditation standards look like if teachers were expected to teach students the skills of disagreement, deliberation, and perspective-taking? What might federal reporting regulations include if the definition of teacher persistence included persistent efforts to challenge existing school structures and policies that help reproduce inequality? What private or public advocacy groups and philanthropists might invest their time and resources in evaluating and reporting to the public about teacher education programs' progress toward democratic ends? What if teacher education programs of all kinds were evaluated according to how well they prepared teacher candidates to teach students to live and work productively in an acutely diverse and divided democratic nation? To take up these and other questions that look to the future, this book describes a number of promising practices that are consistent with aspects of democratic accountability in teacher education.

THE DISCOURSES OF ACCOUNTABILITY

We wrote this book with the intention of entering into multiple discourses about educational accountability—discourses related to teacher quality, teacher preparation, teacher preparation program evaluation, teacher education reform, and education reform in general. Three of these discourses are especially relevant.

The first discourse connects teacher quality, teacher education, and education reform. Attention to the connections among these three emerged in developed countries as a response to the late-20th-century shift from an industrial to a knowledge economy that brought unparalleled attention to the quality of education systems, particularly teachers. There has been debate for more than three decades about educational policies and reforms intended to solve the teacher quality problem by boosting the quality of teacher preparation. During the 1990s and well into the mid-2000s, much of the debate in teacher education revolved around two competing agendas related to these issues, often deemed the professionalization agenda and the deregulation agenda (Cochran-Smith & Fries, 2001; Zeichner, 2003). In contrast, however, since the mid- to late 2000s, there has been a shift in the policy rhetoric about teacher quality from focusing on teachers' qualifications and credentials to emphasizing effectiveness (Hess & McShane, 2014). Consistent with this shift, many of today's hottest policy and popular debates linking teacher quality, teacher education, and education reform are about how to "do teacher education better" by establishing new providers and/or formats, including new graduate schools of education unaffiliated with universities, new online and for-profit providers, and new university-initiated approaches, such as urban teacher residencies. There has also been a related push to make teacher education more practice- or clinically based by focusing less on influencing teacher candidates' theories, beliefs, and values and more on training them to enact effectively the core tasks of teaching. This book directly relates to the discourse about these reforms, many of which are highly contested.

The second strand of discourse we aim to enter with this book has to do directly with the complex U.S. teacher education accountability landscape, which is characterized by new accountability demands and multiple competing accountability goals, relationships, and actors. Although accountability is not new, the focus of teacher education accountability has made a dramatic shift. Ushered in with No Child Left Behind (NCLB) in 2002 and intensified by the regulations and requirements of Race to the Top (RTTT) in 2009 (Henry, Kershaw, Zulli, & Smith, 2012), teacher education has been increasingly held accountable for outcomes by state and federal policies as well by professional groups and various advocacy organizations. Some of the scholarly work in this area is intended to sort out different forms of evaluation in teacher education, while other work has the aim of critiquing particular accountability approaches. Still other work in this area is very deliberately intended to intensify the accountability focus in teacher education, critiquing previous failed efforts to reform teacher education and proposing stronger accountability models that utilize better state data and public reporting systems. In contrast, some analyses aim to expose the underlying ideological aspects of accountability policies and raise questions about teacher education for equity, social justice, and democratic education. In short, the teacher education accountability discourse is contentious, and many of the issues are not only highly publicized but also highly politicized. This book enters these debates, offering an analysis of how accountability came to be so central, the impact it is having on the field, and what a different approach to accountability committed to the democratic project and the public good might look like.

The third discourse this book addresses has to do with the rise of accountability in education more generally and in the public sector. Since the 1980s, accountability has emerged as a major strategy for improving not only teacher education but also K–12 education, higher education, and work in the public sector. An important topic in the accountability discourse is critique of heightened auditing, monitoring, and surveillance of education and other public sectors, which are perceived by many as having an increasingly negative impact on workers' motivation, sense of trust, and actual improvement of their work. Some scholars have conceptualized new alternative forms of accountability that utilize multiple measures of knowledgeable judgment about professional work, enhance trust among participants, and/or recast accountability as the mutual responsibility of all stakeholders.

This book is intended to enter into all three of these discourses related to accountability and teacher education. The book does so in part by connecting accountability issues in K–12 education, higher education, and the public sector to accountability issues in teacher education.

A NEW POLITICAL CLIMATE FOR EDUCATION?

As we were completing the analyses for this book, the acrimonious 2016 presidential campaign came to its conclusion with the election of Donald Trump as the 45th U.S. president. To say that the outcome was unexpected and unprecedented would be an understatement in the extreme. To say that the outcome stoked fear about the future of public education and about the very core of American democracy would not be an exaggeration.

Education was not a major emphasis for Candidate Donald Trump, the consummate campaigner. From time to time, he railed against the Common Core, claiming that it let Washington tell local schools what to do and what their students should study. Sometimes he asserted that he might drastically reduce the power and reach of the U.S. Department of Education (DOE) because of its one-size-fits-all approach to education that he said encroached on local control. Although Trump's scattershot campaign comments about education did not add up to anything close to an articulated education policy, his "signature proposal" in education was the provision of $20 billion in federal funds for school choice (Saul, 2016). Without offering any details, this proposal generally had to do with a choice/voucher system wherein low-income families and students would be encouraged to choose among schooling options, including many non-public options such as private schools, religious schools, homeschooling arrangements, online schooling, for-profit schools, and public and private charter schools, some of which are run by for-profit management companies. Both teachers' unions and public education advocates opposed the idea, claiming it would diminish resources for public schools. Indeed, Randi Weingarten, president of the American Federation of Teachers (AFT), said the proposal would bring about the "decimation of public education" (Brown, 2016).

Just as education was not a major focus for Candidate Trump, it was also not a major focus for President Trump during his first year in office, which was just coming to a close as this book went to press. Trump's first important action in education was to nominate as Secretary of Education billionaire Republican donor and longtime school choice advocate Betsy DeVos, whom the Senate confirmed by a razor-thin margin. Although DeVos has by now developed supporters among mainstream Republicans and the Business Roundtable (Mintz Levin Strategies, LLC, 2017), it is telling that she has no experience as a student, teacher, or parent in public schools. Her confirmation hearings revealed her stunning lack of knowledge about public education, including the purpose and safeguards of major legislation such as the Individuals with Disabilities Act (IDEA) and the racialized context in which certain educational institutions originated, such as historically black colleges and universities. Trump's choice of DeVos, who has referred to public schools as a "dead end" and a "monopoly" (Strauss, 2017), does not bode well for public education.

Trump's proposed federal budget for 2018 was also telling with regard to what his approach to education policy would be (Johnson, Campbell, Spicklemire, & Partelow, 2017). Although actual reductions will likely not be as extreme, the proposed budget included massive cuts to education (some $9 billion, or 13% of the Department of Education's funding) in student loan funds, Medicaid services to poor and disabled students, teacher education, class size reductions, and after-school programs. In sharp contrast, the proposed budget also included major new funds for school choice ($1 billion for choice for poor students, $250 million for vouchers for private schools, and $167 million for charters).

At about the same time the proposed budget was released, Congress and Trump used the arcane Congressional Review Act to rescind the new federal reporting requirements of the Higher Education Act (HEA)/Title II—enacted at the end of the Obama administration—that required states to rate teacher preparation programs on graduates' performance (Iasevoli, 2017). Although there had been enormous opposition to these regulations from the teacher education profession, there had also been support from various professional groups. At the same time, Trump also rescinded new rules regarding how states were to carry out the Every Student Succeeds Act (ESSA) along with two other Obama-era bills. At a signing ceremony at the White House, Trump applauded Congress (and himself) for the education repeals, boasting that they "remov[ed] an additional layer of bureaucracy to encourage freedom in our schools" (as quoted in Brown, 2017, para. 2). These education bill repeals were part of Trump's broader agenda to dismantle as many as possible of the policies and programs put in place by Obama (Baker, 2017)—an action some have referred to as repeal without replacement.

Outside of repeal of the HEA/Title II regulations and the new ESSA accountability requirements, the Trump administration has done little in education, although the PROSPER Act that was being debated as this book went into final production would make important changes in teacher education reporting regulations and in funds available for students, as we discuss in Chapter 4. It is clear that the Trump administration favors more states' rights and less federal oversight of education as well as more choice, including charters and vouchers. But the USDOE continues to have many key posts unfilled, and education is clearly not a priority. It is not clear what this means for the accountability era. Perhaps the most certain thing that can be said is that the future of education policy under Trump, including the future of teacher education policy, is uncertain. However, it is important to remember, as Spring (2011) has argued and Ravitch (2017) reiterated, that the development of human capital education policies in the United States has long been a bipartisan project, led by Clinton in the 1990s, Bush in the 2000s, dueling branches of the Democratic party in campaign platforms in 2008, and Obama from 2008 to 2016. The assumptions underlying these policies reflect a neoliberal, market-based approach to education reform, including consumer choice, charter schools, alternative routes into teaching, competition among schools, data-driven decision making, high-stakes testing, and other forms of accountability, with severe consequences for failure to meet expectations. Although Trump rescinded Obama's new HEA/Title II and ESSA accountability regulations in order to—rhetorically, at least—shift regulatory power to the states, it is not clear what the Trump administration stance will be on the neoliberal frames that feed the accountability paradigm. However, because neoliberal reform is tied to conservative agendas (Apple, 2006), it is unlikely that the underlying assumptions and ideas behind accountability will disappear from the national political discourse or from decision making.

In short, this is an unprecedented—and, some would say, dangerous—moment in time. Some people fear that public education itself, which is critical to the future of a democratic society, is being undermined and—worse—is at risk of being dismantled. This book, which focuses on teacher education accountability, enters the conversation at this uncertain time and speaks directly to the pressing concerns of many people in the educational community. The book makes a case for a new kind of teacher education accountability—an accountability that has been "reclaimed" in support of the democratic project and that emphasizes the obligation of teacher education programs in a democratic society to prepare teachers to enact deliberative democratic education and work with others to challenge inequities. This approach is built on the premise that in a democratic society, the work of teachers and teacher educators ought to be a public enterprise for the common good rather than a market enterprise based on individual competition for private goods.

READING THIS BOOK

The purpose of *Reclaiming Accountability* is to explain how accountability came to be so central to teacher education, to deconstruct and critique current U.S. accountability policies and initiatives, and to make the case for a new approach to teacher education accountability consistent with the democratic project. To do so, the book is organized into three major parts.

Part I, "Teacher Education in the Era of Accountability," describes the scope, purpose, and national and global contexts of teacher education and locates the book within larger discourses about teacher quality, educational reform, democratic education, and the rise of accountability regimes in education. Its three chapters, including this one, characterize the current teacher education landscape in the United States, particularly the accountability landscape. Chapter 2 describes the policy and political contexts of teacher education in the United States, where teacher quality—and with it teacher education—have been defined as public policy problems since the early 1980s. Unlike many other developed countries, however, each of the 50 states has its own regulatory policies regarding teacher preparation and teacher licensure that criss-cross with federal reporting and funding policies, national accreditation standards and regulations, and, increasingly, with critiques disseminated by various think tanks, research institutions, and new education reform advocacy organizations. The quality—and widely perceived inadequacy—of U.S. teacher education has been the target of unprecedented attention over the last few decades, and the field has changed rapidly. This chapter argues that the current context can be described as teacher education's era of accountability and describes five professional, policy, and political developments that prompted the emergence of the era.

Chapter 3 connects teacher education's accountability era to the emerging focus on accountability in education more broadly (both K–12 education and higher education). In each of these areas, there has been an intensification of accountability as well as a growing sense of dissatisfaction and concern about the impact of accountability schemes featuring increased scrutiny and monitoring of professional work. This chapter is informed by some of the rich scholarship about accountability in these various sectors. Drawing on this work, the chapter provides a new framework for deconstructing teacher education accountability initiatives and reclaiming accountability. The *eight dimensions of accountability in teacher education* framework is used to unpack selected cases of teacher education accountability in the next part of the book and also to organize the new approach of democratic accountability in teacher education that we propose in the final part.

Part II of this book, "The Problem with Accountability: Four Cases," is comprised of four chapters, one for each of the four most widely publicized, highly politicized, and dramatically impactful national-level accountability policies and initiatives proposed and/or implemented in the United States during teacher education's era of accountability. The four accountability initiatives are: Obama administration–approved federally mandated and state-enforced reporting regulations stipulated in Title II of the HEA; the accreditation system and procedures of the Council for the Accreditation of Educator Preparation (CAEP), teacher education's single national accreditor; biennial evaluations of teacher preparation programs and pathways conducted and widely disseminated by the National Council for Teacher Quality (NCTQ); and the Educative Teacher Performance Assessment (edTPA), a nationally available teacher candidate performance assessment now used in multiple programs and states.

Drawing on hundreds of policy documents, position statements, website information, media responses, and professional critiques, these chapters treat each initiative or policy as a highly visible case of a controversial approach to accountability in teacher education. Informed by ideas from policy studies and frame theory, each case chapter provides multiple analyses and critiques, including the initiatives' history, the broader agendas or organizations to which they are attached, the political and professional contexts in which they emerged, and their sponsors, advocates, and opponents. Each chapter provides an eight-dimensional analysis and also evaluates existing evidence for the claims its advocates make about how it will presumably improve teacher education quality and, ultimately, teacher quality. Finally, each chapter discusses the impact and implications of the initiative.

Part III of the book, "Reclaiming Accountability," is the final and in some ways the most important section. It has two chapters that speak to teacher education practitioners, candidates, researchers, graduate students, evaluators, policymakers, advocates, critics, and social entrepreneurs who are part of the expanding and diversifying teacher education community. Chapter 8 offers cross-case analysis of the major initiatives listed above, pointing out commonalities and differences, evaluating the quality of the evidentiary warrant of the initiatives individually and collectively, and assessing their overall impact on teacher education, teaching, and the democratic project. This chapter argues that despite differences, there is a *dominant accountability paradigm* in teacher education that has generally reified test scores as the primary measure of students' learning and has had a subtractive impact on the work of teacher education.

Chapter 9, the final chapter in this book, focuses directly on reclaiming accountability by conceptualizing and elaborating a new approach—

democratic accountability in teacher education. The chapter offers three basic principles that are consistent with the democratic project and elaborates these by drawing on democratic theory, critical policy analysis, and teacher education studies. Chapter 9 also considers promising teacher education accountability practices that are relevant to the task of reclaiming accountability and consistent with one or more aspects of democratic accountability, as we conceptualize it in this book. These promising practices are drawn from different levels and forms of accountability. This chapter also raises questions about what accountability policies and initiatives might look like if democratic education were considered a worthy goal of teacher education and if teacher education programs were accountable for preparing teachers to teach their students to be free and equal participants in a diverse democracy. The chapter concludes that we need democratic accountability now more than ever, given the uncertain policy and political climate and growing fears about the future of democratic education.

CHAPTER 2

Teacher Education's Era of Accountability

In this chapter, we make two assertions. First, we argue that the decades between 1998 and 2017 have constituted an "era of accountability" in U.S. teacher education. What we mean is that during this period many federal, state, and professional accountability initiatives used the same three-part logic: "holding teacher education accountable" will boost the quality of teacher education programs and institutions; boosting the quality of teacher education programs will increase the overall level of teacher quality, defined primarily in terms of students' achievement; and higher levels of student achievement will ensure both individual prosperity and the long-term economic health of the nation. The key accountability assumption in this string of claims is that the way to "fix" what was repeatedly referred to as the "broken system" of teacher education (Duncan, 2009; U.S. Department of Education [USDOE], 2002) is systematic, vigilant public evaluation and monitoring of teacher education programs' and graduates' impact.

The second assertion we make in this chapter is that the language and logic of accountability have become so deeply embedded in the everyday discourse and practice of teacher education that they are now difficult to discern as policy and practice alternatives. Instead they are often presumed to be self-evident and inevitable, more or less a "baked-in" part of teacher education. In this chapter, we try to get to the bottom of all this. We unpack the assumptions, language, and logic that have defined teacher education's era of accountability. And, just as importantly, we identify the major policy, political, and professional developments that contributed to its emergence and its staying power.

In the chapter's conclusion, we briefly consider the future of teacher education accountability policy and politics at this unique moment in our nation's history following the surprising election of Donald Trump as president. We acknowledge that it is probably too early to predict what will happen with accountability given our great national uncertainty about nearly all policies in the public domain, including education. Nevertheless, we try to speculate a bit. Could teacher education's accountability era be over? Could it be in the beginning stage of a long, slow death, ultimately replaced by a new "choice" or "voucher" era? Or is it the case that accountability will now evolve into a new form? If the latter turns out to be the case, is it possible that that new form could be more constructive and more in keeping with the democratic project, or is it more likely to create further divisions in an already acutely divided society?

THE ERA OF ACCOUNTABILITY

We begin with what we mean by teacher education's "era of accountability." During the 1980s and 1990s, the entire educational enterprise in the United States was "awash" in standards. There were standards for teaching the subject areas, standards for constructing assessments, and even standards for standards (Ericsson, 2005). Standards were so pervasive in the development of teacher education licensure, certification, and accreditation policies and practices that during this time, Roth (1996) described it as "the era of standards." What we are suggesting, however, is that very soon after this, teacher education's era of standards began to evolve into what we call the "era of accountability (and standards)," with the emphasis squarely on accountability for outcomes. That is, many initiatives designed to improve (or even replace) university-based teacher preparation from the late 1990s onward led with the idea that the key to reform was heightened accountability for teacher and student outcomes through close scrutiny, ongoing monitoring, large-scale data systems, and highly public evaluation and reporting (Cochran-Smith, Stern, et al., 2016; Lewis & Young, 2013). Over two decades, the accountability focus has become so pervasive and so normalized in teacher education that it warrants the label "the era of accountability."

As we noted in Chapter 1, accountability was not a new phenomenon in education or teacher education during the late 1990s. Rather, the emerging era of accountability was part of a larger sea change (Cuban, 2004) that cut across education levels—from K–12 through higher education—and across professions (Ginsberg & Kingston, 2014). The shift was from accountability primarily for inputs, resources, and processes to accountability for what Ambrosio (2013) called "auditable" (or measurable) outcomes representing results, effectiveness, and/or efficiency. Some have described this shift in educational accountability in simpler terms—from inputs to outcomes. This is an apt description for teacher education, as we show below.

The roots of teacher education's accountability era were in the accountability requirements of the Elementary and Secondary Education Act (ESEA) of 1965, which for the first time tied the distribution of federal education funds to results. But the presumed need for accountability related to teaching and teacher preparation was brought into sharpest relief by the famously alarming predictions of *A Nation at Risk* (National Commission on Excellence in Education, 1983). This galvanizing report linked mediocre student performance to sluggish global economic performance. In particular, the report charged that the quality of teachers and teaching in the United States was at such a low level that the workforce the schools produced was not going to be able to compete in the emerging global economy, which in turn threatened national security (Lagemann, 2000). *A Nation at Risk* and the slew of national and international reports that accompanied or followed it conveyed the same message: teachers matter, not just in the classroom, but in terms of the robustness and health of national economies (e.g., Furlong, Cochran-Smith, & Brennan, 2009; McKinsey and Company, 2007; Organisation for Economic Co-operation and Development [OECD] 2005; World Bank, 2010). This message prompted unprecedented concern about teacher quality almost universally and marked the emergence of a new "education policy paradigm" in the United States (Mehta, 2013) that focused on teacher quality, defined in terms of students' achievement, and accountability.

Grounded in these roots, teacher education's accountability era was ushered in with the 1998 reauthorization of HEA, which was by then the single most important legislation affecting higher education (Hannah, 1996). HEA's Title II provisions stipulated mandatory federal reporting requirements for states and teacher education institutions, linked state grants to the revision of certification, and provided funding for alternative certification routes (Cochran-Smith, 2005; Earley, 2004). With the new Title II regulations, institutions of higher education were required to report annually to their states about the results of teacher tests and other certification requirements. States, in turn, were required to report to the USDOE about state certification and licensure requirements, disaggregated by institution and by gender, race, ethnicity, and pass rates. In addition, the U.S. Secretary of Education was required to report annually to Congress on the status of the "teacher quality problem" in the nation. For teacher education, the new accountability approach was intensified by the Bush administration's NCLB act (Cochran-Smith, 2002, 2005; Elmore, 2002) and exacerbated by the Obama administration's RTTT policies and the proposed new HEA/Title II requirements (Cochran-Smith, Piazza, & Power, 2013; Lewis & Young, 2013), which we take up in Chapter 4.

In the remainder of this chapter, we suggest that teacher education's "era of accountability" emerged from five broad developments: (1) unprecedented global attention to teacher quality, tied to neoliberal economics; (2) a continuous public narrative asserting that "traditional" university-sponsored teacher education was failing to produce effective teachers who were prepared to respond to the demands of contemporary classrooms; (3) the conceptualization of teacher education as a public policy problem wherein it was assumed that getting the right policies in place would boost teacher quality and the national economy; (4) the teacher education establishment's turn toward accountability, which was consistent with a conception of teacher quality defined as effectiveness and linked to the human capital paradigm; and (5) the belief that the reform of public education, rather than other social policies, was the major tool for redressing inequality and eradicating poverty in the United States.

Our intention in this chapter is to describe the contexts and conditions within which the accountability emphasis in teacher education emerged and try to explain why it took hold so firmly. However, there is always more than one way to tell a story. We are not suggesting that the story of teacher education's accountability era in terms of the five developments we consider below includes everything that could be said. We are also not suggesting that these developments "caused" the accountability era. Rather than proposing a comprehensive and linear chain of events, we are suggesting that the five developments we identify were interrelated and more or less co-occurring aspects of the emerging accountability era, with each shaping and fortifying the others. As Taubman (2009) suggests in his analysis of accountability and standards in education writ large, there are no "easy causal narratives" in this domain.

UNPRECEDENTED GLOBAL ATTENTION
TO TEACHER QUALITY TIED TO NEOLIBERAL ECONOMICS

The emphasis on accountability in teacher education emerged as part of the decades-long shift from an industrial economy based on manufacturing and material goods to a global knowledge economy based on the production and distribution of information. In the United States and elsewhere, the shift to a knowledge society was also a shift to neoliberal economics wherein individualism, free markets, and private good(s) took precedence over other goals (Cochran-Smith & Villegas, 2016). Neoliberal economics favored policies related to privatization, deregulation, free trade, increased roles for the private sector, and decreased social protections for citizens (Hickel, 2012). Although it is beyond the scope of this chapter to examine why and how neoliberalism emerged, it is worth noting here that there were social, political, and economic factors—such as inflation and economic stagnation—that made neoliberalism more appealing to top-level policymakers and to corporate America than the post–World War II liberalism that was dominant until the late 1970s (Harvey, 2005; Hickel, 2012).

At this point it's worth reiterating that our purpose in this chapter is to explain how teacher education's era of accountability emerged and took hold. Our aim is not to explicate and critique the tenets of neoliberal economics and human capital theory or to evaluate the general impact of market-based interventions on schooling. Many scholars have offered trenchant critiques about the impact of these ideological shifts on education politics and policies, and we refer readers to their work (e.g., Apple, 2006; Au, 2016; Hill, 2007; Hursh, 2007; Leyva, 2009; Lipman & Hursh, 2007; Mehta, 2013; Sleeter, 2007; Torres, 2009).

For our purposes in this chapter, one of the most important things to emphasize about neoliberal ideology is its conceptualization of human beings as rational, individual economic actors. This viewpoint is consistent with the logic of human capital theory, as Tan (2014) makes clear in an extensive review of human capital theory and criticism: "In essence, human capital theory suggests that education increases the productivity and earnings of individuals; therefore, education is an investment. In fact, this investment is not only crucial for individuals but it is also the key to the economic growth of a country" (p. 412). According to human capital theory, education is the central source of economic development. This means that the capacity of education systems to meet the demands of the global market is paramount. Tan emphasized that "economy-driven education policies," which are based on neoliberal understandings of individuals as economic actors, are intended to enable citizens to "contribute to production rather than relying on the social welfare state" (p. 429).

So what do the logic of human capital theory and neoliberalism's emphasis on the individual as an economic actor have to do with teacher quality and accountability? The connection is crystal-clear in the work of Eric Hanushek, senior fellow at the conservative Hoover Institute and arguably one of the most influential contemporary voices about the economics of public education policy. Hanushek (2002) defines teacher quality simply: teachers who produce large gains in students' achievement. He asserts that the key to effective education policy is accountability in the form of performance incentives for teachers and schools rather than policies that try to change school conditions, such as decreasing class size. Hanushek and colleagues (Hanushek, Peterson, & Woessmann, 2013; Hanushek & Woessmann, 2015) argue that nothing is more important to the long-term future of the United States than the cognitive knowledge and skills (or human capital) of those being educated today. Based on econometric analyses of international data, they assert that the level of human capital acquired by school students has a direct causal effect on a nation's long-term economic growth. They also suggest that enormous financial and security benefits would accrue to U.S. citizens over a lifetime if the schools could be brought to world-class standards through policies establishing effective accountability, choice, competition, and direct rewards for good performance.

It is important to note that neither the human capital paradigm nor market-based education reforms are partisan agendas. Along these lines, Spring (2011) pointed out that presidents and candidates from both U.S. political parties have used the language and logic of human capital education for decades, including Clinton in the 1990s, Bush in the 2000s, both parties in campaign platforms in 2008, and Obama throughout his two terms. Similarly Au (2016) demonstrated that reforming public education through market-based interventions has involved the enactment of policies over almost two decades. These include school choice, vouchers, deregulation of teacher education, decreases in democratic oversight of schools, contracting public school services to private industry, and, most importantly, high-stakes testing, which provides a system for the "objective" evaluation of students, teachers, and schools and establishes the justification for choice and competition.

Given the purpose and limits of this chapter, we conclude this section with just three critical points about neoliberal economics, human capital theory, and teacher education. First, although the link between a knowledge society and neoliberal economics has come to be considered more or less inevitable (Hickel, 2012) and although alternative explanations have been marginalized in the United States (Hursh, 2007), this link is not a given (Castells, 2010). There are competing perspectives. And some education practitioners, scholars, and policymakers in the United States and elsewhere have managed (or at least are trying hard) to resist the neoliberal paradigm (Scott, 2016; Tatto et al., 2016). Examples include schools like Central Park East in New York City and the Mission Hill School in Boston; alliances such as the Coalition of Essential Schools and Expeditionary Learning schools; parent and teacher collectives explicitly organized to resist high-stakes testing, such as the Opt Out movement; teacher education programs and groups that focus on social justice and community needs, such as STEP-UP in Chicago and the alliance of Education Deans for Justice and Equity; and the national education/teacher education models operating in Finland and Scotland.

Our second point is that the shift to a competitive knowledge economy wherein individualism and private good(s) take precedence over other goals involves a narrow and problematic notion of educational equity, which we take up in some detail in the final section of this chapter. And third, we believe that a neoliberal or human capital approach to education policy ultimately undermines a democratic vision of society. Market ideology, which is about individual competition for private goods (Labaree, 1997), is fundamentally inconsistent with a vision of strong democratic education, understood as a public enterprise for the common good (Earley, 2000; Engel, 2000). We return to these ideas in detail in the third part of this book, which is about democratic accountability for teacher education.

CONTINUOUS PUBLIC NARRATIVE ABOUT
THE FAILURE OF TEACHERS/TEACHER EDUCATION

A second important influence on the emergence of teacher education's era of accountability was a continuous public narrative alleging that university-sponsored teacher education had failed and was continuing to fail despite reforms. To be sure, this was not the only narrative about teacher education during this time, but it was the dominant one. The failure narrative was constructed by various individuals and constituencies, including representatives and spokespersons for the U.S.DOE, conservative think tanks, private advocacy and philanthropic organizations, leaders from the business community, emerging educational entrepreneurs and reformers, and some education scholars and professionals. These assorted critics were not joined in a formal alliance. But they were loosely united by sentiments consistent with neoliberal ideology and human capital theory, as outlined above, and with the idea of teacher education as a policy problem, as discussed below. Because of these shared bases, the failure narrative was extremely powerful. It was comprised of different but broadly consistent charges about teacher education's presumed failure that built on one another and gained momentum from relentless repetition.

In fairness, we acknowledge that university teacher education *did* have genuine problems during the period we are discussing (and both prior to and following this period), not the least of which was markedly uneven quality across programs and institutions and its general failure to address structural aspects of inequity. But the failure narrative was about something more than calling attention to legitimate problems and debating the evidence. It was comprised of multiple themes, including teacher education's alleged ineffectiveness and bias, its supposedly cumbersome certification procedures, its lack of attention to the "science" of education, the presumed superiority of alternate recruitment and certification pathways, and its alleged lack of a strong accountability system based on effectiveness. Below we provide illustrations of the major arguments and sources of the teacher education failure narrative to convey its scope and consistency and to suggest its cumulative weight and power. As these examples show, the failure narrative was often conveyed in inflammatory, condescending, or alarming rhetoric. It was made up of a potent concoction of contested empirical assertions, unsubstantiated normative claims, name-calling, and hyperbole, all wrapped up in politics.

- Teacher candidates' completion of university-based teacher preparation makes no discernible difference in the achievement of students (Abell Foundation, 2001a; Ballou & Podgursky, 1999, 2001; Kanstoroom & Finn, 1999).
- Teacher education programs are out of step with the public interest because of the "liberal" bias of teacher educators (Farkas, Johnson, & Duffett, 1997).
- Teacher education programs are preoccupied with theory (Greenberg, McKee, & Walsh, 2013; Kamenetz, 2016) as well as multicultural ideology and "touchy-feely self awareness" (Schrag, 1999).
- Certification is an unnecessary hurdle that precludes entry into the profession of academically able young people who want to teach but don't want to "waste time" on "trivial" education courses (Hess, 2001).

- The regulatory apparatus for teacher certification and licensure is a "broken" system; alternate entry and certification routes are superior to university programs and provide a policy model for improving teacher quality (Duncan, 2009; USDOE, 2002, 2003).
- Schools of education do not embrace the science of education, are resistant to change, and ought to be "blown up" (Lyon, 2002).
- University teacher preparation is based on social justice and other progressive "ideologies" rather than "objective" standards, "core knowledge," and the "science" of education (National Association of Scholars, 2005; Walsh, Glaser, & Wilcox, 2006).
- Existing reforms don't focus on what really matters for teacher quality—regulatory oversight and accountability for teachers' effectiveness and students' learning (Crowe, 2010; Deans for Impact, 2015; Hanushek & Woessmann, 2015).

Importantly, despite its lack of evidence and largely ideological bases, this failure narrative constituted a major portion of what the public heard and what people came to "know" about the work of teacher education. This was often without the benefit of information about the political agendas, funders, methods, or histories of the individuals and groups behind the charges and without any way to sort out substantiated from unsubstantiated claims and allegations.

There was extensive resistance and pushback to the failure narrative from a variety of individuals and groups in the teacher education community. But the failure narrative was very effective. It helped to establish a new "common sense" about university teacher education and its alleged inability to do the job of producing the workforce the nation needed (Scott, 2016). This commonsense viewpoint was a major part of the rationale for new accountability schemes designed to produce compliance and uniformity across university teacher education programs. The failure narrative also supported the proliferation of alternate pathways, new nonprofit and for-profit providers, and test-only entry routes into teaching intended to sidestep or replace university teacher preparation programs.

So why was the failure narrative so effective? Part of the reason is that it built on the already strong international consensus that "teachers matter," a phrase that was inflated and repeated endlessly in the policy world by both opponents and advocates of university teacher education (e.g., Darling-Hammond, 1997, 2000a, b; National Commission on Teaching & America's Future [NCTAF], 1997; OECD, 2005; Sanders, 1998; Sanders & Horn, 1998). In the United States, the highly seductive assertion that teachers were the most important factor in students' achievement was a double-edged sword. This was the case in part because this assertion lived alongside the received wisdom—since at least the time of *A Nation at Risk*—that *teachers and schools* were failing. Although this conclusion was challenged, the "fact" that the performance of America's students was substandard compared to the performance of students in many other nations was documented in report after report, and the blame for failure was laid squarely at the feet of schools, teachers, teacher unions, and teacher education (Hanushek, Peterson, & Woessmann, 2013; Hanushek & Woessmann, 2015; Teaching Commission, 2004). The logic here was crystal-clear: if teachers are the most important factor in students' achievement and U.S. students' achievement is substandard, then U.S. teachers are the culprits, as are the people and institutions that prepare them.

Clearly the failure narrative was consistent with the larger neoliberal discourse about why and how to improve education through market-based reforms that enhance educational systems' capacity for producing human capital, as we discussed above. Just as importantly, the failure narrative zeroed in almost exclusively on schools, teachers, and teacher education as both the cause and the cure for social and educational inequality, which took other needed social reforms off the table and took policymakers off the hook for devising and implementing these reforms.

TEACHER EDUCATION AS A POLICY PROBLEM

Concurrent with the two developments discussed above, a third factor that influenced the emergence of the accountability era in teacher education was the construction of teacher education as a public "policy problem" (Cochran-Smith, 2004, 2005). When teacher education is defined as a policy problem, the goal is to determine which of the broad parameters that can be controlled by policymakers is most likely to enhance teacher quality and thus have a positive impact on desired outcomes (Kennedy, 1999). Toward the beginning of the accountability era, the policy parameters in question generally had to do with the structural arrangements and regulations governing teacher education programs and certification, such as subject-matter and fieldwork requirements, 4- or 5-year programs, alternate entry routes, and teacher testing. As the accountability emphasis gained momentum, the policy parameters in question increasingly zeroed in on policy requirements regarding outcomes, such as students' achievement, teacher performance in the classroom, and teacher persistence.

As noted above, the Bush administration's NCLB act intensified the policy approach to improving teaching and teacher education by ushering in a broad testing mandate for K–12 schools and stipulating that all teachers be "highly qualified." Coupled with the HEA/Title II 1998 reporting requirements, which we describe in detail in Chapter 4, NCLB also established a new approach to teacher education as a policy problem—high-stakes accountability managed by the states, but mandated and controlled by the federal government (Kumashiro, 2015).

The accountability focus of NCLB was sharply exacerbated by the Obama administration's RTTT policies and funding. RTTT signaled what Hess and McShane (2014) referred to as a shift in policy rhetoric from a demand for "highly qualified teachers" to a clamor for "highly effective teachers." As we have suggested, the distinction here is between what many people have called teacher quality "inputs," on the one hand, and "outputs" or "outcomes" on the other. So-called inputs include such things as teachers' qualifications and credentials, their subject-matter knowledge, and the characteristics of their preparation and entry routes. Inputs have to do primarily with the selection and recruitment of teachers, the assumption being that establishing policies that attract the right people into teaching—usually, those who are "smarter" because they have stronger academic records and have attended more prestigious colleges and universities—will substantially improve students' achievement. In contrast, teacher quality "outcomes" include teachers' classroom performance, their retention in schools, evaluations of teachers by administrators and students, and—most controversial and some would argue most important—evaluation of teacher preparation programs based on program graduates' impact on the learning of their students, using value-added or student growth measurement models. Policies focused on outcomes are much less concerned about teachers' qualifications and instead concentrate on results.

The wording of RTTT funding guidelines, which determined cash-strapped states' eligibility for federal funds and for NCLB waivers, made the policy shift to outcomes very clear. In a policy report on RTTT funds and teacher preparation, Crowe (2011) pointed out that RTTT very clearly defined teaching effectiveness in terms of students' test scores. He made this point by quoting from the guidelines:

> effective teachers are those whose students achieve acceptable rates of student growth . . . student growth [is] the change in student achievement . . . between 2 points in time . . . student achievement [is] a student's score on the state's assessments . . . (p. 2)

In short, RTTT established that effective teachers were those who raised test scores, a definition perfectly aligned with Hanushek's perspective on teacher quality. To be competitive for RTTT funds, states promised to implement new accountability measures that tied teacher education program evaluation to teacher evaluation based in large part on students' achievement as indicated by scores on standardized tests (Crowe, 2011; Henry et al., 2012).

The perspectives implicit in the RTTT guidelines were consistent with market-oriented, neoliberal values and concepts. As Scott's (2016) analysis of the politics of market-based education reform suggests, this is not surprising. Scott argues that conservatives and neoliberals have dominated the framing of the problem of the schools in the United States for decades. They characterize schools as wasteful, inefficient, and inattentive to results, thus exacerbating the failed potential of students and the protection of inefficient and overpaid teachers and school leaders, all resulting in the declining ability of the United States to compete globally. Meanwhile, as Scott notes, progressives' framing of the problem of schools—too much focus on tests, unequal funding, unequal distribution of well-qualified teachers, curricula that don't include citizenship and democratic education—has been marginalized.

In K–12 schooling in general, as in teacher education, the framing of problems goes hand in hand with the framing of solutions. Scott (2016) pointed out that under Obama, the federal approach to education "emulated venture philanthropy" (p. 10). That is, its solutions to the policy problem of education/teacher education included competition, privileging strategies that "work," emphasizing private-sector funding, and favoring diverse providers such as charter schools and the participation of private-sector actors in the operation of schools. This take on the problem of teacher education has been very clear during the last decade as more and more new nonprofit and for-profit teacher preparation providers have emerged (Cochran-Smith, Carney, & Miller, 2016; Cochran-Smith, Carney, Miller, & Sánchez, 2017). Many of these have had ongoing funding or at least initial support from New Schools Venture Fund and other venture capitalists, and/or from the Gates Foundation, the Walton Family Foundation, the Broad Foundation, and other private philanthropic organizations (Zeichner & Pena-Sandoval, 2015).

Although policymakers' attention to teacher preparation as a policy problem was not new during teacher education's accountability era, three things were. First, there was great faith in federally mandated, state-enforced regulatory policy as a key to fixing teacher education. Second, the enlarged federal role in education brought the attention of high-level state and federal policymakers and politicians, including presidents and governors, to teacher education. And third, policy matters became a major part of the discourse within the teacher education community itself, although this had not been the norm during most of its history (Kennedy, 1999). During the two decades of teacher education's accountability era, the control of teacher education shifted away from local and toward state and federal levels (Bales, 2006). The majority of the hotly contested issues about and within teacher education revolved around state and federal accountability policies, the policy tools used for their implementation, and the accountability initiatives and expectations of new education reform advocacy organizations and philanthropies.

THE TEACHER EDUCATION ESTABLISHMENT'S ACCOUNTABILITY TURN

The fourth factor in the emergence of the era of accountability is the teacher education "establishment's" own turn toward accountability. We begin with the ready admission that the enterprise of teacher education is complicated, with many players involved (Cochran-Smith & Fries, 2011a; Wilson & Tamir, 2008). However, we would argue that there are two major national organizations that have been centrally concerned about teacher education policy for the last 70 years. First is the National Council for the Accreditation of Teachers (NCATE), which was the major national professional accreditor from 1954 until 2013. As we recount in Chapter 5, in 2013 NCATE merged with the smaller Teacher Education Accreditation Council (TEAC) to form the Council for the Accreditation of Educator Preparation (CAEP), to become the single accreditor of teacher education providers in the United States. The second organization is the American Association of Colleges for Teacher Education (AACTE), an institutional membership organization that is the major professional alliance of teacher education institutions in the United States. The leaders of these two organizations, which for most of their histories were very closely tied to one another, are often cast as spokespersons for teacher education in emerging policy and political developments. Thus we use them to talk about the "teacher education establishment's" turn toward accountability.

NCATE/CAEP and AACTE have been close collaborators and mutual professional supporters for years, with AACTE serving as a key major financial backer of NCATE. Although they played somewhat different roles in promoting teacher education's emerging accountability agenda, with few exceptions their roles were consistent and interlocking. Given that the history of CAEP, its accountability processes and procedures, and its emerging support of teacher education's accountability agenda is analyzed in detail in Chapter 5, we focus here on NCATE and AACTE.

In 2000, NCATE announced new teacher preparation program accreditation standards, which were described by AACTE leaders (Schalock & Imig, 2000) as "a paradigm shift from inputs to outcomes." NCATE's new system required schools of education to provide performance evidence of candidate competence, including state licensing examination results as well as performance evidence of candidates' knowledge and skill (Cochran-Smith, 2001; Wise, 1999). The 2000 NCATE standards were consistent with both the movement to professionalize teaching and with other professions where the emphasis was shifting from inputs to outcome measures (Dill, 1998). But the NCATE standards were also consistent with the accountability push by the larger educational establishment (Ambrosio, 2013; Taubman, 2009). This was particularly evident in the matching language and logic of the teacher education professional discourse and the larger state and federal policy discourse about teacher quality and the knowledge economy (Cochran-Smith & Fries, 2011a; Taubman, 2009).

NCATE'S turn toward accountability was not surprising, given the ongoing failure narrative about teacher education, which we described above.

Essentially, NCATE was struggling to redefine itself during the 2000s and early 2010s. As we show in Chapter 5, it was also searching for ways to remain relevant as an accreditor, given the competition of TEAC as an alternative accreditor whose popularity was growing. NCATE's efforts to reestablish relevance occurred during a time when alternate pathways into teaching were also growing rapidly, and there was increasing pressure on university programs to maintain enrollment levels. NCATE's efforts were not only to regain relevance, however. They were also intended to avoid what Earley (2000) described as being "cast as a culprit" in the larger phenomenon of American schools' poor showing on international comparisons. Following the NCATE-TEAC merger, CAEP announced new standards that were consistent in many ways with the HEA/Title II reporting regulations proposed by the federal government under the Obama administration and with the larger policy push for accountability. We continue the story of CAEP's development in Chapter 5.

Meanwhile, AACTE had its own struggles. In his insightful book that deconstructs the discourse of standards and accountability in education writ large, Taubman (2009) suggested that in the early to mid-2000s AACTE made a "rush to support standards and accountability . . . given the threat of privatization on one hand and withdrawal of government funding on the other" (p. 77). To a great extent, we agree with this description. But we would also point out that AACTE's paying membership was made up primarily of deans and other leaders from the same schools and colleges of education that were the butt of excoriating critiques and the targets of new accountability policies based on mistrust of the profession. This rush to support accountability undoubtedly had to do with AACTE's strategy of walking a fine line between carrying the torch for the new accountability era on the one hand and questioning the new accountability in keeping with the concerns of its members on the other.

When Sharon Robinson was named AACTE's CEO in 2005, its banner mission statement became "AACTE—serving learners," which signaled that the organization was not concerned simply with enhancing *teachers'* knowledge but was also committed to boosting *students'* achievement. AACTE's shift was consistent and co-occurred with NCATE's paradigm shift from inputs to outcomes, and both of these were to a great extent in line with the teacher quality policies of the Bush and later the Obama administrations. As we discuss in Chapter 4, the Obama administration's first blueprint for improving teacher education was released in 2011; it called for teacher preparation program evaluation on the basis of the test scores of the students of program graduates as well as job placements and retention rates. In response to this plan, Robinson said: "This is a good thing, to have the Department [of Education] now become a part of our reform effort in teacher education. We need to be able to discern between programs that get it done and those that don't" (as quoted in Grasgreen, 2011, para. 5). Robinson's comparison of preparation programs that did or did not "get it done" seemed intended to convey ownership by the teacher education establishment of the focus on program outcomes and graduates' impact on students' achievement. She also implied that outcomes had always been the establishment's major agenda.

The Obama administration's 2011 plan died in committee, but many of its policies reemerged in starker form in HEA/Title II regulations proposed in 2014, which prompted unprecedented public and professional opposition. At that point, AACTE joined with many other professional organizations to oppose the proposed 2014 regulations. This primarily had to do with the enormous outpouring of objections to the proposal's focus on evaluating preparation programs according to their graduates' impact on students' achievement and the emphasis on establishing minimum grade point averages and national test scores for all teacher candidates. AACTE's stated reasons for opposition were: the regulations represented an unfunded mandate for schools, states, and higher education institutions; they impeded the recruitment of a diverse teacher workforce, particularly in high-need areas; and they tied federal aid to preparation program evaluation based on expansion of an "un-tested" system (AACTE, 2017). When the 2016 approved version of the regulations was rescinded in March 2017, AACTE credited its own organization's "tireless advocacy" for opposing the regulations, although AACTE's opposition likely had little to do with Trump's rescinding of as many Obama-initiated policies as possible.

Today the accountability discourse is pervasive and normalized both within the university-sponsored teacher education establishment and outside it. Most professional/university teacher educators define outcomes more broadly than students' test scores, and many continue to object to teacher preparation program evaluation based primarily on students' test scores. Nevertheless, it is now a fact of life that nearly everybody in teacher education focuses on outcomes either willingly or reluctantly, and there are far fewer questions raised about accountability.

EDUCATION REFORM AS THE CURE FOR INEQUALITY

The final factor we consider in the emergence of teacher education's accountability era is the belief that education reform is the cure for inequality. What we mean by this is that over time it has come to be assumed by policymakers and others that poverty and income inequality are problems that can be solved by education reform *without* reforms addressing other social, economic, and political conditions and without recognition of the knowledge perspectives and values of historically marginalized students, families, and communities.

Kantor and Lowe (2016) made this argument very clearly in their insightful essay about the evolution of social policy in the United States since the New Deal. They argued that:

> Belief in the capacity of public education to redress unequal opportunity and eliminate poverty is one of the most distinctive features of American social policy . . . [E]ver since Lyndon Johnson prioritized education over the project of building on the New Deal to create a robust welfare state, educational reform has been the federal government's favored solution to the problems of poverty, inequality, and economic insecurity. (p. 38)

Kantor and Lowe acknowledged that, on the plus side, belief in the power of education has historically been the rationale for greater access to schools for low-income and children of color. On the minus side, however, they also pointed out that:

> The idea that inequality and poverty are susceptible to educational corrections . . . has reduced pressure on the state for other social policies that might more directly ameliorate economic distress, but, because education's capacity to redistribute opportunity has been limited by absence of social policies that directly address poverty and economic inequality, it has fueled disillusionment with public education itself for its failure to solve problems beyond its reach. (p. 38)

Kantor and Lowe (2016) argued that the impact of the belief that education reform could solve the problem of inequality was far-reaching. It relieved policymakers of the burden of developing the social policies that, coupled with education reform, might actually reduce inequality, such as those related to employment, housing, transportation, early childhood services, and health care (Broader, Bolder Approach to Education, 2008). This belief also exacerbated disillusionment with public education and supported the turn away from public schools and toward "diverse provider models," including charter schools and school choice (Scott, 2016).

For teacher education, this belief ratcheted up what policymakers and the public expected from teachers and teacher educators. Increasingly in the United States and elsewhere, teachers were expected not only to teach all students to world-class standards in order to produce a competitive labor force, but also to play a key role in responding to rising social expectations and achieving greater social equity (Furlong, Cochran-Smith, & Brennan, 2008). Consistent with these high expectations for teachers, teacher education programs were expected to produce teachers who were prepared to do all these things on "day one" in the classroom. The belief that education reform could eradicate inequality also led some people to conclude that anyone who said teachers and schools *could not* solve the nation's social problems were self-interested insiders who supported the status quo, wanted to lighten their own workloads, and were simply making "excuses" for the ineffectiveness of schools, teachers, and teacher educators (Hanushek, 2002; Haycock, 2005). Overall, the belief that education reform was the cure for inequality bolstered support for market-based teacher education accountability schemes intended to enhance the capacity of the U.S. workforce to compete.

It is important to note here that—at least rhetorically—nearly all contemporary U.S. teacher education accountability initiatives have as one of their goals promoting equity by ensuring that students have access to good teachers. However, what we have found is that underlying most accountability initiatives is "thin" rather than "strong" equity (Cochran-Smith, Stern, et al., 2016), a distinction we have developed that borrows language from democratic theory, particularly Benjamin Barber's (1984) classic distinction between "thin" and "strong" democracy. Barber criticized "thin democracy" (that is, liberal democracy), which he said was based on both a rights or "radical individualistic" perspective that protects private property and on market capitalism. In contrast, he defined "strong democracy," which is participatory, in terms of a "self-governing" community wherein dependent private individuals are transformed into free citizens and partial and private interests are transformed into public goods.

When we talk about teacher education accountability, we use "thin equity" to refer to initiatives that assume that equity has to do with individuals' equal (or the same) access to "high-quality" teachers, curriculum, and school opportunities. Thin equity's individualistic focus is consistent with the neoliberal view that human beings are rational, individual economic actors responsible for taking action for themselves (Tan, 2014). Consistent in some ways with notions of distributive justice (Fraser & Honneth, 2003), a thin equity perspective assumes that assimilation into "shared" school goals is the bottom line in the education of minoritized students, not recognizing the point that King (2006) rightly asserted—equal access to a faulty curriculum is not justice. Here "faulty" refers in part to a curriculum that does not reflect the knowledge traditions and values of minoritized families and communities who traditionally have not had a voice in the development of the knowledge and perspectives the schools value.

In contrast, a "strong equity" perspective acknowledges the complex and intersecting historical, economic, and social systems that create inequalities in access to teacher quality in the first place (Anyon, 2005; Gadsden, Artiles, & Davis, 2009). A strong equity perspective assumes that equity cannot be achieved by teachers and schools alone. Rather, it requires educators, working with policymakers, activists, families, and communities to challenge the structural and systemic aspects of schools and society that reproduce inequity. The idea of strong equity also explicitly acknowledges the racialized nature of teacher education accountability initiatives that focus on high-stakes testing to evaluate teacher candidates and preparation programs. As Au (2016) has argued, high-stakes testing regimes have consistently reproduced racial inequality in the United States by assuming objectivity and thus masking the structural nature of racial inequality within a neoliberal ideology of "individual meritocracy" (p. 40), which denies the structural and material aspects of racism. We elaborate our distinction between "thin" and "strong" equity in Chapter 9 as part of our discussion about democratic accountability in teacher education.

There are many teacher education scholars and practitioners, ourselves included, who work from critical and social justice perspectives that are consistent with the idea of strong equity as we have elaborated it here. But this is not the dominant view operating in accountability policies and initiatives in teacher education. As we demonstrate above, all five of the developments that have shaped teacher education's accountability era have assumed that teacher quality is the single most influential factor in the success of individuals and in national economic prosperity, and all five reflect primarily a "thin equity" perspective.

WHITHER THE ERA OF ACCOUNTABILITY?

Throughout this chapter, we have made it clear that teacher education's era of accountability was not precipitated by a singular event or development in the field, nor was it the final point in a causally linked chain of chronological events. Rather the accountability era emerged from multiple interrelated and contemporaneous developments, including but not limited to those we have described. Teacher education accountability was also not a new phenomenon in the late 1990s. Rather, as we have shown, the accountability era was related to the larger change in educational accountability writ large that was part of the shift to a global knowledge economy, and to a belief that teacher quality was the primary determinant of students' achievement and of the capacity of nations to compete successfully in the global economy.

Finally, the accountability era was not something that was imposed on teacher education by accreditors, state and federal regulators, and reform advocacy organizations. It is true that large elements of the teacher education community opposed federal proposals regarding reporting systems and the imposition of accountability expectations by private organizations with anti-teacher education agendas. For the most part, however, and partly in response to relentless critique and expanding competition from new providers, key players in the teacher education establishment came to embrace standards and accountability in ways that were broadly consistent with larger state and federal trends in social policy wherein it was assumed that public education could eliminate inequalities and mitigate poverty.

As we have shown, the five policy, political, and professional developments we have talked about in this chapter are closely interwoven in terms of logic and language, and they were co-occurring in terms of chronology.

These developments shaped but also reinforced one another. Considering these five developments together helps explain the contexts and conditions within which the accountability emphasis in teacher education emerged and took hold. Collectively what they have added up to in teacher education over the last two decades is that accountability—of the type we have described in this chapter—has come to be perceived as "common sense" in education rather than as a policy or professional alternative (Apple, 2006; Au, 2016; Kumashiro, 2012), which would imply that other policy and professional choices are possible. What this means is that the language of accountability has come to be heard as a "natural" part of education policy and practice, and its underlying logic and assumptions about relationships between knowledge and power and the ways particular policies and practices produce and reproduce inequalities have come to be largely invisible.

As we noted at the beginning of this book, given the results of the 2016 U.S. presidential election, the future of education policy in all areas is uncertain. Uncertainty notwithstanding, based on Trump's campaign and other statements and on the education budget his administration proposed for 2018, it seems reasonable to say that his administration favors more states' rights and less federal oversight of education, including teacher education, as well as more voucher plans and consumer choice about schools. The future will likely also include more support for charter schools, alternate routes into teaching, and new schools of education unaffiliated with universities (Cochran-Smith, Carney, & Miller, 2016). In addition, as we noted, early in his term, Trump rescinded Obama's new HEA/Title II reporting regulations as well as the accountability regulations of the ESSA. However, so far there has been little indication about the Trump administration's stance on the neoliberal ideology that underlies the accountability paradigm. In addition, as we noted earlier, because neoliberal reform is tied to conservative agendas (Apple, 2006), it seems unlikely that the underlying assumptions and ideas behind teacher education accountability will disappear from the national political discourse or decision making.

Our position in this book is that even if we could, we should not abandon accountability in teacher education, nor should we champion radical localism, although we believe that all federal, state, and professional accountability policies and initiatives should work from a position of respect for local values and commitments. We believe that this may be a time for new ideas about accountability that bring together some of those who have resisted the emphasis on surveillance, monitoring, and high-stakes testing of the accountability era. Instead of abandoning accountability, then, we are calling for a new approach—democratic accountability in teacher education—that is consistent with the democratic project and is based on strong equity. We elaborate this concept as well as existing conditions that serve as either obstacles or supports for this idea in Chapters 8 and 9.

CHAPTER 3

The Eight Dimensions of Accountability

During the two decades from 1998 to 2017, accountability emerged as the major approach to reforming teacher education in the United States. But this was true not only in teacher education. Ushered in by NCLB, accountability was also the major mechanism for enhancing the quality of K–12 education, and during the same period, accountability became more important in higher education, the public sector, and other professional fields. As we have shown, this rise in accountability regimes across public domains reflected the broad shift to a global and competitive knowledge society shaped by principles and policies derived from neoliberal economics and from the business world. However, in teacher education, as in other domains, the contemporary accountability landscape is complex. There is not just one approach to accountability, but multiple co-existing accountability strategies and initiatives. There are multiple—and sometimes competing—accountability demands and expectations. And there are new accountability forms and mechanisms superimposed over existing ones.

This chapter presents "the eight dimensions of accountability," a new framework for teacher education comprised of eight interrelated dimensions that build on and extend cross-disciplinary conceptions of accountability. In this chapter we argue that all teacher education accountability policies and initiatives can be analyzed according to these eight interrelated dimensions, whether or not they are explicitly stated in policy documents and tools. We also suggest that in order to fully understand the practices and implications of any teacher education accountability policy or initiative, all eight of the dimensions have to be taken into account.

So why do we need another framework in teacher education? As we showed in Chapter 2, for many years university-sponsored teacher education was the target of harsh critique—some of it deserved—from critics both within and outside the field. Many of today's accountability initiatives were shaped by—and contributed to—that critique, especially the assertion that the only way to fix teacher education was either to replace it by sidestepping universities or control it through accountability schemes centered on uniformity and compliance. To survive in this climate and to meet mounting state, federal, professional, and public accountability demands, many university-sponsored teacher education programs had little choice but to comply, regardless of the questions they might have had about the broader goals and purposes of the new demands. In some contexts, compliance with very time-consuming and complex accountability demands meant little time and few opportunities for the participants in teacher education programs to drill beneath the surface of requirements and regulations. In other contexts, the perspectives of some teacher educators and their leaders were more or less in sync with the "common sense" of new accountability initiatives—that the primary goal of teacher education is and should be preparing teachers who can boost students' achievement. The eight dimensions of accountability, which we elaborate in this chapter, is a tool for educators, researchers, and policymakers who want to unpack and interrogate accountability regulations and policies by drilling beneath the surface level of rhetoric and highly politicized debate.

One of the major arguments of this book is that at this uncertain time for education policies and politics, teacher education needs to reclaim accountability for the democratic project. We can't even begin to do this, however, without in-depth understanding of the current accountability context, which requires interrogating the multiple and interrelated dimensions of accountability policy and practice. That's what our new framework is intended to do. Applying the framework not only unpacks the nuts and bolts of an accountability initiative's operation but also exposes its underlying values and principles, its theory of change, and its relationship to larger political and policy agendas. Examining two or more accountability initiatives in terms of our framework highlights not only their similarities but also the critical differences among them. Looking across multiple examples of accountability policies and initiatives can reveal common patterns and assumptions about how accountability is intended to work as a tool for teacher education reform.

Before we turn to our eight dimensions of accountability framework, it is important to clarify what is *not* the purpose of this chapter. We do not provide a typology of current approaches to preparation program evaluation, nor do we analyze the strengths and weaknesses of existing accountability schemes. Others have taken up these tasks and produced useful analyses (e.g., Coggshall, Bivona, & Reschly, 2012; Crowe, 2011; Feuer, Floden, Chudowsky, & Ahn, 2013; Plecki, Elfers, & Nakamura, 2012). In addition, our purpose in this chapter is *not* to propose a new kind of accountability for teacher education. We take up this task in Chapters 8 and 9 wherein we identify the dominant accountability paradigm in teacher education and contrast it with democratic accountability for teacher education, which is consistent with the larger democratic project of education for the common good.

In contrast to these other tasks, our purpose in this chapter is to present the eight dimensions of accountability framework by explaining the meaning of each dimension, the conceptual and practical issues that are involved, and how the dimensions relate to one another and to the whole. In the next part of this book (Chapters 4–7), we use this framework to analyze and critique the four most visible and widely known accountability initiatives and policies that co-exist in U.S. teacher education today. One of the things our analysis reveals is that different dimensions of accountability are emphasized in public policy debates and controversies about teacher education, depending on power relationships, political developments, and jurisdictional issues. Another finding is that there is now a common approach to teacher education accountability in the United States that is consistent and widespread enough in concepts and practices to be thought of as an accountability paradigm. We elaborate these findings in Chapter 8.

THEORIZING ACCOUNTABILITY
IN EDUCATION AND THE PUBLIC SECTOR

Scholars in a number of fields have worked to define, theorize, compare, and critique key aspects of accountability, including variations in its underlying rationale and assumptions, forms, dimensions, and impact. We found Trow's (1996) basic definition of accountability in higher education to be a useful starting place:

> Accountability is the obligation to report to others, to explain, to justify, to answer questions about how resources have been used, and to what effect. Accountability to others takes many different forms in different societies, with respect to different actions and different kinds of support. The fundamental questions with respect to accountability are: who is to be held accountable, for what, to whom, through what means, and with what consequences. (p. 310)

Even though Romzek (2000) theorized accountability in the public sector rather than in higher education, she defined accountability along lines similar to Trow's. Romzek said that accountability is "answerability for performance" (p. 21), emphasizing that this includes answerability to whom, for what, and how.

Starting with basic definitions of accountability more or less consistent with those above, some scholars have enumerated multiple conceptions or types of accountability in various domains. We mention a few of these to give a sense of their variation in language and function and to help illustrate why we need a new framework. For example, Darling-Hammond (2004) specified five conceptions of accountability related to K–12 education—political, legal, bureaucratic, professional, and market—and suggested that each had its own strengths and weaknesses. Mayer (2005) applied these five conceptions to teacher education, also noting strengths and weaknesses.

Along somewhat similar lines, Howe and Murray (2015) critiqued state "report cards," which grade states' efforts to improve educational services, and other state-level education policies in terms of a contrast between direct bureaucratic accountability and indirect market accountability. Finally, in their pamphlet about educational accountability internationally, the International Academy of Education (IAE) and the International Institute for Educational Planning (IIEP) (Anderson, 2005) stated that there were three types of accountability systems: "compliance with regulations, adherence to professional norms, and results driven" (p. 1).

One takeaway from these different schema is that there is probably more than one useful way to conceptualize and parse the larger notion of teacher education accountability. Another possible takeaway, however, is that accountability typologies are somewhat problematic. They tend to treat accountability as a unitary and one-dimensional concept, suggesting that it is a more or less straightforward task to classify any given initiative within one category. This may not be the case. Take, for example, the case of a teacher test created by a group of teacher education researchers and practitioners at a university but subsequently required by certain states for all new teacher certifications. Is this an example of professional accountability or bureaucratic accountability, or does it blur the lines between the two? Here's another example: Is the creation and dissemination of a state-level database indicating ratings of teacher preparation programs in that state—and available to prospective teachers, employers, and the general public—an example of market accountability, bureaucratic accountability, or professional accountability? We can't answer these questions without knowing more about the other elements or dimensions of these initiatives. Along somewhat different lines, some lists of accountability types mix together various aspects of accountability in rather confusing ways. The IAE/IIEP pamphlet mentioned above, for example, explicitly stipulates three accountability types. However, their type, "compliance with regulations," seems to concentrate on what an education institution or entity is to be held accountable *for*, while "adherence to professional norms" has more to do with *who* has the jurisdiction to establish expectations and standards, and "results driven" focuses on *how* evidence is to be used within a given accountability system to prompt improvement. While each of these issues is important, they are jumbled together in the IAE/IIEP list of types.

Rather than a typology, then, what we propose in this chapter is a multi-dimensional framework, which allows for a complex and nuanced analysis of accountability policies and initiatives. With this goal in mind, what we found most helpful in the existing literature on accountability in education and the public sector were discussions that tackled multiple aspects of accountability and considered how key dimensions combined and interacted, such as those by Carnoy, Elmore, and Siskin (2003), Powell (2000), Romzek (2000), and Trow (1996). Romzek's ideas about accountability in the public sector were particularly useful. Drawing on this work and on our own analyses of teacher education accountability initiatives (Cochran-Smith, Stern, et al., 2016; Cochran-Smith, Baker, Burton, et al., 2017; Cochran-Smith, Baker, Chang, Fernández, & Keefe, 2017; Cochran-Smith, Burton, Carney, Sánchez, & Miller, 2017), we came to several important conclusions that guided the development of our eight dimensions framework. First, it was clear that we needed to go well beyond labels if we wanted to sort out accountability in teacher education. The same terminology—words like "audit," "self-review," or "professional"—are used by different individuals and organizations to refer to very different processes, procedures, or entities, while similar approaches and processes sometimes have dissimilar labels. Second, we found that applying a single dimension, such as source of accountability expectations or autonomy/trust, was not sufficient for clarification and deep interrogation of accountability approaches. Although two-dimensional frameworks like Romzek's (2000) were more helpful than single dimensions, we found that two dimensions also did not suffice for sorting out the messy teacher education accountability context, with its shifting web of approaches.

Last, we concluded that there were several aspects of accountability that appeared to be central and needed to be taken into account in any accountability framework with conceptual power, although we also found that most of these had not been fully specified in the previous literature or considered in relation to one another. Essential aspects include at least the following: the idea of obligation, which usually distinguishes accountability from a sense of individual responsibility; the question of agency, which gets at issues related to jurisdiction, control, and autonomy; the notion of substance, which has to do with the assumed fundamental purpose of the entity or organization being held accountable; the issue of values, which gets at the principles and ideologies animating an accountability scheme; and the question of mechanism, or how an accountability scheme is expected to operate to yield the desired consequences. The next section, which introduces the eight dimensions of accountability framework, reflects these and other central issues.

THE EIGHT DIMENSIONS OF ACCOUNTABILITY: A FRAMEWORK FOR MAKING SENSE OF ACCOUNTABILITY IN TEACHER EDUCATION

It would be an understatement to say that the teacher education accountability landscape in the United States is complex. As Romzek (2000) pointed out about public-sector accountability internationally, Western democracies tend to use multiple accountability strategies, and new accountability forms are often layered on top of existing forms, which results in "the weaving of a thick web of multiple, overlapping accountability relationships" (p. 23).

Teacher education is no exception to this trend. Over the last two decades, there have been multiple co-existing accountability initiatives, policies, and mechanisms characterized by:

- differing goals and targets
- contrasting historical and institutional contexts
- multiple (and contested) jurisdictions
- differing political affiliations, sponsors, and funders
- new (and old) regulatory, professional, and advocacy actors
- criss-crossing local, state, national, and global influences

This means that the individuals, programs, and institutions associated with the preparation of teachers have had to deal with shifting and sometimes conflicting expectations, uncertainty about the consequences of accountability, and multiple sources of legitimate authority. They have also had to contend at times with would-be sources of authority that they themselves did not regard as legitimate.

The eight dimensions of accountability is a framework intended to help make sense of this messy landscape. As Figure 3.1 illustrates, the basic idea behind the framework is that accountability is not a unitary or one-dimensional construct. Rather, it is a complex and multifaceted concept consisting of eight core dimensions. Starting at the top of the figure and reading clockwise, the eight dimensions are: (1) *the values dimension,* (2) *the purpose dimension,* (3) *the concepts dimension,* (4) *the diagnostic dimension,* (5) *the prognostic dimension,* (6) *the control dimension,* (7) *the content dimension,* and (8) *the consequences dimension.*

These dimensions are intricately interwoven with one another, and no accountability initiative can be fully understood without unraveling all of them and their interrelationships. This means that although a given accountability initiative or policy might be similar to another policy in terms of one or more dimensions, the two policies could nonetheless be dramatically different in overall import and impact because they differ in terms of other dimensions. For example, many aspects of the content dimension (what teacher education programs and pathways are actually held accountable for) of the HEA/Title II teacher preparation reporting requirements proposed in 2014 (Office of the *Federal Register,* 2014) and the content dimension of CAEP's 2013 accreditation requirements (CAEP, 2013a) were very similar. Both policies required preparation programs and pathways to demonstrate impact on student learning as well as employers' and graduates' program satisfaction and employment information about graduates. Despite content similarities, however, these two policies differed significantly in terms of the control dimension—who has or should have jurisdiction over how programs and pathways are assessed and held accountable. As we elaborate on in Chapters 4 and 5 in the next part of this book, the HEA/Title II reporting

Figure 3.1. The Eight Dimensions of Accountability in Teacher Education

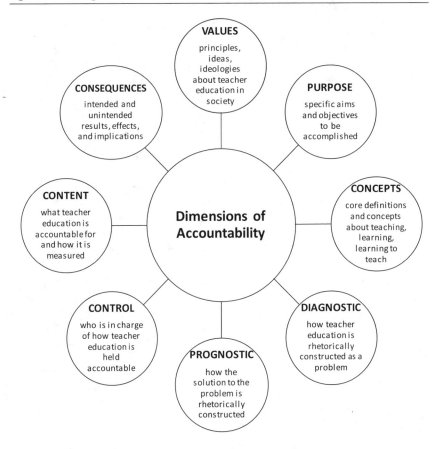

requirements, which were approved with revisions in 2016, were designed to set up state-enforced federal control of teacher preparation. In contrast, CAEP's accreditation system was intended to establish professional control of teacher preparation. These differences matter.

In addition to the multidimensional aspects of accountability that the above examples illustrate, certain dimensions in the eight dimensions of accountability framework cluster together to constitute larger themes and issues in accountability, as Figure 3.2 shows and as we elaborate on in the following pages. The first three dimensions—values, purpose, and concepts—form a thematic cluster that has to do with the "foundations of accountability," or the underlying ideas, ideals, aims, and ideologies of any accountability initiative or policy. The next two—the diagnostic and prognostic dimensions—form a thematic cluster that focuses on what we

Figure 3.2. Thematic Clusters and Dimensions of Accountability in Teacher Education

Thematic Cluster	Description of Cluster	Dimension	Key Question and Description of Dimension
Foundations of Accountability	This cluster is based on the assumption that neither teacher education accountability nor teacher education itself are value-free or neutral. Rather, these are in part about ideas and ideals. This cluster thus has to do with the values, principles, intentions, and concepts underlying accountability.	Values	*Why?* Stated or implied cultural ideas, ideals, beliefs, and principles about the broad purposes and roles of teaching, schooling, and teacher education in the larger society.
		Purpose	*For what?* Stated aims and objectives of a particular accountability initiative and what it is explicitly intended to accomplish in teacher education.
		Concepts	*What's common sense?* Core definitions and key concepts about teaching, learning, and learning to teach that animate a given accountability policy or initiative and represent its "commonsense" worldview.
The Problem of Teacher Education	This cluster is based on the assumption that policy problems don't exist "out there," waiting to be taken up by policymakers. Rather, problems and solutions are constructed as part of larger debates about educational ideas, ideals, and worldviews.	Diagnostic	*What's the problem?* How the language and rhetoric of an accountability initiative construct or diagnose the teacher quality/teacher education problem, including who or what "caused" the problem and what kind of problem it actually is.
		Prognostic	*What's the fix?* How the language and rhetoric of an accountability initiative construct the prognosis or solution to the perceived problem, including what the theory of change is about how the accountability mechanism or system will "fix" the perceived problem.

Power Relationships in Accountability	This cluster is based on the assumption that teacher education accountability policies, like all teacher quality policies, are political, not neutral, in the sense that they involve power relationships and contestations. This cluster has to do with distribution of power and how power and control are related to stipulations about the content and consequences of accountability.	Control	*Who decides?* Jurisdictional issues involved in an accountability initiative, including who is in charge/should be in charge of how institutions, programs/pathways, and/or individuals are assessed and held accountable for particular requirements, processes, or results.
		Content	*What counts?* What an accountability initiative actually holds teacher education accountable for, as well as what counts as valid and reliable evidence that teacher education programs/pathways are being accountable for the requirements, processes, or results stipulated.
		Consequences	*What happens?* Intended—and unintended—results, effects, impacts, and implications of an accountability policy or initiative for the institutions, programs/pathways, and/or individuals that are their targets and implementers.

call "the problem of teacher education." This has to do with how teacher preparation is conceptualized broadly as a policy and practice problem as well as how solutions to that problem are operationalized. The last three dimensions—control, content, and consequences—form the thematic cluster of "power relationships in accountability." This thematic cluster gets at the politics of accountability, including what expectations and evidence for claims are stipulated, who stipulates them and whom they affect, and both short- and long-term implications of the policy for the direct targets of the initiative and the broader enterprise of teacher preparation.

The eight dimensions in this framework accentuate the essential elements of any particular accountability policy or initiative and highlight both similarities and differences from other initiatives. Just as importantly, grouping the dimensions into clusters that are part of a larger whole underscores how the dimensions operate together systemically. In the remainder of this chapter, we elaborate the interrelated dimensions that are part of the eight dimensions of accountability framework and the clusters these dimensions form. In Chapters 4 through 7, we then use these dimensions and clusters as part of our interrogation of teacher education's most prominent and far-reaching national-level accountability schemes.

THE FOUNDATIONS OF ACCOUNTABILITY:
VALUES, PURPOSE, AND CONCEPTS

As Figure 3.2 shows, we refer to the first thematic cluster in the eight dimensions framework as the "foundations of accountability." This cluster is based on the assumption that neither teacher education accountability nor the broader enterprise of teacher education itself is value-free or neutral. Rather, accountability in teacher education, like all other social and cultural practices in education and teacher education, emerges from values, ideas, and ideals. The "foundations of accountability" cluster thus has to do with the fundamental values, principles, intentions, and concepts that underlie any given accountability initiative. Understanding these is essential to understanding what is behind a policy or initiative. This cluster has three dimensions. The *values dimension* focuses on stated or implied cultural ideas, ideals, beliefs, and principles about the broad purposes and roles of teaching, schooling, and teacher education in the larger society. The *purpose dimension*, which is related to values but is more specific, has to do with the stated aims and objectives of a particular accountability initiative and what it is explicitly intended to accomplish in teacher education. The *concepts dimension* refers to the core definitions and key concepts about teaching, learning, and learning to teach that animate a given accountability policy or initiative. We take up each of these below.

The values dimension has squarely to do with ideas and ideology. Here we do *not* mean ideology in the narrow sense of a closed system that walls out other points of view. Rather, we mean this in the nonpejorative sense that all approaches to teacher education accountability are based on some set of cultural ideas, ideals, beliefs, and principles, whether or not these are stated explicitly (Gee, 1996).

One way to elaborate the values dimension in teacher education accountability is in the terms some scholars have used to describe the major ideologies underlying most current education reforms in the United States. Lipman (2011), for example, argues that today's dominant "ideological project" is the "neoliberalization of public education" (p. 115). With this approach, she points out, teaching is driven by testing and performance outcomes, school leaders are regarded in managerial terms, learning equates with test performance, market mechanisms and business practices are used to ramp up the production of human capital, and teachers, teacher education, and parents are held accountable for failure. These values are more or less consistent with the assumptions underlying what Mehta (2013) refers to as a new "education policy paradigm" (p. 286) focused on economic success and identifying teachers and schools—rather than outside factors, such as poverty—as responsible for school failure. Lipman's neoliberalization ideology and Mehta's policy paradigm share many values and beliefs about the role of teaching and teacher education in producing the workforce the nation presumably needs to compete in the global economy, which have superseded values and beliefs related to citizenships and participation in a democratic society.

To understand the values dimension, consider two recently formed national associations of education deans—"Deans for Impact" and "Education Deans for Justice and Equity." Neither is a teacher education accountability policy or initiative per se, but both directly aim to influence accountability policy and its underlying values and ideologies. The policy agenda of "Deans for Impact" (2017) is twofold: to urge states to produce better data for preparation programs about the impact of their graduates and to emphasize that preparation programs are fully on board with the agenda of producing teachers who are effective. In contrast, "Education Deans for Justice and Equity" (2017b) is an alliance committed to collectively influencing education policy and reform in line with democratic and social justice principles, including the need to dismantle structures of poverty and inequality and resist policies and practices that reproduce discrimination and exclusion. These two deans' groups work from sharply contrasting ideologies related to the purposes of education in society, the causes and cures of inequality, and the role of education schools (and deans) in influencing policy.

The *purpose dimension* is the second dimension within the "foundations of accountability" cluster. Although the values dimension deals with the purpose of education and teacher education in society in a very broad sense, the purpose dimension is more specific. It centers on the stated aims and objectives of any given accountability policy or initiative and what it is designed to accomplish in teacher education.

The National Academy of Education's (NEA) report on teacher preparation program evaluation (Feuer et al., 2013) suggests that there are three basic purposes for evaluating teacher education programs: "holding programs accountable, providing consumer information to prospective [teacher preparation program] students and their potential employers, and supporting program self-improvement" (p. 4). Although this discussion of the purposes of teacher education accountability is helpful, it suffers from the same failings we discussed earlier with regard to typologies that treat accountability as a unitary and one-dimensional concept. The differences among accountability initiatives are not captured simply by understanding their purposes. Rather, this depends on understanding the interrelationships of purpose and other dimensions of accountability, including values, discussed above, and content, control, and consequences, discussed in the final section below.

A second aspect of the purpose dimension of accountability has to do with the consistency (or not) of stated and covert purposes. For example, in some states that use value-added approaches for the evaluation of teacher preparation programs or with program accreditation systems that require such evidence, the stated purpose is teacher preparation program improvement. Thus, we would expect that implementation of the policy would yield well-founded and effective evidence and feedback that could be used for the improvement of individual programs. However, this has not been the case, and even major supporters of value added–type approaches for assessing teacher preparation programs acknowledge that the information produced is not usable for improvement at the program or institutional level (Henry et al., 2013). This raises questions about whether the covert purpose of the initiative is something other than program improvement.

The *concepts dimension* is the third dimension within the "foundations of accountability" cluster. As noted, this dimension has to do with the core definitions and key concepts about teaching, learning, and learning to teach that animate a given accountability policy or initiative and add up to its "commonsense" view of the world and how it works. Our assumption here is that every accountability policy or initiative is animated by certain conceptions and operating assumptions about the role and image of the teacher; the nature of teaching, learning, and schooling; the meaning of teacher quality and teacher education quality; definitions of effectiveness and success in teaching and teacher education; what it means to learn to teach and to teach someone to teach; the knowledge teachers need to teach well; and the assumed nature of relationships among teacher preparation, teacher performance, school outcomes, and larger goals.

It is not possible to describe all the important concepts that are part of the foundations of various teacher education accountability policies and initiatives. Thus, to elaborate the concepts dimension, we raise questions about a few of the most important concepts. For example, accountability policies vary considerably in terms of their underlying images of the teacher and the assumptions they make about the nature of teaching and learning. Along these lines, we need to ask to what extent "the teacher/teacher candidate" who is implied in a given accountability policy is assumed to be a professional with professional expertise. Similarly, is teaching portrayed as a complex or technical activity? Is good teaching (or teacher quality) defined primarily as raising students' test scores, or does it involve other facets? Answers to these questions are related directly to an accountability initiative's underlying concepts about what constitutes the success (or failure) of a teacher education program. Some teacher education accountability initiatives, for example, value above all else what Miller (2017) calls the "teacher effectiveness doctrine," or the idea that the ability of the graduates of teacher education programs to boost students' test scores is more important than anything else and is the primary signal of success. When this concept of preparation program success is operating, then similar concepts follow, such as the idea that learning to teach is defined as learning to demonstrate specific behaviors that are assumed to lead to student achievement.

THE PROBLEM OF TEACHER EDUCATION: DIAGNOSTIC AND PROGNOSTIC DIMENSIONS

As summarized in Figure 3.2, what we call the *diagnostic dimension* and the *prognostic dimension* form a second thematic cluster in teacher education accountability. This cluster, which we refer to as the "the problem of teacher education," is based on the assumption that policy problems related to education (and other public domains) do not exist "out there," waiting to be discovered by policymakers or reformers. Rather, policy problems and solutions are constructed politically and rhetorically as part of larger debates about educational (and other) ideas, ideals, and worldviews and thus are related to the values dimension above (Snow & Benford, 1988; Stone, 2011). The *diagnostic dimension* refers to how the language and rhetoric of an accountability initiative construct or diagnose the teacher quality/teacher education problem in the United States (or elsewhere), including who or what "caused" the problem and what kind of problem it actually is. The *prognostic dimension* generally goes hand in hand with the diagnostic dimension. The prognostic dimension has to do with how the language and rhetoric of an accountability initiative construct the prognosis and the solution to the perceived problem, including the general underlying theory about what specific accountability mechanism or system presumably will "fix" the perceived problem and how that mechanism will work.

To develop these two dimensions, we borrowed concepts and language from frame theory and frame analysis, particularly the idea of "diagnostic" and "prognostic" frames, which highlight the rhetorical strategies reformers and policymakers use to connect and align their positions with the "commonsense" perspectives of their presumed audiences (Gamson, 1988; Snow & Benford, 1988). As Entman (1993) suggests:

> Framing essentially involves selection and salience. To frame is to select some aspects of a perceived reality and make them more salient in a communicating text, in such a way as to promote a particular problem definition, causal interpretation, moral evaluation, and/or treatment recommendation for the item described. (p. 52)

By including attention to symbols, meanings, and discourses, framing approaches emphasize that cultural meanings are constructed, not fixed. This includes ideas and meanings about justice/injustice, blame- and praiseworthy individuals and organizations, and central problems and solutions.

Applying these ideas from frame analysis to teacher education accountability policies and initiatives rejects the notion that accountability initiatives are the result of a straightforward and nonpolitical "technical-rational" process of choosing among clearly defined alternative strategies to address consensual and fixed goals (Datnow & Park, 2009). Instead, the assumption here is that accountability policies and initiatives, like other policies related to teacher education and teacher quality, occur within ongoing struggles over ideas among multiple actors and at multiple levels. This means, as noted above, that "the problem of teacher education" does not exist independently, waiting only to be discovered and taken up by policymakers and others, but rather that policy problem formation is itself an argument-making process wherein various political actors construct or diagnose what "the problem" is and also construct its prognosis and the preferred strategies and tools that will solve the problem (Stone, 2011).

To illustrate how we are using the ideas of diagnostic and prognostic frames to talk about teacher education accountability, we refer to *Our Future, Our Teachers*, which was the original Obama administration-proposed plan for improving teacher preparation. In the Foreword to this report, then–U.S. Secretary of Education Arne Duncan explicitly diagnosed the problem of teacher education, suggesting that the vast majority of teacher preparation programs were not up to the task because they "operate partially blindfolded, without access to data that tells them how effective their graduates are in elementary and secondary school classrooms after they leave their teacher preparation programs" (USDOE, 2011, p. 1). The report then offered the prognosis and solution for this problem—implementation of reforms that tracked "the academic growth of a teacher's P–12 students back to the preparation program from which that teacher graduated" (p. 7).

During teacher education's accountability era, the dominant construction of "the problem" of teacher education has not only been the perceived ineffectiveness of university programs to produce quality teachers, but also their alleged unwillingness to do anything about it. During the first part of the accountability era, the diagnosis, or cause, of this presumed failure was usually constructed as teacher education's inability to recruit and prepare teacher candidates with the background, knowledge, and aptitude that would allow them to be successful. Accordingly, the solution during this period was often seen as the privileging of alternate entry or preparation routes like Teach for America or the New York City Teaching Fellows Program, which were designed to attract a teaching pool with stronger academic qualifications. In short, the idea was to solve the teacher quality problem by recruiting "smarter" teachers. During the second half of the accountability era, however, as the Duncan quote above suggests, construction of the cause of teacher education's failure shifted from teachers' characteristics to lack of systematic data about their effectiveness. Accordingly, "the solution" to the problem was the creation of state, federal, or professional data systems assessing graduates' performance and programs' impact on students' achievement. The logic of diagnosis and prognosis went like this: With sophisticated, large-scale data systems about program impact and student-level outcomes, everything would work better—states would better decide which preparation programs needed to improve (or be closed down), schools would make better hiring decisions, and prospective "consumers" would make better choices about which preparation programs to attend.

POWER RELATIONSHIPS IN ACCOUNTABILITY: CONTROL, CONTENT, AND CONSEQUENCES

As Figure 3.2 indicates, we refer to the final cluster in our framework as "power relationships in accountability." This cluster is based on the assumption that teacher education accountability policies, like all teacher quality policies (and education policies and practices in general), are political, not neutral (Bruner, 1996), in the sense that they involve issues of power and power relationships and, often, contestations about power and jurisdiction. This cluster, then, has to do with the distribution of power and with who has the power to stipulate the content and consequences of accountability. Within the "power relationships in accountability" cluster, the *control dimension* refers specifically to jurisdiction and jurisdictional issues, including who is in charge and who should be in charge of the way teacher education institutions, programs/pathways, and/or individuals (e.g., teacher candidates) are assessed and held accountable for particular requirements, processes, or results. The *content dimension* has to do with what a given accountability initiative actually holds teacher education institutions, programs/pathways, and/or individuals accountable for, as well as what counts as valid and reliable evidence that teacher education is actually being accountable for the things stipulated by the policy. Finally, the *consequences dimension* refers to the intended—and unintended—results, effects, and implications of an accountability policy or initiative for the institutions, organizations, and individuals that are its targets and implementers and also for the broader enterprise of teacher preparation. We take up these dimensions below.

The control dimension focuses squarely on power and jurisdiction. Teacher preparation programs have many masters, and teacher education is a complicated enterprise with many moving parts. It has been characterized as the object of a "tug of war" (Bales, 2006) between federal and state control and as a crowded "social field" (Wilson & Tamir, 2008) wherein the establishment, its challengers, and boundary-crossers vie for power. What these descriptions suggest is that in order to understand any accountability initiative, we need to identify which agencies or organizations are in control over how, why, and for what reasons programs are held accountable and, just as importantly, the authority by which they claim and seek to maintain that control.

Romzek (2000) suggests that the source of authority regarding the expectations of accountability schemes in the public sector ranges along a continuum—from internal to external—to those occupational groups being held accountable. Other scholars have also zeroed in on the internal-external distinction in accountability for K–12 or higher education (e.g., Carnoy et al., 2003; Fullan, Rincon-Gallardo, & Hargreaves, 2015; Trow, 1996). With teacher education, however, the internal-external issue is especially tricky. It is certainly possible to conceptualize the source of authority regarding accountability expectations for teacher education along a continuum from internal to external. But the question—internal or external to what?—matters a great deal. This could mean internal or external to the programs, institutions, and individuals who are the actual targets of accountability, which is what the K–12 and higher education scholars cited above were talking about. However, with teacher education, this could also mean internal or external to "the profession" of teacher education.

By way of illustration, many people would agree that although they are very different from one another, *both* the 2016 HEA/Title II reporting requirements for teacher education institutions and states (Office of the *Federal Register*, 2016) *and* the NCTQ "Teacher Prep Reviews," (Greenberg et al., 2013), which began grading teacher education programs across the nation in 2013, are external accountability schemes. (These initiatives are elaborated on in Chapters 4 and 6, respectively.) That is, even though the former is a federal initiative, while the latter is the project of a private advocacy organization with no regulatory standing in teacher education, both of these accountability initiatives were developed externally to teacher education institutions and programs and with minimal participation from the groups they sought to control. In contrast, consider CAEP's accreditation standards (discussed in Chapter 5) and the use of edTPA by institutions or states as a teacher certification requirement (described in Chapter 7). Some members of the teacher education community consider both CAEP's accreditation standards and the adoption of edTPA by institutions or states as accountability initiatives that were created "by and for" the profession, and thus they see these initiatives as internal to the profession. However, some other members of the teacher education community think of these two accountability initiatives as external because they are inconsistent with local institutional/program values, they were developed without local participation, and evaluations are made by those external to the local context. We elaborate on these issues in Chapter 8, where we look across the four policy initiatives. Our point here is that there are major—and not easily resolvable—questions about who or what constitutes the teacher education profession, who speaks for the profession, and how local control and internal control are related conceptually and practically. These issues can't be dealt with by conceptualizing the control dimension of accountability as a matter simply of internal or external source of accountability expectations for teacher education. Rather, these have to be considered along with issues related to content and consequences.

Like issues related to control, the content dimension of teacher education accountability policies and initiatives is contentious. As noted, this dimension has to do with what an accountability policy holds teacher education accountable for, as well as what counts as evidence that it is being accountable for those things. In describing public-sector accountability in Western democracies, Romzek (2000) treated content in terms of what she called accountability "orientations," including inputs (i.e., resources and resource management), processes (i.e., appropriate procedures), outputs (i.e., quantity and quality of services), and outcomes (i.e., quantity and quality of results). She identified a major shift in the private sector since the 1980s toward outcomes-based accountability, which, as we have shown, is also reflected in K–12 and teacher education accountability in the United States.

The content dimension gives us a lens for considering the inputs, processes, outputs, and/or outcomes stipulated by an initiative as well as the measurement tools deemed appropriate for assessing those things. Many of the most acrimonious debates about teacher education accountability over the last two decades have had to do with the content dimension. In particular, there have been major disagreements about whether the content of teacher education accountability should be defined primarily in terms of outcomes, especially teacher education programs' impact and program graduates' "effectiveness" at boosting test scores. At the same time, there have been enormous controversies about whether value-added or related statistical measures of program graduates' effectiveness based on their students' test scores are appropriate and valid means for measuring this outcome.

The content dimension also gives us a way to consider what is omitted or marginalized in accountability policies. For example, with a given accountability initiative, we need to ask whether teacher education programs and graduates are accountable only for their impact on students' academic achievement, or whether they are also responsible for students' social, emotional, civic, critical, and democratic learning? Is the impact of programs measured only through graduates' impact, or are there also measures of teachers' practices, beliefs and expectations, ethics, moral values, ability to make judgments, and perspectives on justice and equity? It is important to ascertain what content has been emphasized and what has been left out during teacher education's accountability era.

As we noted above, the consequences dimension has to do with the intended—and unintended—results, effects, and implications of an accountability policy or initiative for the institutions, programs/pathways, and individuals that are the targets and implementers of the policy, and also for the broader enterprise of teacher preparation. Some teacher education accountability initiatives, such as statewide teacher tests or performance assessments, actually hold teacher candidates accountable, given that the consequence of the policy is the granting or denial of teacher certification or licensure to individual candidates. Many of today's accountability initiatives, however, hold teacher educators and their programs and institutions directly accountable. Here the intended consequences are far-reaching—the granting of state program approval (with or without qualification), the granting of national professional accreditation (with or without qualification), the approval or denial of an institution's right to distribute federal grant money to prospective teacher candidates, and/or widely disseminated consumer information and public acclaim or discredit regarding program "quality."

As important as intended consequences are the unintended consequences of accountability policies and initiatives. For example, some approaches to educational accountability diminish trust among stakeholders and/or erode a sense of shared responsibility for the quality of the work being done (Crooks, 2003). This reflects the culprit-savior dilemma in teaching/teacher education reform (Cochran-Smith, 2005). That is, teachers and teacher educators are regarded as both the major problem that has to be solved in order to improve effectiveness but also as the problem's most likely solution. Years ago, Elmore and McLaughlin (1988) offered an insightful point along these lines: "The use of policy as an implement of reform grows out of a fundamental distrust of professional judgment. But the dilemma that accompanies this use of policy is that the fate of reforms ultimately depends on those who are the object of distrust" (p. 34).

In addition to the unintended consequences mentioned above, there have been major concerns that particular teacher education accountability initiatives and policies narrow the teacher preparation curriculum. The concern is that in order to ensure program and candidate success, the curriculum is revised over time so that it concentrates primarily on those aspects of teacher performance that are assessed by the measurement tools that accompany the initiative. The concern is that this ignores other important aspects related to teaching students to think critically, preparation for democratic participation, social justice, and equality. Along similar lines, policies that assess teacher effectiveness in terms of students' achievement or student growth may discourage teacher education graduates from taking jobs in high-need and/or low-income areas where historically students have had less support and opportunity to succeed on tests of academic achievement. Likewise, policies that zero in on teacher candidates' academic credentials, like grade point averages or scores on national college aptitude tests, may reduce the number of teacher candidates of color.

In this chapter we have presented a comprehensive framework for teacher education: the eight dimensions of accountability. This consists of eight interrelated dimensions for making sense of teacher education's complex and messy accountability context. We have made two arguments about this framework. First, we've shown that it is necessary to consider all eight dimensions and their relationships to one another in order to gain a full understanding of the import and implications of a given initiative. Second, we've suggested that any teacher education accountability initiative or policy can be unpacked using this framework.

In the next parts of this book, we use the eight dimensions of accountability framework in two ways. Chapters 4, 5, 6, and 7 each take up one major national-level teacher education accountability initiative or policy that is widely disseminated, impactful, and controversial. One of the analyses we offer in each chapter involves using the dimensions framework to provide an eight-dimensional analysis of the initiative by deconstructing its major elements. Applying the dimensions framework allows us to produce a systematic and critical analysis of the values and cultural meanings implicit in the initiative, its underlying language and logic, how it constructs teacher education as a problem with a preferred solution, and the general theory of change behind the initiative. For each initiative, we explicitly identify the power relationships—and jurisdictional disputes—that are explicit and implicit, including new and old policy actors and policy "influencers" (Cochran-Smith & Fries, 2011b), such as education reform advocacy organizations, corporations, and foundations that provide extensive financial and other forms of support.

The second way we use the eight dimensions framework is to guide a cross-case analysis of the four accountability initiatives discussed in Chapters

4 through 7. The cross-case analysis appears in Chapter 8. Informed by the eight dimensions, we argue that an "accountability paradigm" has emerged over the last 20 to 30 years and is now dominant in this country despite the fact that the current times are mightily uncertain for education policy and politics. We suggest that the major teacher education accountability reforms that emerged from this paradigm have reshaped teacher education's goals and expectations in what we think are subtractive ways. To a certain extent, they have redefined how teacher educators understand their roles by placing great emphasis on test-based accountability and reducing the spaces for discussion and advocacy related to equity and social justice. This is similar to the way K–12 testing has reshaped the work of teachers and school leaders, in many places reducing their work to raising test scores and undermining the importance of preparation for participation in a democratic society wherein there are deep divides and sharply differing viewpoints.

Part II

THE PROBLEM WITH ACCOUNTABILITY:
Four Cases

CHAPTER 4

Tug of War

Federally Mandated Reporting Requirements for Teacher Education

In the United States, regulation and oversight of teacher education have been the object of a tug of war between the federal government and the states for some time (Bales, 2006). During the era of accountability, teacher education came under increasingly intense federal scrutiny, and the USDOE created new mechanisms to hold both states and teacher preparation institutions accountable for program impact and graduates' effectiveness. As we noted in Chapter 2, in 1998 the Higher Education Act (HEA), which is the major federal legislation that governs and provides student funding for higher education programs, included new Title II reporting regulations for states and teacher education providers. These regulations, often referred to simply as "Title II," required states to assess the quality of teacher preparation programs on an annual basis and report to the USDOE (Earley, 2002). We have suggested that this marked the starting point of the accountability era in teacher education.

In 2016, following highly politicized debate, the Obama administration released the final version of its new Title II teacher preparation reporting regulations, entitled *Teacher Preparation Issues* (Office of the *Federal Register*, 2016). These regulations established a federally mandated, state-enforced data system designed to measure teacher education quality by requiring significant and controversial new methods of scoring, ranking, and funding teacher preparation programs. The first draft of these regulations, proposed in 2014, prompted an unprecedented number of highly polarized responses from teacher educators, professional organizations, and education researchers. Concerns ranged from the regulations' concepts of equity to their underlying theory of change and how they would be implemented. The majority of the critiques, however, had to do with controversies about who should have jurisdiction over teacher education accountability. In particular, those who wanted to curtail the federal role in teacher education charged that the new regulations overstepped the boundaries between federal and state jurisdiction and undermined the autonomy of teacher preparation programs and institutions. In response to many highly publicized concerns, the final version of the Title II reporting requirements reflected somewhat more authority and flexibility for states regarding how to measure and weigh the results of the evidence regarding program performance. However, many of the major requirements that had appeared in early versions of the regulations remained in place in the final version approved in 2016.

In this chapter we suggest that the unexpected outcome of the 2016 presidential election transformed the Obama-era Title II regulations into a moving target for both states and teacher education programs. Many stakeholders were caught off guard when the Trump administration abruptly rescinded the regulations after only two months in office without offering an alternative, and there was a great deal of uncertainty about what states and institutions would be required to do. As this book went to press, a proposal for the overdue reauthorization of HEA, titled the "Promoting Real Opportunity, Success, and Prosperity Through Education Reform" Act (H.R. 4508, [PROSPER, 2015]) was introduced by the bipartisan congressional Committee on Education and the Workforce. If approved as proposed, PROSPER would completely repeal HEA's Title II, which would not only mean major changes in how teacher education is regulated, but would also end funding for Teacher Quality Partnership grants, TEACH grants, and teacher loan forgiveness (AACTE, 2018). We return to PROSPER at the conclusion of this chapter.

Using the eight dimensions of accountability framework, this chapter deconstructs the highly controversial Title II teacher preparation regulations approved in 2016, unpacks USDOE claims and evidence about how to boost teacher education quality, and considers the impact of the federal grip on teacher education, which steadily increased during the era of accountability, even though it now may be undone. While a certain degree of federal regulation of states and teacher preparation programs is inevitable, given the structure of federal funding for teacher candidates, we argue in this chapter that the 2016 Title II teacher education reporting requirements prompted resistance and opposition in part because they represented an extreme effort to control teacher education externally.

This chapter also shows that there is little evidence that externally incentivized, outcomes-based accountability mechanisms like those stipulated by the 2016 Title II regulations result in positive outcomes for students or in the strengthening of the profession. Furthermore, our analysis reveals that the 2016 Title II regulations—even though now rescinded—had an important impact on the field and left many lingering concerns about the complex consequences of external control of the profession and its negative impact on equity and democratic values in education. The chapter shows that the USDOE has the capacity to have a significant influence on the way public discussions about accountability are framed and on the public's conceptions of teacher quality and teacher education quality.

CONTEXT: FEDERAL INVOLVEMENT IN TEACHER EDUCATION

In 2014 the Obama administration proposed a new version of the Title II teacher preparation regulations included in the HEA. The reform context in which the new teacher preparation regulations were debated was similar in some ways to the context preceding the 1998 HEA reauthorization, when concerns about teacher quality were also central (Earley, 2002). The 1998 Title II reporting regulations were intended to help recruit highly qualified persons into teaching, hold institutions of higher education accountable for preparing skilled teachers, improve the quality of teacher preparation and professional development, and boost student achievement. These regulations cemented into policy the idea that teacher education accountability was part of the federal purview regarding education. The 2016 Title II regulations were very similar in goals and intentions to the 1998 Title II regulations, but the new regulations extended the federal reach into education and stipulated highly controversial methods of measuring the impact of teacher preparation programs and graduates. These new regulations, approved by the Obama administration in 2016 but rescinded by the Trump administration just a few months later, are a dramatic illustration that the tug of war between states and federal oversight is ongoing.

The History of Authority and Power Under HEA

While the 2016 Title II reporting regulations triggered an avalanche of critique, their origin can be traced to a much earlier time in the history of federal legislation regarding education. Since the post–World War II era, the quality of the nation's education system has been linked to the nation's economic health, and accountability has shifted from a focus on resources and inputs to a focus on outcomes.

In 1964, then President Johnson declared "unconditional war on poverty in America" (Johnson, 1964, p. 212), which was related to the signing of the ESEA in 1965. This was the same year that the HEA was signed, providing, among other things, federal financial aid to low-income students to attend postsecondary institutions (Cohen-Vogel, 2005). At the point of their origins, both the ESEA and the HEA were part of a strategic network of policies instituted to eradicate the origins and ramifications of poverty in America by not only offering "better schools" but also "better health, and better homes, and better training, and better job opportunities" (Johnson, 1964, p. 212). HEA has been reauthorized eight times since its establishment in 1965. Unfortunately, however, the idea that multiple social policies would need to be implemented simultaneously in order to eradicate poverty was abandoned soon after that time. This was replaced by a new policy approach that zeroed in on educational policies rather than broader social policies related to health, housing, transportation, and jobs. The new assumption was that public education itself could "ameliorate economic distress" (Kantor & Lowe, 2013, p. 25).

Over time, issues of economic inequality and injustice were framed as education problems, in particular as problems related to teacher quality. Despite concerns about teacher quality, after the Education Professions Development Act (1967), which aimed to decrease teacher shortages and improve teaching, it is not far-fetched to say that federal policy more or less neglected teacher education until the 1990s (Cohen-Vogel, 2005). As we argued in Chapter 2, the 1998 reauthorization of the HEA with its new Title II reporting regulations regarding teacher quality was precipitated by a discourse that emerged with *A Nation at Risk* in 1983, blaming teachers and schools for presumed threats to the nation's economy and its ability to thrive (Earley, 2000; Mehta, 2013).The 1998 reauthorization of the HEA included contested reporting requirements for teacher preparation programs, influenced in part by both the National Commission on Teaching & America's Future (NCTAF) and by congressional leaders. The critiques were many, including the charges that: the quality of teacher education programs was grossly uneven across institutions and programs, teachers were not well prepared in the subject areas, preparation standards were not consistent with certification and licensure requirements, and there was a disconnect between teacher preparation and K–12 education (Earley, 2000; NCTAF, 1996). Under the 1998 HEA reauthorization, "all states and colleges or universities that directly or indirectly receive any federal dollars through the HEA [had to] provide the secretary of education with data on teacher preparation standards and licensure procedures" (Earley, 2000, p. 34). These data included information about numerous inputs, such as how many students were in each teacher preparation program, what the faculty-to-student ratios were, the average number of hours of supervised practice teaching required by programs, and whether the state had accredited each program or deemed it low-performing. These new reporting requirements marked an increasingly stringent federal approach to accountability in teacher education that only intensified in the years that followed.

Reflecting the assumptions implicit in the new regulations, teachers and teacher educators were perceived as the primary culprits in the alleged failure of America's schools to produce a competitive workforce, and they were the targets of many educational reforms, especially NCLB in 2001 and RTTT in 2009, both of which included important provisions regarding teacher quality and teacher preparation. In 2011, thirteen years after Title II reporting regulations were first required, the USDOE released *Our Future, Our Teachers*, a report that outlined the Obama administration's initial plan to improve teacher quality and teacher education under the broad umbrella of economic recovery. This plan represented a shift from the 1998 Title II reporting requirements, which focused on program inputs. Instead the 2011 plan called for "meaningful data" about outcomes, with "meaningful" defined in terms of program effectiveness and graduates' impact on students' achievement (USDOE, 2011). This plan also called for the collection of data in the areas of student growth outcomes, teacher placement and retention, and teacher candidate and principal surveys to ascertain perceptions of program success and classify programs that fell short as "low-performing" (USDOE, 2011). The Obama administration's plan aimed to revise the federally funded Teacher Education Assistance for College and Higher Education (TEACH) program, renaming it the "Presidential Teaching Fellows" program and allocating funds only to "the best programs for the best students with a priority on those with financial need" (USDOE, 2011, p. 11). Although the administration's 2011 plan never became policy, it formed the basis of most of the Title II regulations proposed in 2014 and finalized in 2016.

The Basics of HEA/Title II:
The Pursuit of "Meaningful" Data and Effective Incentives

In December 2014, the USDOE proposed a new version of HEA/Title II federal reporting requirements for states and teacher preparation programs. The argument was that previous requirements had failed to determine the effectiveness of programs because indicators were defined by each state and were not "meaningful" in that they did not measure program and graduate impact (Office of the *Federal Register*, 2014). The proposed regulations were intended to change significantly the way teacher education programs were annually evaluated and ranked by states. Also, for the first time, the results of these evaluations were to be tied to federal funding.

The proposed regulations required that states score all teacher preparation programs based on each program's performance according to a set of outcome measures for teacher quality designated by the federal government (Office of the *Federal Register*, 2014, 2016). The outcomes included the highly controversial use of value-added measures, which linked students' test scores to teacher performance and linked teacher performance to teacher preparation programs. The regulations also called for the use of surveys of teacher education programs' "consumers" (i.e., teacher candidates and teachers) and of their potential employers (i.e., the school administrators who hired them). In addition, the regulations concentrated on whether institutions recruited teacher candidates with high-level GPAs and competitive academic standing according to scores on national tests of the college-going population. The idea with the regulations was that teacher preparation programs would be scored at the state level according to the above criteria, and then would be ranked relative to one another using state-selected cutoff scores for classifying programs as "exceptional," "effective," "at-risk," or "low-performing." Last, the proposed regulations stipulated that programs that were consistently classified as "low-performing" would become ineligible to offer federally funded grants to prospective teachers and would face closure by their states if they continued to fail to show gains.

In the two years that followed the 2014 release of the proposed Title II revisions, the USDOE solicited public feedback and commentary, made some revisions in response to a huge outpouring of public comments, and approved the final version of the regulations in 2016 (Office of the *Federal Register*, 2016). The approved regulations were released by the Secretary of Education during the last few months of the Obama administration in October 2016 and then, as we noted above, they were revoked just a few months later under the Trump administration. The regulations were highly controversial, as this chapter reveals. We also show that the evidence does not support the claim that this accountability approach is an effective mechanism for change.

2016 HEA/TITLE II REPORTING REGULATIONS: AN EIGHT-DIMENSIONAL ANALYSIS

In this section, we unpack the 2016 HEA/Title II regulations using our eight dimensions of accountability framework to dig deeper into this purportedly "commonsensical" yet highly controversial initiative (see Figure 4.1). We take up each of the framework's dimensions and thematic clusters below.

Foundations of Accountability

Next we consider each of the three dimensions that are part of the "foundations" cluster. As noted in the previous chapter, the values dimension has to do with an accountability initiative's implicit or explicit ideas, ideals, beliefs, and principles about the roles of teaching, schooling, and teacher education in the larger society. We show below that the ideology behind the 2016 Title II regulations reflects the values inherent in global capitalism and neoliberalism that dominated this era of educational reform (Taubman, 2009).

The values orientation of the 2016 Title II regulations is explicitly stated in the language of the policy and similarly reflected in its rhetoric. Policy documents explain that there is a "need for regulatory action" regarding teacher education quality because "recent international assessments . . . have revealed that the United States is significantly behind other countries in preparing students to compete in the global economy" (Office of the *Federal Register*, 2014, p. 71850). The language of the regulations reflects concern about the standing of the United States in the global economy as well as the USDOE position that regulating teacher education would help to solve the problem. Repeated statements like the one quoted above helped to solidify the idea that the value of teacher education rests in its ability to produce

Figure 4.1. Dimensions of Accountability: USDOE

Thematic Cluster	Dimension	2016 HEA/Title II: Reporting Regulations
Foundations of Accountability	Values	• Securing the United States's standing in a globally competitive, knowledge-based economy
	Purpose	• Identifying teacher preparation programs as high- and low-performing • Dispensing awards and punishments
	Concepts	• Student learning as equivalent to, and adequately measured by, students' test scores • Teacher and teacher preparation quality as equivalent to the results of value-added or similar statistical procedures
The Problem of Teacher Education	Diagnostic	• Teacher preparation programs fail to prepare teachers who boost students' test scores and thus make the United States less able to compete globally • Preparation programs fail because programs and states lack sophisticated data systems that provide meaningful feedback about program quality
	Prognostic	• Data systems that identify high- and low-performing programs can be established by linking student test scores to teacher performance and linking teacher performance to teacher preparation programs • These data systems will provide a continuous feedback loop that bolsters high-quality programs and identifies low-quality programs for remediation or closure
Power Relationships in Accountability	Control	• Federally mandated policies, enforced by state departments and agencies • External to programs and the profession
	Content	• Programs and states held accountable for preparing teachers who boost students' test scores satisfy employers and students, and stay in the profession • Evidence for accountability is multiple, quantifiable outcomes
	Consequences	• Distribution of federal TEACH funds granted or denied based on program performance • Program praise/closure as the result of successive high/low evaluations on mandated outcome measures • Narrow conceptions of teacher quality/teacher preparation promoted • System based on mistrust of the profession prompts low morale and lack of motivation among teacher educators

teachers who can prepare students for a globally competitive market, and frame teacher education quality as a matter of national economic security (Cochran-Smith, Baker, et al., 2017).

The many policy documents and tools used to support the 2016 Title II regulations also link concerns about global competition with concerns around equality. For example, the Obama administration's publication *Our Future, Our Teachers* outlined the USDOE's mission to "promote student achievement and preparation for global competitiveness by fostering educational excellence and ensuring equal access" (USDOE, 2011, p. 1). This connection between teacher education quality and equality for students is echoed in the rhetoric used to promote the Title II regulations. In 2015, Secretary of Education Arne Duncan explained that "few issues in education are more important than ensuring equitable access to high-quality teachers . . . access to great teachers makes a big difference for all students, and even more so for students facing the challenges of concentrated poverty and racial isolation" (USDOE, 2015, p. 1). This statement and many others like it suggest that equitable access to teachers who know how to prepare students to compete in a global economy will counter the impact of economic and racial injustice.

Documents and public discourse advocating the 2016 Title II regulations indicate that the value placed on economic security is tightly related to the value placed on equity. As we've noted, equity can be framed in significantly different ways across policy discussions (Stone, 2011). In the case of the Title II regulations, equity meant all students having equal access to high-quality teachers, which was assumed to mean that students would then have equal opportunities for educational success. Even though the language of the Title II regulations acknowledged poverty and racial isolation, as the quotation above makes clear, the assumption was that these problems could be resolved by ensuring equal access to quality teachers. Furthermore, the discourse surrounding the new Title II requirements presumes that the nation could develop a globally competitive workforce and minimize the impact of inequality without addressing the systems and root causes that perpetuate poverty and injustice.

The "thin equity" perspective underlying the 2016 Title II regulations is considerably different from the kind of equity President Johnson was promoting when HEA first became law in 1965. As noted above, the original HEA was instituted as part of a set of social policies related to jobs, housing, health care, and education to address the *roots of inequity,* with the understanding this would alleviate the impact of poverty and therefore lead to the nation's prosperity. In the 2016 Title II regulations the logic is very different—even reversed. The regulations were intended to achieve a globally competitive workforce through the mechanism of an accountability system that would produce better teachers and schools *in spite of* inequity's deep roots, thus masking the impact of poverty and the causes of inequity.

The contrast in values between the first HEA and the regulations proposed in 2016 also relates to the purpose dimension of accountability, which has to do with an accountability policy's stated aims and objectives in terms of what it explicitly intends to accomplish. Again, the purpose of the 2016 Title II regulations stands in stark contrast to the purpose the Johnson administration initially upheld. With the 2016 regulations, teacher education is framed as a means to restore the nation's global preeminence through enhanced student achievement. This means that there must be effective teacher education programs that produce effective teachers who can boost student achievement as measured by standardized tests. To accomplish this, the USDOE aimed to reward teacher preparation programs they identified as highly rated and punish programs they identified as underperforming. Underperforming programs would lose federal funding and could eventually face closure by the state. These values and purposes promoted by the 2016 Title II regulations closely align with the definitions of teaching and learning (concepts dimension) that the initiative promoted, which we discuss below.

In terms of the concepts dimension of accountability, the 2016 Title II regulations were based on the assumption that school students' low standardized test scores were the result of low-level teacher quality, which was in turn the result of low-level teacher education quality. The regulations narrowed the concept of student learning to what could be captured by standardized test scores and used for state, national, and international comparisons. This helped to establish a commonsense rationale for improving teacher education by linking a very narrow conception of student learning to an equally narrow view of teacher quality and teacher education quality, all measured primarily by value-added or similar statistical procedures.

The use of standardized test scores to represent student learning, value-added assessments to represent teacher quality, and a series of state data systems to link these outcomes to teacher education quality reflects the values underlying the proposed 2016 Title II regulations. The foundation of the proposed regulations is a relatively simplistic chain of causal relationships: boost teacher education quality, which will boost teacher quality, which will boost students' achievement, which will boost the nation's economy. Beneath this chain of reasoning are the assumptions that equity means access for all students to the same things and that equity will be achieved when all students have the same access to highly effective teachers—that is, teachers who can increase students' performance on standardized tests.

The Problem of Teacher Education

The second thematic cluster in our eight dimensions of accountability framework is what we call "the problem of teacher education," which has to do with how the discourse promoting a given accountability initiative frames teacher education as a problem to be addressed through policy. This includes assumptions about who is considered to be blame- or praiseworthy, what kind of a problem teacher education is, and what the preferred solution to the problem is. This cluster has two closely related dimensions, the diagnostic dimension and the prognostic dimension.

In keeping with its neoliberal values and its reflection of ideas from human capital theory, the discourse promoting the 2016 Title II regulations diagnosed the problem of teacher education as U.S. students' low achievement on international and national standardized tests, which constituted a problem of national economic security. Along these lines, the proposed regulations explicitly stated:

> The United States is significantly behind other countries in preparing students to compete in the global economy. Although many factors influence student achievement, a large body of research has used value added analysis to demonstrate that teacher quality is the largest in-school factor affecting student achievement. (Office of the *Federal Register*, 2014, p. 71850)

As this statement shows, students' low achievement was linked to concerns about the nation's ability to produce a workforce that would maintain the nation's competitive ranking in a global, knowledge-based economy. This problem was further framed in terms of the causal logic we talked about above. USDOE documents promoting the new regulations argued that too many U.S. students' scores fall below those of their global counterparts because too many teachers are ill-prepared, especially teachers in schools with large concentrations of marginalized student populations. Furthermore, the USDOE argument is that teachers are ill-prepared because states fail to use complex data systems that link student test scores to teacher performance and link teacher performance back to teacher preparation programs. With this logic, the USDOE's mistrust of teachers' and teacher preparation programs' ability to prepare students who can compete in the global economy justifies the need for more sophisticated state data systems about teacher and teacher preparation quality.

Framing the problem of teacher education in terms of a simplistic and more or less linear relationship from students' test scores to national economic security provided a platform for the USDOE to propose its solution to the problem. As we have said, the prognostic dimension of accountability has to do with how the discourse promoting an accountability policy constructs the solution to the perceived problem. The language supporting the proposed USDOE regulations indicates that the economic security of the nation is seriously at risk because of the lack of complex data systems linking student performance to teacher performance and teacher performance to teacher preparation programs. Therefore, the logical solution to this problem is the development and implementation of sophisticated outcomes-oriented data systems in every state, which previous versions of the Title II regulations lacked.

According to the USDOE, the 1998 Title II reporting requirements for teacher preparation programs had not succeeded at controlling teacher education and boosting teacher quality. The charge was that although Section 205 of the HEA/Title II required states to report on the criteria they used to assess "whether teacher preparation programs [we]re low-performing or at-risk of being low-performing . . . it [was] difficult to identify programs in need of remediation or closure because few of the reporting requirements ask[ed] for information indicative of program quality" (Office of the *Federal Register*, 2014, p. 71820). Along these lines, the USDOE drew sharp attention to the fact that in the prior 12 years, 27 states had not identified even one teacher preparation program as "low-performing" (Office of the *Federal Register*, 2014). Furthermore, states required programs to report on more than 600 indicators every year without focusing on program effectiveness linking programs, teachers, and student scores (Office of the *Federal Register*, 2014). According to the USDOE, these excessive but irrelevant data prevented states from properly assessing teacher education quality and identifying low-performing programs. As a consequence, the public had no way of knowing how effective teacher education programs and teachers were. With this line of logic about the flaws and failures of the existing Title II reporting requirements, the proposed 2016 regulations were supposed to "fix" the problem of teacher education with new sophisticated state data systems linking teachers, students, and teacher preparation programs. The idea was that new data systems would remedy the problems of inefficiency and ineffectiveness caused by the lack of meaningful and systematic data.

In other words, the problem of teacher education that was diagnosed and constructed in the policy discourse supporting the 2016 Title II regulations was perfectly aligned with the solution that was offered—bigger, more sophisticated, outcomes-based data systems that could be used as the basis for meting out program incentives and punishments. As we have noted, this approach reflected the larger shift in accountability—away from a primary focus on inputs and toward "auditable" (or measurable) outcomes (Ambrosio, 2013). In short, the 2016 Title II prognosis was that fixing teacher education required the construction of data systems that linked student achievement data to teacher data to preparation program data, thus creating a "feedback loop" (Office of the *Federal Register*, 2014) to facilitate program improvement. The proposed regulations pointed out that "the final regulations address shortcomings in the current system . . . including more meaningful indicators of program inputs and program outcomes, such as the ability of the program's graduates to produce gains in student learning" (Office of the *Federal Register*, 2014, p. 5). These data systems were expected to function as a solution because they held programs accountable for outcomes that had previously been ignored.

Power Relationships in Accountability

As we noted in Chapter 3, the power cluster of dimensions gets at the politics of accountability, including who stipulates accountability expectations and evidence, whom they affect, and what the implications are for both the direct targets of the initiative and the broader enterprise of teacher preparation. Power and control issues are arguably the most critical and controversial features of the 2016 Title II regulations and are critical to understanding the trajectory of the regulations. Because the regulations were intended to be enforced by the states but controlled by the federal government, they would have reduced states' and institutions' autonomy to define and evaluate teacher preparation quality. Many teacher educators and professional and activist organizations argued that the regulations constituted federal overreach beyond the USDOE's jurisdiction. For example, the National Association for Equal Opportunity in Higher Education (NAFEO, 2015) asserted:

> The proposed regulations are overly broad and would result in a substantial expansion of federal authority into matters heretofore reserved to states and institutions . . . The approach of the Department is curious in some regards because it is so broad and intrusive that it may be deemed to be "executive overreach" by inviting political (departmental) oversight of scholarly and educational work and thus, be deemed violative of Academic Freedom. (p. 1)

As a teacher education accountability initiative, the 2016 Title II regulations established control external to teacher education programs and institutions, and they used federal funding to force compliance. Participation was not optional for states or teacher preparation programs. Rather the regulations were unavoidable and inescapable—until they were suddenly rescinded in 2017. Interestingly, when Congress and Trump rescinded these regulations, restoration of states' rights was one of the stated rationales for the action. But in an interesting twist, this swift and unexpected political turn also emphasized the impact of federal control in teacher education accountability by showing just how easily expectations and mandates regarding preparation programs could be changed without consulting states or teacher educators. The rescinding of the 2016 Title II regulations altered in one fell swoop what teacher educators were to be held accountable for by reverting to the Title II regulations that were already in place, but the change also made it undeniably evident that the USDOE had strong control over who was accountable for what.

The content dimension in our accountability framework has to do with what teacher education is accountable for and what counts as evidence. The content of the final approved 2016 Title II regulations varied somewhat from the content of both the first version of the regulations released in 2014 and the revised 2015 version. The 2014 proposal explicitly named value-added assessments as the main evaluation tool to be used by programs and states to provide evidence of student learning, which was the chief indicator of programs' and graduates' effectiveness. In contrast, revisions to the regulations called for a multiple measures approach to providing evidence of student learning. According to those revisions, in addition to the scores of graduates' eventual students on standardized tests, institutions would be required to include at least one additional measure of teachers' impact on student learning. Additional measures could include student work and/ or information about student learning goals and growth, and they could be teacher-generated, reported by parents, or students' perceptions of their own learning and their teachers' support, among other options.

Another difference between the 2014 and 2016 versions of the regulations had to do with the criteria to be used by states to rank teacher preparation programs. The 2014 proposed regulations stipulated four categories to classify programs based on impact data. In contrast, the final regulations stated:

> Several commenters objected to the Department's proposal to establish four performance levels for States' assessment . . . These commenters stated that these provisions of the HEA give to the States the authority to determine whether to establish more than three performance levels. . . . We have revised SS 612.4(b) (1) to remove the requirement for States to rate their teacher preparation programs using the category "exceptional" [the fourth category]. (Office of the *Federal Register*, 2016, p. 75497)

These changes were in part a response to criticisms from teacher educators and educational organizations during the proposal rule-making processes. While this shift may indicate some nuance in the power relationships in play, it is important to note that the USDOE remained firmly in control as the entity that ultimately decided the content of accountability.

The 2016 Title II regulations were designed to have significant consequences for teacher preparation programs. The regulations proposed a system of rewards and punishments based on program rankings that relied on the performance-level classifications note above. The logic here was that highly ranked programs would be rewarded with the opportunity to distribute federal TEACH grants and by the positive publicity of public rankings. In contrast, poorly ranked programs would be required to

> immediately notify each student who is enrolled in or accepted into [the program] . . . and who receives title IV, HEA program funds that the institution is no longer eligible to provide such funding . . . and disclose on its web site and in promotional materials that . . . the teacher preparation program has been identified as low-performing. (Office of the *Federal Register*, 2014, p. 71842)

The logic behind this public shame approach was that this would motivate programs to improve or ultimately face the threat of closure.

In his review of the proposed regulations, Kumashiro (2015) pointed out that above all else, they were a federally mandated but state-enforced accountability initiative. Kumashiro's description emphasizes the tug of war between federal and state jurisdiction regarding teacher education and teacher quality that lay just beneath the surface of the proposed regulations. In the next section, we examine the evidence that does/does not support the claims made by advocates of the new HEA/Title II regulatory system about its viability as a mechanism for change in teacher education.

2016 HEA/TITLE II REPORTING REGULATIONS: THEORY OF CHANGE AND THE RELATED EVIDENCE

In this section, we offer two kinds of analysis. First we identify the central stated or implied claims about how the federal Title II regulations would presumably work as a mechanism to bring about improvement in the quality of teacher education programs. This has to do with the logic underlying the policy or the theory of change behind the regulations and the accountability system that they would have put into place. The second part of the analysis has to do with the validity of the Title II regulations as a policy instrument—that is, whether or not there is evidence that the regulations actually had the capacity to meet their stated aims.

The first claim underlying the 2016 Title II regulations is that an accountability system controlled by the federal government but implemented by the states is an effective strategy for improving teacher education and teacher quality. Interestingly, this claim mirrors the accountability rationale established by the 1998 Title II reporting requirements. However, after almost 20 years of implementing those original Title II requirements, the USDOE itself identified the lack of efficiency and effectiveness inherent in their design and used this assertion to promote stricter and fewer outcomes-based requirements in the proposed regulations. "The Department's existing Title II reporting system framework has not, however, ensured sufficient quality feedback to various stakeholders on program performance . . . struggling teacher preparation programs may not receive the technical assistance they need" (Office of the *Federal Register*, 2016, p. 75494). The USDOE also pointed out that more than 50% of states perceived the Title II requirements as not useful for assessing their teacher preparation programs (United States Government Accountability Office, 2015).

The 2016 Title II regulations were intended to overcome previous shortcomings by using more powerful rewards and punishments as consequences for program performance. Incentives included positive publicity for high-ranking programs and authorization to distribute TEACH grants to prospective teachers. Sanctions included denial of the opportunity to distribute TEACH grants to prospective teachers and putting pressure on states to close persistently low-ranking programs. Clearly the proposed Title II regulations were not informed by the existing evidence based on implementation of NCLB, which indicated that high-stakes sanctions and rewards were an ineffective mechanism for improvement. In fact, tight federal accountability systems with high-stakes consequences for institutions have not proved to be effective in fostering improvement of teachers' practices or students' learning opportunities. Rather they have promoted superficial adjustments oriented at improving test scores (Supovitz, 2009).

The second accountability claim underlying the 2016 Title II regulations was that evaluating and classifying programs based on student learning outcomes would contribute to the improvement of teacher education programs. Although the final version of the proposed regulations allowed institutions and states to report multiple types of evidence, it was clear that the preferred evidence was graduates' impact on students' achievement as measured by standardized tests:

> Whether using student scores on State assessments, teacher evaluation ratings, or other measures of student growth, under the regulations States must link the student learning outcomes data back to the teacher, and then back to that teacher's preparation program. The costs to States to comply with this requirement will depend, in part, on the data and linkages in their statewide longitudinal data system. (Office of the *Federal Register*, 2016, p. 75594)

Highly recognized approaches linking teacher preparation programs with students' test scores via value-added assessments, such as the systems used in Louisiana and Tennessee, were lauded in the proposed Title II regulations as exemplary data systems for determining teacher preparation quality and improving programs (Office of the *Federal Register*, 2014). For example, the narrative in the final Title II regulations asserted that Louisiana's data system was able to identify programs in need of improvement and that those programs then changed their practices and improved their previous classifications within two years: "This is one example, but it suggests that States can use data on student learning outcomes for graduates of teacher preparation programs to help these programs identify weaknesses and implement needed reforms in a reasonable amount of time" (Office of the *Federal Register*, 2014, p. 71866).

However, there have been major critiques of the use of value-added measures, including the difficulties involved in isolating the effects of teacher preparation programs on graduates and, subsequently, on school students. Also, value-added measures have been criticized because of the small differences in graduates' impacts on student learning for programs rated as high versus programs rated as underperforming (Boyd, Grossman,

Lankford, Loeb, & Wyckoff, 2009; Chiang et al., 2011; Goldhaber, Liddle, & Theobald, 2013; Koedel, Parsons, Podgursky, & Ehlert, 2012; Mason, 2010). Along these lines, after evaluating Missouri teacher preparation programs based on Louisiana and Tennessee's methodology, for example, Koedel and collaborators concluded:

> The measureable differences in effectiveness across teachers from different preparation programs are very small. The overwhelming majority of the variation in teacher quality occurs within programs. We encourage policymakers to think carefully about our findings as achievement-based evaluation systems, and associated accountability consequences, are being developed for TPPs. (p. 22)

Scholars also criticized the great variability in the conclusions of studies using value-added measures of teachers' impact on students' learning based on variation in the multiple methodological decisions involved at different stages of estimation and interpretation of effects (Henry et al., 2012; Lincove, Osborne, Dillon, & Mills, 2014; Meyer, Piyatigorsky, & Rice, 2014; Mihaly, McCaffrey, Sass, & Lockwood, 2012). For these and other reasons, many scholars and scholarly organizations have cautioned that value-added assessments should not be used for high-stakes decisions about programs. The lack of reliability involved in efforts linking teacher preparation programs with school students' achievement casts great doubt on the potential effectiveness of the Title II regulations for identifying strong and weak programs and providing valuable information for their improvement (Cochran-Smith, Stern, et al., 2016).

The third claim related to the 2016 Title II regulations has to do with its underlying market logic—that is, the Title II reporting regulations assumed that teacher preparation programs would be driven to improve because prospective teachers, employers, and the public would make decisions based on program classifications (i.e., low-performing, at-risk, and effective). While the final version of the regulations minimized the importance of the state public rankings, it remained that a key goal of the regulations was to provide public information about program quality: "The availability of these data in State reports, which States and the Secretary would make available to the public, can help guide potential employers in their hiring decisions and prospective teachers in their application decisions" (Office of the *Federal Register*, 2014, p. 71831).

According to the USDOE, public information would drive consumers' decisions, and this pressure would foster program improvement or force programs to close due to low enrollment. Few studies have explored the connection between public information about rankings of teacher preparation programs, on one hand, and the decisions made by prospective teachers' or the school leaders who hire them, on the other, an issue we discuss further in Chapter 6. Additionally, there is little evidence that teacher preparation programs actually improve in response to potential consumers' decisions based on public information. Huang, Yi, and Haycock (2002) explain:

> Many institutions, even whole states, have 100% pass rates on teacher licensure tests. . . . However, pass rates on licensure tests can provide a misleading picture of quality. . . . Nearly half the states that require teacher candidates to pass basic skills tests actually require those tests for program entry and/or prior to completion. . . . In these states and institutions, then, those pass rates are automatically 100%. (p. 6)

As the example above indicates, in the past, when there was pressure to demonstrate positive outcomes on teacher tests according to the 1998 Title II reporting requirements, some programs did what skeptics referred to as "gaming the system." That is, they made passing scores on the state teacher test an admission requirement rather than an exit requirement. As a result, many teacher preparation programs did indeed report 100% pass rates on their state's teacher test, making the information meaningless for consumers' decisions. The evidence about gaming the system is limited— and cynical—but it raises reasonable doubt about the contribution of public reports on teacher preparation programs as a valuable tool for shaping both consumers' decisions and program improvement.

IMPACT AND IMPLICATIONS

We conclude this chapter with a discussion of the impact and implications of the 2016 Title II regulations. Even though these regulations were rescinded before they were actually put into effect, they have very real and far-reaching implications for preparation programs, institutions, and the broader enterprise of teacher education. As we have shown, the reporting regulations were designed to establish a federal system of control of teacher education programs and institutions based primarily on graduates' and programs' demonstrated outcomes, as defined and stipulated by the USDOE. This established new power relationships between the federal government and the states and new obligations for states and local programs. As we have argued, much of the opposition to the regulations had to do with issues of power and control—who had the authority to decide who was accountable to whom, for what, and for what purposes when it came to assessing and evaluating teacher education.

Implicit in the 2016 Title II regulations was the assumption that teachers and teacher education programs are both the cause of and the cure for not only the problem of national security, which depends on a competitive workforce, but also the problem of inequity. As we noted above, when HEA was originally established under President Johnson, it was part of a network of public education, health, and housing policies designed to address the impact of poverty and inequity in America with the aim of economic recovery (Johnson, 1964). Johnson considered it a federal responsibility to establish and implement policies to protect the well-being of the nation's citizens and called for a collaborative approach to alleviating poverty. Over the years, however, HEA was reconfigured as an accountability policy that targeted the quality of teacher preparation programs at colleges and universities, which was constructed as a major obstacle to equal educational access and opportunity for all students (Kumashiro, 2015). Instead of exercising federal authority to take up responsible action to dismantle the systems and structures that reproduce inequity in multiple facets of society, the USDOE used policies like the Title II regulations to establish blame and hold teacher education accountable for achieving broad education outcomes and for redressing inequities.

With the Title II reporting requirements approved in 2016, the USDOE extended its authority by allocating or denying funds to teacher preparation programs through forced compliance. However, when the Title II regulations were publicly released, Lamar Alexander, chairman of the Senate Education Committee, stated (U.S. Senate Committee on Health, Education, Labor & Pensions, 2016):

> Today's regulation appears to violate the Higher Education Act, which specifically says that states—not bureaucrats at a distant department in Washington—are responsible for evaluating whether a college's program gives teachers the skills they need for the classroom. The regulation also effectively mandates teacher evaluations and forces states to focus on students' test scores in a way that Congress explicitly rejected just months ago when we fixed No Child Left Behind and its unworkable National School Board approach. (p. 1)

This statement illustrates some of the many criticisms surrounding the 2016 Title II regulations and again reflects not only the tug of war between the federal government and the states, but also the range of viewpoints at the federal level specifically about imposing federal authority over teacher education and more or less bypassing state jurisdiction. Interestingly, criticisms about the overreach of the federal government came not only from Republicans, including Alexander, who historically had advocated for less government regulation, but also from teacher educators who wanted more institutional autonomy and more attention to local needs and goals.

The theory of change underlying the 2016 Title II reporting regulations was also controversial. The assumption behind the regulations was that a high-stakes accountability initiative with serious incentives and punishments would drive change and foster compliance with federal requirements. This theory of change was highly criticized by scholars, teacher educators, and activists who argued that punitive accountability principles were already known to be ineffective at producing substantive change. Along these lines, Lin Goodwin, the Vice President of the American Education Research Association for Division K (Teaching and Teacher Education) at the time issued a public statement:

> This punitive approach to reform will surely result in deform instead of reform. Fear of "the big stick" typically results in compliance versus transformation. Paradoxically then, the proposed rules provide an incentive for narrowly defined, superficial change, certainly not real or meaningful change. (Goodwin, 2015, p. 1)

By compelling teacher preparation programs to comply, the 2016 Title II regulations would have coerced teacher educators to work from premises many of them did not support, such as the idea that "the lack of student learning is solely the result of having an ineffective teacher" or that a novice teacher should be expected "to perform as effectively as a teacher with multiple years of accumulated wisdom" (Kumashiro, 2015, p. 6). Along these lines, the National Council of Teachers of English (NCTE) issued a statement about problems with the outcomes-based criteria for the allocation of TEACH grants:

> Until criteria for TEACH Grants come closer to the NCTE guidelines for candidate preparation that support comprehensive professional learning—including ample feedback to candidates and early-career practitioners from experienced and well-qualified local and regional educators—it seems unlikely that TEACH Grants will achieve their laudable purposes. (NCTE, 2014)

Other public feedback concerning the 2016 Title II regulations had to do with their underlying definition of the knowledge teachers need in order to teach well. According to the responses collected during the public comment period by the federal government, many people found the view of teacher knowledge implicit in the regulations very narrow, failing to include things like "a teacher's ability to factor students' cultural, linguistic, and experiential background into the design and implementation of productive learning experiences" (Office of the *Federal Register*, 2016, p. 75502). Along similar lines, the American Federation of Teachers (2016) also argued that "teacher prep programs need to help ensure that teachers are ready to engage their students in powerful learning and creating an environment that is conducive to learning. These regulations will not help achieve that goal" (p. 1). In response to critiques like these, the USDOE simply replied that their definition of teacher knowledge was "sufficiently broad to address, in general terms, the key areas of content and pedagogical knowledge that aspiring teachers should gain in their teacher preparation programs" (Office of the *Federal Register*, 2016, p. 75502), a response that did not address the root of the critiques.

As we have argued, embedded in the 2016 Title II regulations was a notion of equity that assumed that all students' equal access to quality teachers would mitigate school and societal inequalities and ultimately enhance the nation's economic health. This is a narrow view of both equity and teacher education quality (Cochran-Smith, Stern, et al., 2016). As Kumashiro (2015) stated:

> Within the proposed regulations, student learning is presumed to be marked by high test scores; teaching is presumed to be the raising of test scores; and teacher preparation is presumed to enable teachers to increase test scores. But, as commonly agreed, this is not the end goal of education. If, as John Dewey said, the purpose of education is to strengthen our democratic society then the proposed regulations should expand and enrich . . . how the nation thinks about and advances the promises and purposes of public education. (p. 9)

The 2016 Title II regulations framed the purpose of education in terms of economic priorities and subverted the critical purposes of democratic education, an issue we discuss at length in the third part of this book.

There are many additional concerns about the values and concepts implicit in the Title II regulations and in the rhetoric that promoted them. As we noted above, many teacher educators and assessment scholars have voiced concerns about the emphasis on test scores as a measure of teachers' effectiveness because research has shown that value-added measures are unreliable and that they should not be used to establish consequences for teachers and teacher preparation programs.

Additionally, during the period for public feedback about the proposed Title II regulations, representatives of many states and teacher education programs/institutions pointed out repeatedly that they did not have in place the elaborate data systems needed to implement the regulations, and they expressed concern about the absence of federal funds to establish such systems (Office of the *Federal Register*, 2016). For example, the American Council on Education (ACE) (2016) asserted that the USDOE "dramatically underestimated the cost of complying with the rules" (p. 1). Many commenters also stated that "the implementation costs . . . would require States either to take funds away from other programs or raise taxes or fees to comply" (Office of the *Federal Register*, 2016, p. 75501). The USDOE's response was that the "preparation program reporting system established in Title II of the HEA provides an important tool for understanding whether these programs are making good" on the nation's "billions of dollars of public funds it spends producing novice teachers" (Office of the *Federal Register*, 2016, p. 75502). This response did not address states' concerns about the implications of the regulations, including its lack of funding. If anything, this response added insult to injury by stating, "We assume that a State would want to provide such technical assistance rather than have program[s] continue to be low-performing" (Office of the *Federal Register*, 2016, p. 75501). Many responses during the public comment period expressed concern about the burden on teacher educators of collecting and analyzing data that undermined the pursuit of other critical work. These comments made it clear that the consequences and costs of the short-lived accountability system established by the 2016 Title II regulations would fall to teacher preparation programs and states, while control over the process and content of accountability would be determined externally by federal regulators.

These criticisms illustrate stakeholders' concerns about the impact of the proposed regulations as an unfunded, federally mandated and state-enforced initiative that did not reflect the values and commitments of local teacher preparation programs and did not uphold the rights of states to regulate teacher preparation. Even though the 2016 Title II reporting regulations were proposed, approved, and finally rescinded all within a 3-year period, they have had a strong impact on teacher preparation programs and continue to have important implications for equity in education. They demonstrate the power of federal authorities to influence public discussions about teacher education quality and to attempt to control the work of states and teacher preparation programs.

As this book went to press, the House of Representatives introduced the PROSPER Act—proposed major legislation to reauthorize HEA, which has been due for reauthorization since 2013. Among its sweeping changes to HEA, a main priority of the PROSPER Act is a paring back of regulations, including Title II, which the Act targets for complete repeal (AACTE, 2018). Instead, PROSPER promises to hold institutions accountable by requiring accreditors to focus on student learning and educational outcomes as a part of their review and have a system in place to annually identify institutions that may be experiencing difficulties accomplishing their missions (United States House of Representatives Committee on Education and the Workforce, 2017, para. 8). There is bipartisan support for reform of HEA, which is expected to head toward a vote in 2018. It remains to be seen what the outcome of the reauthorization will be, but it is fairly certain that the tug of war between federal oversight, states' rights, and teacher education program autonomy will continue.

CHAPTER 5

A Would-Be Watchdog

CAEP's Problematic Approach to Professional Accountability

In 2013, amid mounting concern about U.S. teacher quality and growing skepticism about university teacher preparation's ability to produce effective teachers, a new national accreditation agency was born. CAEP was the result of the strategic union of two federally recognized accreditors: NCATE, in operation since 1954, and TEAC, founded in 1997. Historically these two teacher education accreditors had markedly different philosophical approaches to accreditation, leading to sometimes rancorous public disagreements, with NCATE focused on program alignment with standards and TEAC more interested in program improvement and internal accountability. But as blame for the nation's "failing schools" shifted to teacher education, including widespread doubt about the profession's ability to police itself, leaders of the two groups eventually concluded that a merger would present a unified front and give more structure to the field (Sawchuk, 2010). We suggest in this chapter that the merger was also motivated by the need for self-preservation and professional control of the field.

This chapter argues that CAEP was designed to be a "watchdog" of teacher quality and accountability by marshaling professional control of teacher education while maintaining "external objectivity" regarding individual programs. The NCATE-TEAC merger aimed to strengthen teacher education quality and elevate the profession by improving the accreditation process, restoring the legitimacy of national program accreditation, and regaining public confidence through transparent accountability requirements. Yet as CAEP publicly positioned itself as the "single voice" of the profession (Cibulka, Gollnick & Cohen, n.d.; NCATE, 2010a), it became clear that its new accreditation standards and procedures lacked the complete support of the profession (AACTE, 2015; Feuer et al., 2013). To the contrary, since its founding, CAEP's processes have been fraught with criticism from both within *and* outside of the profession, seriously undermining its ability to elevate the status of the teacher education profession.

CAEP ACCREDITATION:
A BEACON FOR UNIFIED PROFESSIONAL ACCOUNTABILITY?

As we discussed in Chapter 2, during the 1990s and 2000s, a sea of critics perpetuated the narrative that U.S. schools were failing, teachers were centrally responsible, and preparation programs were to blame for not producing effective teachers. The establishment of an internal-to-the-profession single national accreditor was intended as a strong signal that the profession itself (and *not* an external regulator such as USDOE) could and should be fully accountable for teacher quality. The concerted effort to establish this collective accountability was intended to recapture the relevance of professional accreditation by merging two systems instead of having what TEAC president Frank Murray referred to as two independent accreditation organizations "viewed as antagonistic" (Sawchuk, 2010).

The History of CAEP: Born to Reform

CAEP aspired to be a credible, transparent evaluator, well positioned to laud programs that met CAEP standards and to compel weak programs to improve through better alignment with those standards. Accreditation as a means of ensuring accountability internal to the profession, though, was not a new idea during the emerging era of accountability in teacher education. The motivation for the establishment in 1954 of CAEP's forerunner, NCATE, was very similar when it was founded by five organizations, most notably AACTE (NCATE, 2010b), whose membership currently includes nearly two-thirds of the nation's teacher education colleges, departments, and schools of education. Like CAEP, NCATE billed itself as "the profession's mechanism to help establish high quality teacher preparation" (NCATE, 2010b, para. 2) and identified its dual mission as "accountability and improvement in educator preparation" (NCATE, 2010b, para. 1).

NCATE's goal—like CAEP's—was to elevate the status of the teaching profession and improve teacher education quality through rigorous national standards and continuous assessment and improvement (Cochran-Smith, 2001; Vergari & Hess, 2002). NCATE hoped to make professional accreditation critical and meaningful to teacher education programs by comparing it to well-respected specialized professions, such as architecture, engineering, medicine, and law, promoting accreditation as "the bedrock upon which all professions have built their reputations" (NCATE, n.d.). However, by the late 1990s, NCATE had failed to convince more than half of the nation's teacher preparation programs to seek accreditation, including a number of historically elite colleges and universities. Skepticism about NCATE's ability to raise teacher education program quality, disinterest in accreditation

(Murray, 2003; Vergari & Hess, 2002), and dissatisfaction with NCATE's exorbitant costs, especially for smaller colleges (Honawar, 2008; Sawchuk, 2010), prompted the establishment of TEAC in 1997.

While NCATE was focused on "performance-based reform" (NCATE, 2000), TEAC intended to achieve accountability through the "goal of public assurance that teacher education accomplished what it was supposed to accomplish" (Murray, 2003, p. 3). TEAC's system of accreditation allowed institutions to develop internal standards and quality control on the assumption that "program faculties actually knew what they were doing" (Murray, 2011). This stood in stark contrast to NCATE's accountability pathway, which focused on professional standards external to individual programs. In addition, TEAC accreditation was significantly less expensive—less than half the cost of NCATE accreditation. The TEAC accreditation option resonated with many programs, resulting in TEAC successfully accrediting nearly 200 institutions by the time of the NCATE-TEAC merger. The creation of TEAC elevated the appeal of accreditation (Murray, 2005) in part by developing collegial capital within the profession that had been absent during the NCATE-only era. TEAC's creation and popularity seemed to bolster support for the existence of two distinct accrediting bodies among teacher educators and programs.

Although AACTE leaders maintained the stance that its membership desired a *single* accrediting body, their 2007 vote to support only one accreditor ended in a surprisingly narrow margin suggesting something entirely different (Honawar, 2007). What influenced the narrative that soon developed among TEAC and NCATE leaders that merging the two accreditors was necessary to preserve relevancy and internal professional control? Part of the motivation for the NCATE-TEAC merger came from developments outside the two organizations. By 2007 a whopping 20% of the nation's teachers were being trained in "alternative certification" programs (Walsh & Jacobs, 2007). In addition, as we discussed in Chapter 2, scrutiny of teacher education had intensified in the policy arena at both the federal and state levels, propelling the narrative that teacher education was a "broken" system (Cochran-Smith, 2005; Cochran-Smith et al., 2013; Murray, 2011) and that alternative recruitment and/or certification routes were superior. This likely contributed to teacher education stakeholders' interest in self-preservation and tipped favor to the unification of NCATE and TEAC in 2008, when a task force of both accreditors was formed to investigate the possibility of their merger (AACTE, n.d.-a). Thus, as the external threat of alternative certification began to exceed internal differences, CAEP was conceived in 2010, when NCATE and TEAC released a joint statement that they had reached an agreement to merge.

Evidence-Based Accreditation:
The Basics of CAEP's Approach to Accountability

CAEP's new leadership group was the legacy of leadership from the two former accreditors. As CAEP leaders sought recognition from the Council for Higher Education Accreditation and the USDOE as the sole national accreditor of teacher preparation programs, they branded their work through powerful accountability themes intended to appeal to an audience broader than the teacher education community. One strategy was comparison to other fields' high standards, including engineering, law, and medicine (Brabeck & Koch, 2013). CAEP endeavored to appeal to a wide range of stakeholders by campaigning for "public accountability reporting with multiple measures, including those directly linked to student achievement" (CAEP, 2012). These stakeholders included CAEP's critics, traditional and nontraditional programs, practitioners, employers, and the public (Brabeck & Koch, 2013; Ginsberg & Levine, 2013). CAEP asserted that all these entities had a "stake in the effectiveness of educator preparation, and should be involved" (Cibulka et al., n.d.). CAEP posited that the creation and use of a single reconstituted teacher education accreditation system built upon stringent standards would address the problem that Art Levine, former president of Teachers College, had called the "wild west of higher education," where "anything goes, and [there is] no real sheriff to provide order" (Ginsberg & Levine, 2013). CAEP leaders intended to revolutionize teacher education by positioning itself as the new "sheriff" in town (CAEP, 2013b).

CAEP's accreditation system, designed to police the field, is built on five professional standards, which reflect two overarching principles: solid evidence that a provider's graduates are competent and caring educators and solid evidence that the provider has the capacity to maintain a culture of evidence to enhance the quality of the programs they offer (CAEP, n.d.). The five standards, which were designed to "reflect the voice of the education field—on what makes a quality educator" (CAEP, n.d.), include broad domains that the CAEP Commission on Standards and Performance Reporting concluded represented the best thinking about program quality: Content and Pedagogical Knowledge (Standard 1); Clinical Partnerships and Practice (Standard 2); Candidate Quality, Recruitment and Selectivity (Standard 3); Program Impact (Standard 4); and Provider Quality, Continuous Improvement, and Capacity (Standard 5).

The first iteration of the standards was intended to leverage the public's perception of teachers, teaching, and teacher education performance by strengthening their commitment to public accountability and transparency. CAEP asserted that they would publicize annual data reports regarding teacher education programs to ensure that "consumers" (i.e., prospective teacher candidates) were well informed when "shopping" for programs

(Bryk et al., 2013; CAEP, 2015a). This meant that programs seeking CAEP accreditation were accountable for the systematic collection and synthesis of evidence regarding program and graduates' impact and rates of graduation, licensure, hiring, and student loan defaults. It is important to emphasize that CAEP processes and standards were remarkably similar in many ways to the USDOE's 2014 proposed Title II regulations for reforming teacher education. This was unsettling to the many segments of the teacher education community that had protested federal regulations. Along these lines, CAEP was named an exemplar of a "promising practice" in teacher education by the USDOE, and CAEP accreditation was one of four indicators of performance for state rating systems outlined in the proposed teacher preparation rules (Kumashiro, 2015). This entangled CAEP's professional accreditation processes with the federal government in a way that significantly departed from NCATE's and TEAC's descriptions of themselves as nongovernmental (AACTE, 1999; Murray, 2001).

By the end of 2017, the new CAEP accreditation organization had accredited 50 teacher education programs and placed several others on probation. By then, even though it was only two years after they launched their first accreditation visits, CAEP was already in the midst of revising its processes and moving to a single accreditation pathway very reminiscent of the former accreditation process under NCATE. This reflects the difficulties CAEP was having "getting two cultures to agree" (Sawchuk, 2016), and perhaps forecasted the emergence of a competitor in late 2017, which we return to at the end of this chapter.

CAEP ACCREDITATION: AN EIGHT-DIMENSIONAL ANALYSIS

In what follows we use our eight-dimensional framework to unpack CAEP as an accountability mechanism that seeks to hold the profession accountable for teacher education program quality. This analysis is summarized in Figure 5.1.

Foundations of Accountability

The foundations of CAEP's approach to accountability demonstrate the extent to which it sought professional relevance by embracing the ideology of the accountability era. In terms of the values dimension, CAEP's accreditation procedures and processes reflected the neoliberal consensus that higher-quality teacher education programs and teachers are necessary to improve schooling and the country's global competitiveness. In multiple iterations of the *CAEP Accreditation Handbook* (2015a, 2016a, 2017a), for example, CAEP cited the 2010 NCATE-commissioned Blue Ribbon Panel on teacher quality to articulate its ideological rationale: "The education of

Figure 5.1. Dimensions of Accountability: CAEP

Thematic Cluster	Dimension	CAEP
Foundations of Accountability	Values	• Professional accreditation directly linked to student learning and bolstering the United States's global competitiveness
	Purpose	• Using professional accreditation to hold teacher preparation programs accountable for the teaching and learning outcomes the nation desires
	Concepts	• Teacher effectiveness measured by a teacher's ability to positively impact student learning beginning on day one of teaching • Program quality: a program's ability to produce effective teachers
The Problem of Teacher Education	Diagnostic	• Loss of public confidence in teacher preparation programs' ability to produce effective teachers • Lack of data-based evidence that teacher education produces effective teachers
	Prognostic	• National accrediting organization can rebuild public trust in teacher preparation by enforcing tougher standards, public accountability measures, and evidence quality expectations
Power Relationships in Accountability	Control	• CAEP maintains jurisdiction over accreditation decisions, forms partnerships with states to determine overall program quality • Internal to the profession, external to programs
	Content	• Programs accountable for meeting CAEP's five standards regarding program quality inputs and program/graduate effectiveness • Demonstrated through quantitative and qualitative evidence that meets CAEP's evidence quality criteria
	Consequences	• Jurisdictional power struggles between CAEP and state authorities limit CAEP's current impact • Potential closures for programs that do not receive CAEP accreditation in some states

teachers in the United States needs to be turned upside down . . . to help the nation compete in the global economy, today's teachers will have to educate all students—including those from increasingly diverse economic, racial, linguistic, and academic backgrounds—to the same high learning outcomes" (NCATE, 2010a, p. ii). CAEP worked from this logic without question or critique and built an accreditation system based on the human capital perspectives we describe in Chapter 2. This stance also reflects the "thin equity" notion that is at the heart of the current era of teacher education accountability.

In terms of the purpose dimension, CAEP's position is that accreditation is the best way for the profession to ensure that programs fulfill their duty to produce the high-quality teachers the nation needs. CAEP was designed to be a more effective, accountability-driven, profession-wide quality assurance system. As CAEP stated, the purpose is "to assure teacher candidates, parents, employers, policymakers, and the public that the claims and promises a provider makes about its quality are true" (CAEP, 2016a, p. 6). Unlike TEAC, which emerged in response to the perceived limitations of NCATE, CAEP was designed to be a "new direction" (CAEP, 2016a, p. 5) in teacher education accountability, using evidence-based accreditation and thus fulfilling the role that advocates of data-driven accountability had long hoped it would. CAEP's purpose was also "to increase the value of accreditation and to increase participation by providers in the accreditation system" (CAEP, 2016a, p. 5). CAEP's devotion to data was completely consistent with the broader accountability-driven politics of the current era.

There are two central concepts underlying CAEP standards: teacher effectiveness and program efficacy. CAEP defines effective teaching as the ability to have an immediate positive impact on student learning (CAEP, 2016a). This view of teaching draws on other professional positions such as the Interstate Teacher Assessment and Support Consortium (InTASC) standards, which are widely regarded as robust and not beholden to a single ideological stance. However, CAEP's standards go beyond this. Their standards regarding candidates' and graduates' effectiveness reflect the accountability era's premise that teachers are not considered effective unless they are able immediately (i.e., on "day one") to have an impact on student learning as indicated through quantifiable outcomes. Likewise, the concept of program efficacy is defined as the demonstrated capacity of programs to produce effective teachers along with the capacity to collect and interpret evidence of quality continuously and systematically. CAEP's standard regarding program quality assurance stipulates that programs will be accredited only if they demonstrate that they are in fact quality programs according to CAEP's standards. Ultimately, CAEP's core concepts of teacher effectiveness and program efficacy show the extent to which CAEP aligns accreditation with the accountability ideology underlying CAEP's redefinition of what professional accreditation should look like in the accountability era.

In short, CAEP's values, purpose, and concepts are much more in line with the neoliberal and human capital perspectives articulated in Chapter 2 than with either NCATE's or TEAC's prior approaches to professional accreditation. This is the result of CAEP's determination to make accreditation relevant in the new accountability era. In doing so, its leaders and advocates chose not to challenge the accountability logic that was emerging as the consensus during this era. However, this resulted in a definition of teacher and program quality that was inconsistent with the perspectives of many teacher education practitioners, which we say more about in our discussion of power relationships.

The Problem of Teacher Education

In terms of the diagnostic dimension, CAEP constructs the problem of teacher education as the public's low confidence in teacher education because of what CAEP officials call its prior "process-oriented system of accountability" (Brabeck & Koch, 2013), which lacked reliable and valid evidence for assessing appropriate outcomes. CAEP suggests that this lack of public confidence emerged because teacher education programs were not producing teachers capable of educating students who "acquire the knowledge and skills necessary for full and productive participation in our society" (Teacher Preparation Analytics, 2014, p. 1). According to the founders of CAEP, this was exacerbated by the fact that programs were unable and/or unwilling to move away from "theoretical, academic preparation" (Brabeck & Koch, 2013). This construction of the problem of teacher education assumed that there was a yawning gap between what programs had claimed to be doing well already (i.e., rigorous preparation of teacher candidates in the skills of teaching) and what the public perceived as the profession's failure to adequately prepare teachers for the realities of schools.

The prognostic dimension of the CAEP accreditation system—or what its advocates believed should be done to fix lack of public confidence in professional accreditation—followed directly from the diagnostic dimension. CAEP's "fix" for teacher education was establishing accreditation as a data-driven accountability mechanism that was grounded in the assumption that more rigorous standards would discriminate between high- and low-quality programs, improve candidate selectivity, and require classroom assessments and other outcomes measures to evaluate graduates' and programs' performance (Ginsberg & Levine, 2013). CAEP leaders also intimated that this effort would eventually force alternative certification providers, such as TFA, to be accountable to the same rigorous standards once professional consensus was established (Ginsberg & Levine, 2013). In short, CAEP's proposed solution to the problem of teacher education—data-driven accountability—was completely consistent with its underlying values and concepts, particularly in terms of the need to promote a "commonsense" set of metrics that define what constitutes a quality program and an effective teacher.

Power Relationships in Accountability

As we have argued, teacher education accountability policies are inherently political and involve multiple, overlapping power dynamics. In terms of the control dimension of our framework, CAEP positioned itself as an accreditor that had fully embraced the tenets of teacher education's accountability era, especially tougher standards linked to pupil learning outcomes. As the sole authority for professional accountability, CAEP would serve as the profession's "watchdog" and, at the same time, increase the value of national accreditation. But over time the NCATE/TEAC merger that produced CAEP prompted many questions about who should have control over professional accountability, how accreditation for teacher education accountability should be organized, and what organization or entity actually does represent the profession. These unresolved questions led to a series of power struggles that haunted CAEP from the outset of the merger.

The CAEP "Commission on Standards and Performance Reporting," which convened in 2012 to write the five CAEP standards, brought together representatives from a broad array of education reform advocacy groups, including the conservative think tank the Thomas B. Fordham Institute, the alternative certification provider TFA, and charter school champion the New Schools Venture Fund. In addition to this unusual collection of historically anti-university teacher education participants, the Commission also included professionals from more traditional organizations, such as the Harvard Graduate School of Education, the National Association of State Boards of Education, the American Federation of Teachers, the National Education Association, and the Association of Teacher Educators, but did not include representatives from AACTE. The Commission drafted and released the standards for public comment in February 2013. However, in its feedback on this draft, AACTE argued that implementation of the standards regarding candidate selection would reduce the diversity of teacher candidates, and also noted many problems related to the use of value-added measures as a way of assessing program outcomes. This initial critique of CAEP standards by AACTE, which is widely considered the major institutional organization for teacher education, illustrates that there was not a shared understanding that CAEP was capable of representing the single voice of the profession even during its initial development.

Another power struggle occurred between AACTE and CAEP in early 2015 when AACTE passed a resolution claiming a "crisis of confidence" about CAEP's standards, processes, costs, and capacity. In response, then–CAEP President Cibulka posted a "mea culpa" letter written directly to its stakeholders that acknowledged CAEP's shortcomings, aggressive timelines, inconsistency, insufficiency of guidance, and mistakes, and reaffirmed CAEP's interest in reforming old practices. The letter warned that without CAEP, policymakers could "supplant accreditation with other, potentially more onerous alternatives that would completely diminish the power of educators and other looming external threats to relevancy." Another terse public reply to AACTE came from Chair of the Board of CAEP directors Mary Brabeck, which reasserted both CAEP's authority over the profession and the need for an independent accrediting body that could restore the public's trust in university teacher preparation. Brabeck's letter called on AACTE to require CAEP accreditation of its members. Shortly thereafter, Cibulka was ousted as CAEP president and replaced by Vice-Chair of the Board of Directors Christopher Koch, who still held the position of president as this book went to press. The issues of control that continue to plague CAEP reveal what may well be irreconcilable tensions between trying to be both a hardline accreditor and at the same time a responsible professional partner attuned to the concerns and issues of the colleges, schools, and departments of education that prepare the majority of the nation's teachers.

Despite CAEP's claims to be revolutionizing accreditation, in terms of the content dimension of accountability (that is, what teacher education programs are actually held accountable for), CAEP accreditation was similar in many ways to accreditation through NCATE and TEAC, at least on the surface. To a great extent, CAEP maintained the focus on program inputs with which most teacher educators were already familiar. The continuation of input-type standards was aligned with the long-held professional assumption that any evaluation of program quality should include review of the structures, resources, and supports involved in the execution of a teacher education program (Darling-Hammond & Bransford, 2005). However, the new CAEP accreditation procedures *also* required that programs collect valid and reliable evidence about graduates' effectiveness and program impact using quantitative student learning data. CAEP characterized these new outcomes and evidence standards as essential, given the nation's current focus on teacher effectiveness (CAEP, 2013b). CAEP's five standards were consistent with its underlying ideology and its prognosis regarding how to fix the problem of teacher education, but they were also influenced by its battle for control of the profession. The content of the CAEP standards seemed intended to appease both policymakers who worked from the neoliberal logic underlying the era of accountability and members of the profession who were resistant to this logic. This endeavor was fraught with contradictions.

Finally, we turn to the consequences dimension of CAEP as an accountability policy. CAEP's intention was to create a system of accreditation that would reward teacher preparation programs that met its standards and thus encourage further improvement—or, in contrast, the system would publicly discredit programs that did not. However, because national accreditation is not required in most states, the consequences for not achieving CAEP accreditation are ambiguous. CAEP has made an effort to make accreditation a mechanism for boosting public perceptions of the profession through an aggressive marketing campaign signaling that participating institutions have been recognized as institutions of distinction and vetted for quality and excellence (CAEP, 2017a). But in its first year in operation CAEP granted full accreditation to 17 of the 21 institutions that applied (Iasevoli, 2016), including one fully online teacher preparation program. In 2017, CAEP granted full accreditation to 36 programs, and conditional accreditation to nine others (CAEP, 2017c). In its first two years of operation, CAEP denied accreditation to only three institutions (CAEP, 2017d). This seems to signal that the majority of programs are worthy of the CAEP accreditation distinction, a reality that runs counter to much of CAEP's public diagnosis of the problem of teacher education.

CAEP has tried to expand its reach and impact by increasing the number of state agreements that consolidate state program approval and CAEP accreditation into one process. But the tensions that emerged from the power struggles over CAEP as a single accreditor have led to weak consequences for programs not accredited or not seeking accreditation. This has minimized the ultimate impact that CAEP has had in the profession.

CAEP ACCREDITATION:
THEORY OF CHANGE AND THE RELATED EVIDENCE

In this section, we identify three implicit claims related to the overall assertion that the CAEP system of accreditation leads to higher-quality and more accountable teacher education programs. The first assumption is that a national accreditation system developed and managed by the profession is an effective mechanism for raising standards and thus improving the quality of preparation. The second claim is that publicly available consumer information will restore policymakers' and the public's trust in the profession. And the third is that programs' continuous improvement and innovation, based on reliable and valid evidence about outcomes, will enhance the quality of teacher education and teaching. Below, we evaluate the existing evidence that does or does not support these claims.

Claim #1: The Role of Accreditation and Teacher Education Quality

CAEP asserts that reclaiming jurisdiction over teacher education via a profession-developed national accreditation system with tough standards will boost the hitherto low-quality status of the profession "at a pivotal time for education," claiming that CAEP's "new direction for accreditation" responds directly to the public's and policymakers' concerns (CAEP, 2016a, p. 5). The idea here is that CAEP is a professional regulatory body seeking to "raise the bar" and use "tough standards" as a way to establish the rigor of the programs it accredits. Professional jurisdiction, as opposed to external federal jurisdiction, is assumed to be the key to boosting public opinion.

In public documents describing CAEP's approach, CAEP leaders assert that their work builds "upon the decades of institutional knowledge of the sector's previous accreditors . . . which agreed to form CAEP to advance the field of educator preparation" (CAEP, 2016a, p. 5). They claim that their predecessors' years of research about what constitutes a high-quality teacher education program serves as the underpinnings of their standards, which reflect consensus among stakeholders about what constitutes a "quality" program (CAEP, 2013b). However, there is little empirical evidence to support this claim because it is based on the as-yet-untested assumption that systemic implementation of the CAEP accreditation process will lead to improved programs. CAEP documents cite the improvement science work of scholars such as Tony Bryk and his colleagues (e.g., APA, 2014; CAEP, 2013b) as evidence that practitioners who engage in systematic self-study improve program quality. CAEP presents this as a research-proven technique for achieving continuous improvement in educational organizations. But the cited research is not directly related to teacher education, and it suggests only a weak association at best.

Given that the CAEP system is so new, there is no direct evidence about its efficacy as a national profession-managed mechanism for raising standards. It thus makes sense to look at what the evidence says about the impact of accreditation by CAEPs forerunner, NCATE, on program quality. Here, according to reviewers, the evidence is "nearly non-existent" (Tamir & Wilson, 2005, p. 6). There are mixed results regarding the relationship between teacher candidates' completion of an NCATE-approved program and their scores on licensure tests, and there is no evidence about whether completion of an NCATE program predicts teachers' practices or career trajectories (Wilson & Youngs, 2005). The absence of empirical evidence notwithstanding, many groups have theorized the importance of accreditation, including the National Academy of Education (Feuer et al., 2013), the National Research Council (NRC) (2010), and the NCATE-commissioned Blue Ribbon Panel (NCATE, 2010a). These groups have suggested that high standards could be systematically implemented across teacher education and that programs could be evaluated using such standards. But there is little empirical evidence that accreditation is a workable mechanism for creating and sustaining teacher education quality.

It may be that CAEP's assumption—that the public's lack of confidence in teaching and teacher education is the result of the absence of high-stakes accreditation and tough standards—is faulty in the first place. For example, some scholars have argued that teaching and teacher education have been held in low regard in part because of the traditionally low status ascribed to the work of teachers—mostly women—in the United States (Labaree, Hirsch,

& Beatty, 2004; Lagemann, 2000). In addition, despite stepped-up efforts, neither NCATE nor TEAC accreditation succeeded at enhancing the status of the profession, although those systems supposedly reflected the "best thinking" of their time about how to organize and implement accreditation to assess program quality. In short, CAEP's claim that accreditation boosts program quality reflects the rationale for its existence and its struggle for legitimacy. However, there is very little evidence that an accreditation-based accountability mechanism is in fact an effective mechanism for enhancing teacher education program quality.

Claim #2: The Role of Accreditation, Data, and Consumer Trust

A second claim inherent in the argument that accreditation can raise teacher education quality rests on the belief that amassing publicly available consumer information about teacher education programs, including graduation and hiring rates, will help restore public trust in the profession. CAEP's Evidence Guide (2015) suggests that because the "qualities of educator preparation data fall far short of ideal, . . . [CAEP] must play a prominent role to advance evidence-informed accreditation as one of its professional responsibilities" (CAEP, 2015b, p. 7). In short, over time, the CAEP accreditation process is intended to monitor, collect, and disseminate "quality" evidence from teacher education programs. This evidence is intended to reestablish (or establish) the consumer trust that CAEP leaders perceive to be lacking in the profession. As two CAEP board members who served on the commission that set the standards said, CAEP "will require programs to provide better and more comparable performance data and will ensure that they are more forthcoming in providing that information" (Ginsberg & Levine, 2013, para. 12).

The logic here is that consumers and stakeholders will see that the profession is collecting "better" evidence in more systematic ways and those data are informing continuous improvement, peer comparisons, and prospective teachers' choices about "quality" programs and their outcomes. The assumption is that this will increase the public's faith in the profession's ability to "police itself," and that both higher quality and trust will be the results. The major issue with this claim has to do with the quality of the data itself and whether the data really do serve the purpose that CAEP proposes. In order to gain accreditation, programs must collect the kind of evidence legitimized by CAEP, rather than evidence related to the goals and purposes implicit in programs' internal accountability processes. Along these lines, a central focus of CAEP's claim about the relationship between high-quality evidence and outcomes has to do with the use of value-added measures that define teacher quality in terms of student test scores. In CAEP's impact standard (Standard 4), CAEP proposes that value-added measures and/or student growth percentile (SGP) methodologies should be used as evidence that a program has documented an "expected level of student growth." CAEP makes this assertion despite its own admission that "such measures are in their infancy and are controversial" (Ginsberg & Levine, 2013, para. 11) and that research about the use of value-added measures is only loosely linked to teacher preparation effectiveness (CAEP, 2013b; Ewell, 2013; NRC, 2010).

We found no evidence that making data publicly available prompts program improvement. In fact, making data that lacks validity available for public consumption can be misleading and dangerous for education stakeholders. It may also prompt an increasingly technocratic mindset in which CAEP's forms of evidence are accepted and used by the field in high-stakes accreditation and accountability decisions.

Finally it is important to note that there is evidence that an outcomes-based accountability approach, such as the one promoted by CAEP, may—and indeed has—produced negative consequences. One example is the highly controversial "teach to the test" culture that developed in K–12 settings in response to high-stakes testing and accountability demands. This kind of culture can result in teachers and teacher educators losing sight of the complexity of their work and lacking the motivation or wherewithal to engage in the kind of inquiry that addresses complexity (Cochran-Smith & Lytle, 2009; Hargreaves & Fullan, 2012; MacDonald & Shirley, 2009). In addition, programs may remain unmotivated to use accreditation to elevate their status given the lack of incentives to pursue national accreditation in many states. While CAEP has aspired for broader authority and influence (Brabeck, 2015), it has not achieved it.

Claim #3: The Role of Accreditation and Continuous Improvement of Programs

The final claim implicit in the notion of accreditation as an accountability mechanism is that it promotes cycles of evaluation and improvement based on the collection and analysis of "high-quality" evidence about the outcomes of programs. Along these lines, CAEP places great emphasis on "cultures of evidence" as the vehicle for "continuous improvement" in the teacher education profession. As they say, "We believe that the most important aspect of the CAEP process is that [educator preparation programs] engage in continuous improvement and innovation to enhance teaching and student learning" (CAEP, 2016b, para. 19). Of the five components listed as part of CAEP's Standard 5, which has to do with "Provider Quality, Continuous Improvement and Capacity," two are required, both having to do with "regular and systematic performance against goals and standards" using "measures of [graduates'] impact" (CAEP, 2016c, p. 2). Here again there is an emphasis on controversial measures, including value-added measures.

Throughout its documents, CAEP emphasizes the importance of using measurable student learning outcomes to determine program quality, so it is worth noting how strong the criticism of methods such as value-added measures to evaluate teaching has been. For example, an AERA report (2015) concluded that value-added measures were insufficiently developed to be considered for use in educator evaluation systems. Other individual researchers, even Chiang et al. (2011) and Goldhaber (2013) who embrace certain aspects of linking teacher performance to student outcomes, have overwhelmingly concluded that value-added measures of teacher performance are highly flawed. In a particularly severe critique of the methodology, Amrein-Beardsley and colleagues (2013) claim that "few if any researchers have developed compelling or appropriate methods to examine how much of a teacher's impact on student learning can be attributed to the teacher education unit" (p. 5).

In sum, we found that there was very little evidence suggesting that national outcomes-based accreditation is likely to be effective as an accountability mechanism that leads to program enhancement, intentional planning for continuous improvement, or the creation of cultures of evidence in teacher education. This is the case despite the fact that CAEP documents make broad claims that their accreditation system and procedures are consistent with this theory of action.

IMPACT AND IMPLICATIONS: THE JURY IS STILL OUT

As we have shown throughout this chapter, CAEP's intention as a national accreditor is to fix the "problem" of teacher education by establishing jurisdiction over the field and holding teacher education accountable for programs' and graduates' effectiveness. CAEP's efforts have focused primarily on elevating the status of the profession and professionalizing teaching by making their accreditation processes akin to those of other "respected" professions. But thus far, as we have argued, CAEP's attempt to do so through evidence-based accreditation processes has actually hindered its ability to succeed as an internal-to-the-profession accreditor. In this section, we explore three major implications of this approach.

Reactionary Compliance

CAEP has attempted to establish itself as the watchdog of teacher education by countering the charge against its forerunner, NCATE, that instead of being a rigorous evaluator, it became an "in-house" organization "concerned with meeting the needs of its membership . . . [which was] seen by many as a conflict of interest" (Brabeck, 2015, para. 6). Accordingly, CAEP has focused on data-based accountability to legitimize accreditation. CAEP's approach to accountability via data-based accreditation promotes the increasingly dominant "effectiveness doctrine" in teacher education (Miller, 2017), that is, the idea that the purpose of teacher education is creating effective teachers, who are ready on their first day in the classroom to have a positive impact on student learning outcomes in ways that can be measured quantifiably. CAEP's heavy emphasis on data-driven outcomes reflects what we refer to here as "reactionary compliance." What we mean is that CAEP has been both *compliant* in that its structure and processes are fully compliant and aligned with the dominant accountability rhetoric and at the same time *reactionary* in that its approach makes no effort to pursue new directions forward in discussions about teacher education quality. Driven by concern for relevancy, CAEP's reactionary compliance has three indicators: the adoption of quantifiable and controversial student learning outcomes as the primary measure of teacher candidate and teacher education program quality; CAEP's unwillingness to develop and promote alternatives to the accountability rhetoric; and CAEP's demand that all teacher education programs seeking accreditation comply with one set of expectations.

Compliance with the larger accountability regime, which we refer to in Chapter 8 as the "dominant accountability paradigm," undercuts the notion of professional expertise in teacher education by placing low priority on teacher educators' local knowledge, their commitments to preparing preservice teachers through unique program structures/experiences that meet the needs of the families and communities with which they work, and their use of local measures of progress toward meeting their own goals. CAEP's adoption of dominant accountability ideas, presumably in service of guarding the profession, contrasts sharply with the idea that locally generated professional knowledge about what defines a quality teacher and a quality teacher education program is also important. This contradiction has yet to be resolved.

Along these lines, CAEP has suffered many setbacks to its original goals and has struggled to steady itself in new territory, drawing criticism both from inside and outside the profession. Within the profession, critique has focused on a range of controversial issues, including accusations of disorganization and ill-prepared visiting accreditation teams (Sawchuk, 2016), high levels of staff dissatisfaction and turnover, and the exit of many founding members (CAEP, 2015c; Murray, 2016). Most controversially—and perhaps most importantly—CAEP has been critiqued for its apparent myopia about the barriers to diversity that are baked into their standards, including the requirement that programs use high-bar test scores and GPAs as admissions criteria (AACTE, 2013a), which we take up next.

Going Against the Grain: CAEP's Controversial Decisions

CAEP has two standards that have received widespread criticism. The most controversial is its standard regarding candidate quality, recruitment, and selectivity (Standard 3.2), which "uses challenging admissions selectivity criteria and continuous quality monitoring so that completers will achieve greater success with P–12 student learning" (CAEP, 2015a, para. 2). Establishing academic selectivity criteria was intended to push programs to recruit higher-quality candidates to the profession. However, this standard runs counter to CAEP's stated "cross cutting theme" of diversity by overrelying on the results of standardized tests for admissions. It is well known that standardized tests have historically disadvantaged minoritized groups and created significant admissions obstacles for prospective students (Freedle, 2010; Santelices & Wilson, 2010). Pressed to respond to criticism from stakeholders, CAEP acknowledged the controversy regarding admissions standards (Ginsburg & Levine, 2013) but reaffirmed its commitment to selectivity (CAEP, 2015a). This decision generated additional controversy and pushback from programs and AACTE, as well as a congressional resolution calling on CAEP to modify admissions standards to ensure that they would not exacerbate the exclusion of minoritized candidates (Senate Resolution 301, 2015).

CAEP Standard 4, which has to do with "impact on P-12 student learning and development," recommends the use of value-added measures to assess the impact of program graduates on student achievement. As we noted above, this apparently ignored researchers' arguments that value-added measures were insufficiently developed for use in teacher evaluation systems (AERA, 2015; Amrein-Beardsley et al., 2013). In fact, CAEP's own 2013 white paper warned, "Value added measures (VAM) need to be carefully evaluated because their original application was to examine classroom and school performance, not the effectiveness of the programs that prepared the teachers in those classrooms and schools" (Ewell, 2013, p. 1). CAEP's embrace of these two controversial standards has threatened CAEP's credibility with AACTE, AERA, Congress, and teacher educators.

All Bark, No Bite?

In spite of their efforts to improve teacher education through evidence-based accreditation and to "be respected as the arbiter of educator preparation program quality," CAEP has limited power to influence teacher education accreditation. CAEP has no regulatory control, and there is no cross-state requirement for national accreditation. In a sense, CAEP is a watchdog for the teacher education profession with a lot of bark, but not much bite. Despite its efforts to unify teacher education accreditation, CAEP continues to lack professional legitimacy, and there is no evidence yet that it is bringing about positive change. Indeed, CAEP has been reduced to trying to protect its brand by encouraging programs to market their accreditation as an achievement (CAEP, 2017b).

It is clear that CAEP needs teacher education programs to buy into the idea that CAEP accreditation is critical to the profession. However, there has been a steady stream of criticism and many expressions of skepticism from institutions (Coupland, 2011; Sawchuk, 2016), including voluntary institutional withdrawals from accreditation (CAEP, 2017d). These criticisms suggest that CAEP has not been embraced by the profession as the path to professionalization and public credibility. As this book went to press, the Association for Advancing Quality in Educator Preparation (AAQEP), a new teacher education accreditor, to which we return in Chapter 9, was beginning to build momentum. CAEP immediately jockeyed for position against this upstart accreditor, with CAEP president Christopher Koch saying, "This has all been done. Two accreditors didn't work really well" (Loewus & Sawchuk, 2017, para. 6). CAEP's troubling history suggests that its particular approach to data-based accreditation has not been widely embraced by the profession as the path to professionalization and public credibility.

CHAPTER 6

NCTQ

Shame and Blame in
Market-Based Teacher Accountability

During the early 2000s, NCTQ made a dramatic entrance onto the teacher education scene. NCTQ is a private advocacy organization established by the conservative Fordham Foundation to boost teacher quality and to promote alternate routes into the teaching profession (Ravitch, 2012). To this end, NCTQ produces highly publicized ratings and rankings of teacher education programs, aiming to influence consumers and foster competition among teacher education programs. Unlike other accountability initiatives discussed in this book, NCTQ has neither the regulatory power of a federal or state agency nor the professional status of a national accreditation body or assessment. Despite its lack of regulatory or professional standing, however, NCTQ has published numerous widely disseminated and influential reports about the policies and practices of teacher education programs and institutions, including reports on classroom management and teacher content knowledge (e.g., Greenberg & Walsh, 2008, 2012). The most well-known of these are the *Teacher Prep Reviews,* first published in 2013 in collaboration with the *U.S. News & World Report* (USNWR) and now published on NCTQ's Path to Teach website (NCTQ, n.d.-a), which disseminates NCTQ's ratings to the general public online. NCTQ's teacher preparation reports and accountability initiatives have generated an outpouring of critique and ongoing controversy.

In this chapter, we argue that NCTQ's market-based consumer-oriented approach to holding teacher education programs accountable is deeply flawed and inappropriate as an accountability mechanism for improving teacher education. We begin the chapter by delving into the history of NCTQ, connecting its founding purpose to the broader education reform agenda. We then provide some basic information about NCTQ's initiatives, and we use the eight dimensions of accountability framework to unpack and critique NCTQ's work. We follow this with a careful examination of the existing empirical evidence that speaks to NCTQ's underlying theory of change and conclude by considering how NCTQ has impacted the field of teacher education.

CONTEXT: NCTQ'S HISTORY AND APPROACH

How has NCTQ, a private external advocacy organization, come to be such a widely known and controversial presence in teacher education? Since its founding, NCTQ's goal has been to hold teacher education programs accountable to the general public. For this reason, even though NCTQ's reviews are not part of a formal accountability policy per se because NCTQ has no official authority, we consider the NCTQ reviews alongside the other accountability initiatives discussed in this book.

The History of NCTQ

As a private advocacy organization, NCTQ's efforts to shape the teacher education landscape are related to the political agenda of its founding organization, the Thomas B. Fordham Foundation (now the Thomas B. Fordham Institute). Fordham is one of the nation's leading think tank organizations that advocates for education reform based on standards, test-based accountability, and choices for families and other consumers (Thomas B. Fordham Institute, n.d.-a). Much of the foundation's work is grounded in two premises—that the purpose of education is to prepare the nation's workforce to compete in a global knowledge economy, and that the nation's public schools have failed to serve that purpose (Thomas B. Fordham Institute, n.d.-a). The foundation pursues its reform agenda through the publication of research and policy analyses, commentaries, and advocacy for charter schools. Prior to becoming the foundation's president in 1997, Chester Finn co-founded the Educational Excellence Network (Thomas B. Fordham Institute, n.d.-b), a reform network promoting high standards, choices for families, and test-based accountability for schools and teachers (Thomas B. Fordham Foundation, 1996).

The Fordham Foundation's reform agenda centers on the idea that boosting teacher quality will fix the nation's education system. However, according to the foundation, traditional regulatory policies focused on inputs (e.g., prospective teachers' course-taking) are wrongheaded, since teacher ability is "more a function of innate talents than the quality of education courses" (Ballou & Podgursky, 1997, p. 57). Fordham argues that a better solution is to "get rid of most hoops and hurdles," which are the core of university teacher education programs and certification requirements (Thomas B. Fordham Foundation, 1999, p. 2), and open up alternative entries into teaching (Thomas B. Fordham Foundation, 1999, 2002). The same anti-school of education rhetoric appeared in the foundation-commissioned report *Different Drummer: How Teachers of Teachers View Public Education* (Public Agenda, 1997). Surveying 900 education professors about their attitudes toward education and public schools, the report concluded that teacher educators cared too much about ideology and social justice theory and were out of sync with what most parents, teachers, and students said they needed (Public Agenda, 1997).

As part of the Fordham Foundation's national program to boost teacher quality, NCTQ inherited many of the foundation's reform strategies. These include both "standards-based reform," which is focused on academic standards, tests, and consequences for success and failure, and "market-style" reform, which emphasizes consumer choice and competition. According to the Fordham Foundation's *Five-Year Report: 1997–2001*, "Some think these [two] strategies are opposed or incompatible . . . [but] the opposite is true: Each needs the other if it is to have the brightest prospect of succeeding" (2002, p. 6). NCTQ's publications embody the ideas of its founder, tapping into both market-based consumer-oriented reform strategies and a high-standards, test-based approach.

Led by president Kate Walsh, NCTQ's mantra is that "every child deserves effective teachers and every teacher deserves the opportunity to become effective" (NCTQ, n.d.-b). Prior to serving as the first president of NCTQ in 2003, Walsh was the senior policy analyst of the Baltimore-based Abell Foundation and founded the first alternative certification program in Maryland. During her tenure there, Walsh was involved in efforts to promote the deregulation of teacher education and allow alternative programs to supply teachers to under-resourced school districts (Abell Foundation, 2001a, 2001b). Along these lines, the influential and contentious report *Teacher Certification Reconsidered: Stumbling for Quality* (Abell Foundation, 2001a) directly challenged the then-current evidence base supporting the role of coursework in preparing qualified teachers. Walsh's persistent efforts to challenge university teacher education programs and promote alternative routes to teacher preparation have always been consistent with the Fordham Foundation's reform agenda (Cochran-Smith & Fries, 2001; Walsh & Jacobs, 2007).

It is clear that NCTQ's assumptions and its approach to holding teacher education accountable reflect the vision of its founding organization and its leaders. NCTQ's advisory board members include individuals such as Wendy Kopp (founder of Teach for America), Michael Barber (chief education advisor of Pearson International), and Rick Hess (executive editor of *EducationNext*) (NCTQ, n.d.-c). Proponents of NCTQ include organizations such as the Policy Innovators in Education (PIE) network (Porter-Magee, 2015) and Jeb Bush's Foundation for Excellence in Education. Currently NCTQ receives funding from over 40 private organizations, including the Bill and Melinda Gates Foundation, the Walton Family Foundation, and ExxonMobil Corporation (NCTQ, n.d.-d), as well as from individuals. NCTQ was awarded a $5 million grant from the USDOE in 2001 to launch the American Board for Certification of Teacher Excellence, an online low-cost alternative teaching certification program currently recognized in 11 states and in most private schools across the country (American Board for Certification of Teacher Excellence, n.d.). NCTQ's history, funders, and supporters are revealing. It is crystal clear that the work of the individuals and organizations who founded and support NCTQ reflect the neoliberal market ideology that ties teacher quality to the economic competitiveness of the nation with neoconservative perspectives on standards. Apple (2006) referred to this as the "rightward turn" in education

The Basics: NCTQ's Market-Based Consumer-Oriented Approach

In partnership with USNWR, NCTQ released its first review of teacher preparation programs in June 2013 (Greenberg et al., 2013) and its second a year later (Greenberg, Walsh, & McKee, 2014). For seven years prior to the publication of the *Teacher Prep Review*, NCTQ had conducted numerous smaller-scale reviews about teacher preparation programs in specific states and areas of preparation, such as the teaching of reading. NCTQ's *Teacher Prep Reviews* are more ambitious than previous reports. Inspired by the 1910 Flexner Report, which led what NCTQ called the transformation of "a substandard system of medical training into the world's finest" (Greenberg, Walsh, & McKee, 2014, p. 10), NCTQ envisioned that the publication of its review would shine a similar "harsh spotlight" on schools of education (p. 10).

Following its 2013 and 2014 reviews, NCTQ announced that future reviews would be biennial, and it has since published several *Landscapes* reports, each with a specific focus on one area of teacher preparation. After the publication of the 2014 *Teacher Prep Review*, NCTQ discontinued its partnership with USNWR and shifted its efforts to publishing results on its Path to Teach website, which the organization calls "the consumer guide to colleges of education" (Path to Teach, n.d.) wherein all teacher preparation programs are graded, A to F. Visitors to this website in 2017, for example, would find that Stanford University's elementary education program received a grade of "D" from NCTQ, while teacher preparation programs at Dallas Baptist University and Western Governors University (a strictly online program) were both highly rated.

To determine grades, NCTQ uses a set of mostly input-based internally developed standards to evaluate the quality of programs based on documents such as syllabi, textbooks, student teaching handbooks, and state regulations, among others. The 2013 review included 18 standards encompassing candidate selection, content preparation (e.g., reading, mathematics, special education), professional skills (e.g., classroom management, lesson planning, student teaching), and outcomes (e.g., evidence of effectiveness) (Greenberg et al., 2013). However, only key standards (e.g., Selection Criteria, Elementary Content, Classroom Management, Student Teaching, and Instructional Design for Special Education) were used to assign scores based on a five-point system for each standard, with the combination of scores producing the four-star program ratings.

A total of 2,420 university-based programs were rated on a four-star scale in 2013. In 2014, NCTQ rated 2,400 programs, including 85 non-university alternative preparation programs, and shifted from rating to ranking programs. The most recent review, consisting of six separate *Landscapes* reports, evaluated 2,627 programs (NCTQ, 2016a). This time programs were scored, and each was assigned a grade from A to F as an overall program grade. For the purpose of clarity and simplicity, we use the term "ratings" from now on in this chapter to refer to NCTQ's program evaluation results.

NCTQ'S *TEACHER PREP REVIEWS*: AN EIGHT-DIMENSIONAL ANALYSIS

Using our eight dimensions of accountability framework to unpack NCTQ's teacher preparation reviews allows for a nuanced analysis of its underlying assumptions and values (see Figure 6.1). As with the other initiatives in this book, we organize the dimensions into three clusters.

The Foundations of Accountability

What drives the work of NCTQ? In terms of the values dimension, NCTQ documents conceptualize education as the means toward individual and national economic prosperity, and they see the purpose of education as preparing a labor force ready to compete in a global knowledge economy (Greenberg et al., 2013, p. 1; U.S. House of Representatives, 2011). For instance, the 2013 *Teacher Prep Review* stated: "Once the world leader in educational attainment, the United States has slipped well into the middle of the pack. Countries that were considered little more than educational backwaters just a few years ago have leapt to the forefront of student achievement" (Greenberg et al., 2013, p. 1).

While NCTQ documents acknowledge that many factors, such as budget cutbacks and entrenched poverty, contribute to the country's educational decline (Greenberg et al., 2013), they argue that "ensuring that every child has equal access to effective teachers" (NCTQ, n.d.-b), that is, teachers who have received the same, "classroom-ready" training (Greenberg, Walsh, & McKee, 2014, p. 7), can make up for these structural inequities. This suggests that NCTQ's underlying notion of equity has to do with sameness— the same kind of teacher for each child. The values underlying NCTQ's reviews connect education to competitiveness in a global knowledge economy, which reflects the neoliberal reform ideology outlined in Chapters 2 and 3 and are consistent with the core premises of the Fordham Institute.

In terms of the concepts dimension, NCTQ narrowly defines student learning as students' standardized test scores, which presumably provide

Figure 6.1. Dimensions of Accountability: NCTQ

Thematic Cluster	Dimension	NCTQ
Foundations of Accountability	Values	• Preparing labor force to compete in a global knowledge economy • Establishing market forces to drive change
	Purpose	• Rating programs and producing the largest database available on teacher preparation • Making program information available and transparent to consumers
	Concepts	• Narrow view of teaching and learning defined as student achievement measured by standardized test scores and teacher effectiveness measured by improvement in student achievement • Linear relationship between the purpose of teacher education and the production of teachers who raise student achievement
The Problem of Teacher Education	Diagnostic	• Teacher education is an "industry of mediocrity" and one root cause of poor teacher quality • Teacher educators fail to see their role as "training" teachers
	Prognostic	• Rating programs based on NCTQ standards and making program ratings publicly available to consumers will drive program change
Power Relationships in Accountability	Control	• NCTQ, an independent advocacy organization, creates and publishes its rating system • External to programs and the profession
	Content	• Programs accountable for alignment of program inputs with NCTQ-developed program quality standards/criteria • Demonstrated by ratings NCTQ produces showing extent to which a program has certain inputs
	Consequences	• Negative or positive publicity for poorly or highly rated programs • Program closure due to consumer choice, such as prospective teachers' choices to attend highly rated programs

objective educational data, as Walsh made clear in testimony to Congress (e.g., U.S. House of Representatives, 2011). This definition of student learning is coupled with a definition of the effective teacher as one who has an impact on student learning by boosting students' assessment scores (e.g., Greenberg, Walsh, & McKee, 2014; U.S. House of Representatives, 2011). It is important to remember, however, that even though NCTQ defines effective teaching and learning in terms of test scores, NCTQ's methodology for its reviews of teacher preparation programs focuses on measuring program inputs rather than outcomes. The standards used to rate programs reflect a technical view of teaching and learning to teach—that is, teacher candidates acquiring a set of discrete strategies transmitted by teacher educators and then executing them faithfully in the classroom with the goal of improving students' standardized test scores. For example, NCTQ's report on classroom management specifies the "big five" classroom management strategies that they argue every teacher should implement. These five strategies are very specific; for example, the fourth strategy reads, "Consistently impose consequences for misbehavior" (Greenberg, Putman, & Walsh, 2014, p. i). This simplistic and perhaps punitive language overlooks the complexities and nuances that skilled teachers grapple with when working with children to negotiate boundaries and establish trusting, responsive, democratic relationships. In short, the "effective teachers" NCTQ wants teacher preparation programs to produce do not necessarily need to know how to navigate the complex terrain of inequities that impact students' lives, as long as they know how to maintain order in the classroom and transmit knowledge about reading and mathematics.

With regard to the purpose dimension, NCTQ's reviews aim to promote a market-based approach to accountability in teacher education by rating programs and ensuring that the "largest database on teacher preparation ever assembled" (Greenberg et al., 2013, p. 4) is widely available and transparent to consumers (i.e., prospective teachers and employers) and the public (Greenberg, Walsh, & McKee, 2014). In the 2013 *Teacher Prep Review*, NCTQ stated that by making their data available, "We are setting in place market forces that will spur underachieving programs to recognize their shortcomings and adopt methods used by the high scorers" (Greenberg et al., 2013, p. 4). This purpose is aligned with the organization's view that relationships among teacher preparation, teaching, and student learning are linear and causal.

In addition, part of NCTQ's purpose appears to be promoting what we called in Chapter 2 a "continuous failure narrative" regarding university-sponsored teacher education. In fact, nearly all of NCTQ's published reports since 2006 have shared this purpose. NCTQ's first report, released in 2006, was titled *What Education Schools Aren't Teaching About Reading— and What Elementary Teachers Aren't Learning* (Walsh, Glaser, & Wilcox, 2006). Foreshadowing NCTQ's approach of conducting external reviews of preparation programs based on syllabi and document analysis, this highly controversial report, critiqued by Allington (2002), Cochran-Smith and Demers (2007), and many others, used a narrow definition of teaching reading. The focus was on equipping teachers with a technical and discrete set of skills for reading instruction, which the report referred to as the "science" of teaching reading, but is highly controversial among reading scholars (e.g., Allington, 2002; Dudley-Marling, 2015). This scathing report, which evaluated the syllabi for reading courses at 72 schools of education, concluded that there was a "serious failure in adequately preparing teachers in the best practices of reading instruction" (Walsh et al., 2006, p. 3).

In the years since then, NCTQ has published a steady stream of reports, each taking up a different aspect of teacher preparation, each with a catchy and derogatory title (e.g., *Easy A's and What's Behind Them* [Putman, Greenberg, & Walsh, 2014] and *Incoherent by Design* [Greenberg & Dugan, 2015]), and each pounding the same drumbeat of the failure, failure, failure of university-sponsored teacher education programs to make the grade. Although NCTQ's *Teacher Prep Reviews* and Path to Teach website now review alternate routes to certification alongside traditional programs, the standards to which alternate programs are held are fewer and less specific than those used to rate traditional programs (NCTQ, n.d.-e). NCTQ asserts that in creating a separate set of standards, they "considered the essential features of non-traditional certification" and aimed to make the standards parallel to the key standards applied to traditional graduate secondary programs (NCTQ, n.d.-e). This may or may not be the reason NCTQ treads more lightly when it comes to non-traditional programs, but it is certainly the case that the content of NCTQ's additional reports, as described above, focuses almost exclusively on traditional university-based programs.

The Problem of Teacher Education

NCTQ's diagnosis of "the problem of teacher education" is very clear in their *Teacher Prep Reviews*. They describe the current state of teacher preparation in America as "an industry of mediocrity, churning out first-year teachers with classroom management skills and content knowledge inadequate to thrive" (Greenberg et al., 2013, p. 1). According to NCTQ, this problem was caused by education schools' failure to accept their obligation to "train" teachers, select strong candidates, provide them with rigorous student teaching experiences, focus intently on development of content knowledge and classroom management skills, and monitor candidates' effectiveness after graduation (Greenberg, Walsh, & McKee, 2014; Putman et al., 2014). NCTQ asserts that these problems have been exacerbated by a complete lack of systematic and meaningful data about the quality of teacher education programs.

Not surprisingly, NCTQ's solution to the problem of teacher education (its prognostic dimension) is tightly connected to its diagnosis. The solution to the problem, as NCTQ leaders argue, is to rate teacher education programs based on NCTQ standards and make these ratings publically available to all potential consumers. For example, in the 2013 *Teacher Prep Review*, NCTQ explained that the review was "part of our effort to bring as much transparency as possible to the way America's teachers are prepared" (Greenberg et al., 2013, p. 1). By NCTQ's logic, transparency will result in changes to teacher preparation because poor-quality programs will be forced to improve or shut down due to market pressure. Presumably, teacher candidates and future employers will seek out highly rated programs and abandon programs with low ratings. However, as we show later in this chapter, the theory of change underlying NCTQ's approach hinges on an assumption that schools of education and prospective teacher candidates put a great deal of stock in NCTQ ratings and make choices accordingly, an assumption we question.

Power Relationships in Accountability

In terms of the control dimension of accountability, NCTQ assumes that decisions about how teacher education should be held accountable should lie outside of teacher education itself (Greenberg, Walsh, & McKee, 2014). The assumption behind their review is that an external organization like NCTQ is necessary to provide neutral and objective information about the quality of teacher education programs, which are often described by NCTQ as lacking the capacity and motivation to govern and hold themselves accountable (Greenberg, Walsh, & McKee, 2014). However, even though it claims to be neutral, NCTQ's work to reshape the teacher education landscape has very deliberate political intentions and is tied to a clear reform agenda, as discussed earlier in this chapter. NCTQ's reports portraying the failure of the nation's schools of education are very much in sync with the deregulation agenda that picked up steam in the 1990s (Cochran-Smith & Fries, 2001) and with what became the dominant accountability paradigm, as we describe it in Chapter 8.

The teacher education field has not stayed silent about NCTQ's reviews. Rather it has protested NCTQ's efforts to control teacher preparation accountability externally. The publication of NCTQ's reviews has prompted an outpouring of criticism and resistance from professional organizations (e.g., AACTE, 2013b, 2014a; American Federation of Teachers [AFT], 2013), university leadership (e.g., Lowery-Moore, 2013; Mercer, 2013; Underwood, 2013), teacher educators (e.g., Cochran-Smith, Piazza, & Power, 2013; Pallas, 2013; Strauss, 2013a), research/advocacy organizations (e.g., Eduventures, 2013), and the public sector (e.g., Louisiana Board of Regents, n.d.). These organizations have voiced their concern and even outrage that an external organization with no standing in the field of teacher preparation makes un-founded and erroneous claims about teacher education programs.

As we have noted, NCTQ focuses on course syllabi, textbooks, and other so-called inputs of teacher education programs (NCTQ, n.d.-f). This represents the content dimension of the NCTQ reviews, which has to do with what a given accountability initiative holds teacher education account-able for and what kinds of measures and indicators are used as evidence. The inputs-based material NCTQ collects is reviewed against its standards, which have been widely critiqued, most notably from faculty and deans of education schools across the country who wrote open letters of concern (e.g., Chatterjee, Bergeron, & Bordelon, n.d.; Heller, Segall, & Drake, 2013; McLaughlin, 2013), op-ed pieces (e.g., Gonzalez, 2013; Snyder, 2013), and blog posts (e.g., Pallas, 2013), pointing out the standards were developed in-house without a participatory process and without peer review.

Although the titles of NCTQ's standards (e.g., Early Reading, Classroom Management) seem reasonable enough, the specific indicators for each stan-dard reveal that they are simplistic, fail to account for the nuances of teach-ing and teacher education, and are, in some cases, simply not measuring anything meaningful in the first place. Many of the standards are striking-ly narrow in content, aligning closely with the idea of the "classroom-ready," technically equipped teacher discussed above. For example, as we noted above, NCTQ's standards related to teaching reading have been harshly critiqued by literacy experts for taking a narrow and incomplete view (McMunn Dooley et al., 2013; Strauss, 2013b). The language of the indicators for Early Reading Standard reads:

> Indicators that the program meets the standard: 2.1 Coursework lectures and practice adequately cover the five essential components of effective reading in-struction: phonemic awareness, phonics, fluency, vocabulary, and comprehen-sion strategies. . . . 2.2 Textbooks used in reading courses support effective reading instruction (NCTQ, n.d.-f)

Members of the Reading Hall of Fame, a professional association of elected scholars who are reading experts, argued that "With one stroke NCTQ lim-its the teaching of reading to teaching the 'scientific' reading program, the same one which failed for 13 years in NCLB and it limits teacher education programs to training teachers in this one true method" (Strauss, 2013b, p. 2). The Literacy Research Association also objected to NCTQ's Early Reading Standard, stating that it "does not attend to the literacy needs of diverse student populations" (McMunn Dooley et al., 2013, p. 2) due to the rigidity of the language in the standard and its narrow interpretation of how children should be taught to read.

Although previously NCTQ had a standard on equity, the equity stan-dard was never fully used for program rating and is now an "archived" standard. The separate criteria to which alternate-route programs are held are also devoid of any mention of equity (NCTQ, n.d.-e). With or without the equity standard, none of NCTQ's standards focus on content related to teaching about equity, social justice, or helping teacher candidates understand the complex underlying sources of inequity in the United States.

The consequences dimension of NCTQ's market-based approach is closely related to its prognostic dimension, which indicates that the way to fix teacher education is to rate programs based on NCTQ standards and make these ratings widely publicly available. Indeed, according to NCTQ, the intended consequence of the publication of public program ratings is to serve as a consumer guide and prompt programs to improve. The assumption is that this will happen because programs will not want to risk being poorly rated because of the negative publicity or because of fear of program closure if consumers vote with their feet and choose to attend highly rated programs. In short, according to NCTQ, "good programs will thrive," while poorly rated programs will scramble to improve their ratings or put their reputations at risk (Greenberg et al., 2013, p. 6).

Despite NCTQ's pressure on institutions to provide them with information, many private colleges and universities and some public institutions have stood firm in their refusal to release information to NCTQ, voicing a loud and clear distrust of NCTQ's standards and methodology and noting the organization's lack of professional standing in the field (Ingeno, 2013; Jost, 2014; Sawchuk, 2011). Although many of these programs were eventually rated anyway, with NCTQ accessing publicly available documents from institutions' websites, this dissent was an early indication that some schools of education would pay little attention to the ratings. And as we suggest below, we have found no evidence that the consequences NCTQ had hoped for—that programs would be forced to change or shut down if and when they received negative ratings—have actually occurred.

NCTQ: THEORY OF CHANGE AND THE RELATED EVIDENCE

In this section we unpack the claims that NCTQ makes about its approach, and we weigh the related evidence. In defining the problem of teacher education, NCTQ asserts that one root cause of educational decline in the United States is the uneven (and generally poor) quality of teacher education programs. Specifically, NCTQ asserts that teacher education programs are chaotic, out of sync with policy and public demands, and incapable of preparing teachers to perform in the classroom beginning on "day one" (Greenberg et al., 2013; Greenberg et al., 2014; NCTQ, 2016a, 2017). The theory of change behind NCTQ's reviews of teacher preparation programs is that publicly disseminating ratings of programs will solve the problem of teacher education quality. Underlying this theory of change are two claims that go hand in hand. First is a *market claim* that the publication of program ratings will set market forces in motion that will influence consumers' (i.e., prospective teachers') program choices and also drive program improvement. Second is an underlying *effectiveness claim* based on the idea that differences in programs' NCTQ ratings accurately reflect differences in program quality and in the effectiveness of program graduates.

NCTQ's Market Claim

As we have said, according to NCTQ the only way to enforce standards in the vast and uneven field of teacher education is by "fully engaging the unparalleled power of the marketplace" by shining a "harsh spotlight" on individual institutions and programs, which is "highly motivating" to them (Greenberg et al., 2014, p. 10). NCTQ's theory of change is that a national database based on the results of their reviews empowers consumers to choose good programs and, further, that market forces will drive changes among underperforming programs (Greenberg et al., 2013, p. 4). In short, NCTQ's market claim assumes that the publication of program ratings influences consumers' choices, which creates competition among programs and drives program change, ultimately boosting teacher education quality and teacher quality.

To investigate this claim, we conducted a systematic search of two major education databases. We found no empirical studies of the impact of NCTQ's public program ratings on either consumers' or programs' behaviors in the face of published reviews.

We recognize, however, that despite the lack of empirical evidence about its impact, NCTQ widely and directly disseminates its publications to people like university presidents and deans who are concerned about their institutions' reputations and who have the power to influence university admissions policies, practices, and outcomes. We also recognize that NCTQ has a sizable social media presence, with approximately 22,500 Twitter followers. We thus looked beyond empirical research for signs of evidence of impact. Based on our review of university press releases and organization statements, we found mixed evidence regarding NCTQ's impact on teacher education programs' practices. On one hand, we note that there may be an increasing level of complacency among members of the teacher education community concerning the reviews. As we mentioned earlier, when the first NCTQ review was published in 2013, there was an outpouring of criticisms and resistance from universities, professional organizations, and teacher educators. While the release of the 2014 review received some similar criticism from the teacher education community (e.g., AACTE, 2014a; Heller, 2014), some other universities began to leverage their "good results" from NCTQ. For example, the websites of Arizona State University (2016), Maryville College (2014), the University of Dayton (2014, 2017), the University of

Houston (2014), Western Governors University (2014), and Wilmington University (2016) publicly cite their institutions' good rankings from NCTQ with phrases such as "nationally recognized," "programs recognized as one of nation's best," or "ranked number one by NCTQ." In contrast, many other institutions simply made no mention of NCTQ's program ratings even when their programs were rated favorably by NCTQ (e.g., College of William and Mary, n.d.; ED Lines, 2014; Pianta, 2014).

Given that we found no empirical evidence related to whether NCTQ's public program ratings influenced the market, we looked for information about whether *any* public ranking system of higher education institutions influenced the market. The most relevant evidence comes from studies about the USNWR public annual rankings of U.S. colleges and universities. The findings of several empirical studies suggest that USNWR rankings do have some influence on schools' admission outcomes such as acceptance rates, yield, and quality of entering classes as measured by SAT scores or percentage of students from the top 10% of their high school graduating classes (Meredith, 2004; Monks & Ehrenberg, 1999; Sauder & Lancaster, 2006). For example, Meredith (2004) found that moving from the second to the first quartile of rated institutions led to a significant increase in the number of incoming students who were in the top 10% of their high school classes as well as a significant decrease in the institution's acceptance rate the following year. On the other hand, other studies investigated whether this sort of change in the behaviors of institutions actually made sense educationally or were simply attempts to "game the system" to influence rankings (e.g., Ehrenberg, 2002; Hazelkorn, 2015; Luca & Smith, 2011; Machung, 1998). Along these lines, Machung (1998) concluded that because of the benefits for institutions that receive high rankings, there were concerns about whether certain admission decisions and practices made by schools were ethical. Although our searches have not identified similar empirical evidence related to NCTQ's rating system, anecdotal evidence indicates that at least some faculty members have been asked by senior leadership to change course syllabi or website information to better align with NCTQ's review criteria (Crawford-Garrett as cited in Ravitch, 2014).

In sum, first, NCTQ claims that the "harsh spotlight" of public ratings prompts meaningful changes in teacher preparation programs, but there is little evidence that NCTQ's public ratings actually influence the behaviors of prospective consumers. Second, the USNWR studies of U.S. colleges suggest that although external ratings of programs and institutions may encourage them to manipulate the system to boost their ratings, these changes are unlikely to make sense educationally or lead to meaningful improvement in the quality of programs offered. As Sauder and Lancaster (2006) argue, "The relationship between the signal [produced by the rankings] and the quality it is signaling is not always pure" (p. 107). Although there is no empirical evidence to evaluate NCTQ's market impact, the evidence about

USNWR's impact in other areas causes us to doubt that NCTQ's teacher education ratings constitute a market force that leads to real improvements in programs quality.

NCTQ's Effectiveness Claim

NCTQ's second claim is that differences in its program ratings reflect differences in the quality of programs and their graduates. Yet Richard Allington, a well-known reading scholar and former President of the International Reading Association, argues that NCTQ's program ratings are based on flawed methodology and lack of validity.

> Imagine a person reviews the restaurants in your city by examining the menus they found online. Never tasted the food or ever visited any restaurant. How seriously would you take the reviews that were written? That is the NCTQ report on colleges of education. Had NCTQ not already developed a reputation for sloppy "research" perhaps ed schools would have cooperated. Personally, I'm glad they didn't. (Allington as cited in Ravitch, 2013)

Allington's critique is similar to that of many others who have questioned the validity of NCTQ's approach. One way to evaluate the validity of NCTQ's evaluation system is to determine whether or not its ratings correlate with the results of other measures of program quality and/or with evidence showing that teacher education programs highly ranked by NCTQ produce more effective teachers than do those that are not as highly ranked. NCTQ's usefulness as an accountability mechanism depends on this claim. Empirical research that addresses NCTQ's effectiveness claim is limited, but it is direct and consistent. The most relevant evidence comes from a study by Henry and Bastian (2015). The authors used NCTQ-provided data for more than 4,500 first- or second-year teachers in North Carolina to investigate the association between NCTQ's ratings of programs and two measures of teacher performance—teachers' value-added scores representing their impact on students' test scores and their evaluations by administrators based on classroom observations. Overall, Henry and Bastian found that higher NCTQ program ratings did *not* predict either higher teacher value-added scores or better teacher evaluations. They concluded, "With our data and analyses, we do not find strong relationships between the performance of teacher preparation program graduates and NCTQ's overall program ratings or meeting NCTQ's standards" (Henry & Bastian, 2015, p. 1).

Two smaller studies corroborate Henry and Bastian's general conclusions. Fuller (2015) found a nonsignificant correlation coefficient ($r = 0.178$) between NCTQ's 2013 ratings and the percentage of graduates passing the early childhood and elementary teacher licensure exams in Texas. In the same report, Fuller also found that for two programs in the state of

Washington, teacher candidates from one program had value-added scores that were significantly greater than the scores of those in another program in both reading and mathematics. However, both of these programs received the same rating from NCTQ's first *Teacher Prep Review*. As Fuller (2015) argued, the problem is that NCTQ would have consumers believe that two programs that receive the same NCTQ rating have equal quality, yet this may not be the case. Similarly, Dudley-Marling (2013, 2015) found no relationship between the proportion of programs that met NCTQ's Early Reading Standard in individual states and the NAEP reading performance of students in the same jurisdictions. In short, there is evidence indicating that NCTQ's ratings of teacher education programs are *not* a valid and appropriate method for evaluating the quality of teacher education programs.

To dig deeper into this, we sought to understand whether there were positive associations between programs' scores on individual NCTQ standards and program outcomes. The same study as above by Henry and Bastian (2015) also investigated the relationships between program outcomes (i.e., teacher value-added scores and teacher evaluation ratings) and program scores on individual NCTQ standards. They did not find any systematic correlations between NCTQ's program ratings on each standard and program outcomes. Rather, they found that some correlations between teachers' value-added scores or principal evaluations and their programs' NCTQ ratings were positive and significant, some associations were negative and significant, and most associations were not significant (Henry & Bastian, 2015). Tracz and colleagues (2017) confirmed these findings; they found no significant relationships between NCTQ's Selection Criteria Standard and principals' evaluations of teachers. In addition, they reviewed 13 studies described and cited by NCTQ itself as "strong evidence" supporting their Selection Criteria Standard (NCTQ, 2014b). However Tracz and colleagues found that most of NCTQ's citations provided "little or no evidence to support [NCTQ's] selectivity criteria, and many [of the] articles [that NCTQ] cited as evidence did not even address the topic" (Tracz, Torgerson, & Beare, 2017, p. 12). Our own prior work confirms this. For example, we investigated one study (Boyd, Lankford, Loeb, Rockoff, & Wyckoff, 2008) cited by NCTQ as part of its "strong body of research" for establishing selection criteria for prospective teachers such as SAT scores (NCTQ, 2016b). We found that NCTQ had misrepresented the study's nuanced findings about selectivity criteria for teacher candidates. We also concluded in a "think tank review" that existing research did not support NCTQ's selection criteria (Cochran-Smith, Baker, Chang, Fernández, & Keefe, 2017).

Finally, we consider the relevance of the standards NCTQ uses to evaluate programs. In 2006 the International Ranking Expert Group met in Berlin to review principles of quality and best practices for ranking higher education institutions. The result was a set of 16 "Berlin Principles," vetted by an international group of experts representing many different perspectives (Institute for Higher Education Policy, 2006). As Stolz, Hendel, and Horn (2010) suggest, these principles can be a useful benchmark by which to evaluate the validity of a ranking system and have been used elsewhere to consider the validity of ranking systems (Cheng & Liu, 2008). However, we found that NCTQ's approach did not meet the standards set out in the Berlin Principles. For example, the third principle states that ranking systems should "Recognize the diversity of institutions and take the different missions and goals of institutions into account" (Institute for Higher Education Policy, 2006), yet NCTQ applies a blanket set of standards to all institutions and does not consider the goals that the programs themselves may hold. Perhaps even more troubling is that NCTQ's approach, which relies primarily on inputs such as course syllabi, does not coincide with Berlin Principle 8: "[Ranking systems should] measure outcomes in preference to inputs whenever possible." Further, the NCTQ system does not "specify the linguistic, cultural, economic, and historical contexts of the educational systems being ranked," which is Berlin's Principle 5. Thus NCTQ's standards and methods do not meet internationally vetted standards, further calling into question the effectiveness and validity of their approach.

IMPACT AND IMPLICATIONS: NCTQ'S IMPACT ON THE FIELD

For all of NCTQ's efforts to change teacher preparation in the United States, what impact has its teacher preparation reviews actually had on the landscape of accountability in teacher education? Here we explore several trends.

Perpetuating a Failure Narrative

From its inception, NCTQ's mission and its various initiatives were based on the assertion that university-sponsored teacher preparation programs were failing—that is, failing to produce well-qualified teachers whose programs met their standards. As we explained in Chapter 2, the ongoing narrative of failure has become so embedded in popular rhetoric during the accountability era that it is now part of the "common sense" about education and teacher education.

Based on our analysis of NCTQ's work, it is clear that the organization has been quite effective at contributing to a persistent failure narrative. NCTQ's aggressive distribution of reports, press releases, testimony, and public presentations by its leaders all feed the same narrative that teacher education is failing and that market-driven efforts like NCTQ's are the key to reform. For example, in a 2011 address to Congress, NCTQ president Kate Walsh stated that "the selectivity of teacher preparation programs, the knowledge they require teacher candidates to master, and the way these institutions prepare candidates for the rigors of the classroom is, at best, uneven, and often, woefully inadequate" (U.S. House of Representatives, 2011, p. 3). This narrative of failure is damaging and, as we noted above, sometimes has the power to shape the field directly. This is illustrated in an account of the experience of Katy Crawford-Garrett, an assistant professor of literacy at the University of New Mexico. Crawford-Garrett shared her experience of meeting with a senior administrator of her department at the university regarding the syllabus for her reading course on Diane Ravitch's blog. Crawford-Garrett wrote:

> Our university is in the midst of being evaluated by the National Council on Teacher Quality (NCTQ), the highly suspect political organization widely known for having an agenda aimed at dismantling colleges of education nationwide. My syllabus was deemed unacceptable [by the administrator] for a number of reasons. 1) I did not explicitly mention the words "fluency" or "vocabulary" 2) I did not have my students take a final exam and. . . . During the meeting I was told to "fix" my syllabus and to add one of the textbooks NCTQ deems appropriate. (Crawford-Garrett as cited in Ravitch, 2014)

Crawford-Garrett's account is deeply concerning. It exemplifies the danger of programs buying into the failure narrative articulated by NCTQ and tailoring the teacher education curriculum to align, at least on the surface, with NCTQ's questionable and unvetted standards of quality.

Of course, teacher preparation programs have had a range of reactions to the NCTQ rankings, with many choosing not to provide requested syllabi and other documents, to ignore the ratings, or to speak out against them rather than fall into step with their standards and approach. Many teacher educators have spoken out against NCTQ's problematic views of teaching and learning, which—if followed—narrow the teacher education curriculum (e.g., Gonzalez, 2013; Grenot-Scheyer, 2013; International Reading Association, 2013). We support these colleagues. As we see it, perpetuating a narrative of failure and providing one narrow solution to the problem, as NCTQ does, charts a dangerous course. Where in NCTQ's standards are values and concepts related to preparing teachers and students for participation in a divided democratic society? Where are ideals related to teaching for social justice or helping prospective teachers learn about the systems and structures that reproduce inequity and how to work with others to challenge it? What would happen if most teacher education programs simply adjusted the curriculum to boost NCTQ ratings—would the critical ideas in the teacher education curriculum simply fade away? This is a dangerous prospect, not just for schools of education, but for the country writ large.

Missing the Mark on Program Improvement

NCTQ documents suggest that the key to fixing teacher education is rating programs based on external review. But does this lead to any meaningful program improvement? As suggested in many of the critiques detailed throughout this chapter, NCTQ's methodology is flawed. The indicators they stipulate, the kind of data they collect, and their data analyses are false, incomplete, and not rigorous, as we showed with the example of the Early Reading Standard. Despite NCTQ's supposed aim of improving teacher preparation, the validity of program ratings is problematic, which raises the question of whether NCTQ's rankings provide education schools with information that might be useful for program improvement. Teachers College at Columbia University is a telling example. In 2013, Aaron Pallas wrote a blog post in which he pointed out an unusually egregious mistake in NCTQ's first *Teacher Prep Review*: NCTQ had evaluated and graded two programs at Teachers College that did not even exist. This example has been widely used to point out the absurdity of a system that rates programs without ever engaging with those programs and their participants. We stand with the many others who believe that NCTQ's evaluations do little to bring about meaningful improvement in teacher preparation. And, as we have shown above, the existing empirical data simply do not show a correlation between NCTQ's ratings and other common indicators of program quality (Henry & Bastian, 2015). How useful can program ratings be when they are generated by an external advocacy organization whose work is so distant from the local sites of teacher preparation and from the realities of learning to teach in particular local contexts and communities?

Eroding Trust and Discouraging Collaboration

Finally, NCTQ's teacher preparation reviews, along with its other reports and websites, exacerbate competition, erode trust, and discourage collaboration among teacher education communities and other involved parties such as citizens and policymakers. This is intentional and inherent in NCTQ's market-based approach, which is based on competition, not collaboration. We wonder if erosion of trust and enhanced competition are the true intended consequence of NCTQ's approach. Do the organization's leaders hope that fueling competition among schools of education will enable alternative routes to teacher certification to flourish? After all, as we noted at the beginning of this chapter, the original purpose of NCTQ, which was closely aligned with the purposes of the Fordham Foundation and the Abell Foundation, was to disrupt, even dismantle, university teacher preparation programs and to encourage alternative routes.

In sum, we find NCTQ's efforts deeply troubling. Although NCTQ has identified a legitimate problem in the uneven quality of teacher preparation programs, NCTQ's standards and philosophy are guided by a narrow and technical view of teaching, while ignoring the pressing need to consider issues of equity, social justice, and democratic education. Their market-based approach intentionally aggravates competition among schools of education, discourages collaboration, and erodes trust. Along different somewhat cynical lines, one indication of NCTQ's positive impact on the field is that it has encouraged efforts like ours to unpack and critique the flaws in NCTQ's own methods and logic and to propose alternative, more meaningful approaches to accountability. We take up these issues directly in Chapters 8 and 9.

edTPA

Performance, Professionalization, and Pearson

Billed as a way to "emphasize, measure and support the skills and knowledge that all teachers need from Day 1 in the classroom" (AACTE, n.d.-b, para. 1), the Educative Teacher Performance Assessment, known as edTPA, is a nationally available assessment used to evaluate the performance of teacher candidates. Faculty and staff at Stanford University's Center for Assessment, Learning, and Equity (SCALE), in partnership with AACTE, designed the controversial edTPA to assess what teacher candidates do and how they reflect on their work (AACTE, n.d.-c). Currently required for teacher licensure in a number of states and widely used in teacher education programs across the country, edTPA requires aspiring teachers to submit a portfolio of lessons and reflections, which is scored by anonymous external reviewers through an evaluation system managed by the Pearson corporation. The portfolio highlights teacher candidates' knowledge and skills related to planning, instruction, and assessment through classroom video recordings, student work samples, and commentaries (Pecheone, Shear, Whittaker, & Darling-Hammond, 2013).

Like the other approaches we have reviewed in this book, edTPA is an accountability initiative intended to improve teaching and teacher education. edTPA is different from the others, however, in that it holds teacher candidates, rather than teacher education programs or institutions, accountable. The assessment has prompted both enthusiasm and resistance among a range of actors involved in the teacher education enterprise, from teacher education researchers and practitioners to state departments of education. Pearson's role, which we take up in the final section of this chapter, has been among the most controversial aspects of edTPA. What led to the controversy surrounding edTPA? What do its proponents hope it will achieve in terms of teacher quality and teacher education quality? What is it about this assessment that raises so much consternation among its detractors? To address these questions, this chapter unpacks edTPA as a major teacher education accountability initiative by examining the context in which it emerged, the claims made by its proponents, and the impact and implications it has had on teacher education. We argue that while edTPA has stimulated positive change in a number of teacher education programs, there have been multiple concerns about standardization, professionalization, and corporatization that make it unlikely that edTPA will lead to the widespread enhancements of preparation program quality and professional status its promoters envisage. In short, edTPA is a unique accountability initiative that grew out of good intentions to improve the profession from within and allow for locally designed formative assessment opportunities. Good intentions notwithstanding, the management and implementation demands of a national-level summative assessment, coupled with tensions and inconsistencies in edTPA itself, have marred its capacity to be transformative.

CONTEXT: UNDERSTANDING edTPA

Over the past two decades, amidst the calls for greater teacher effectiveness and increased student achievement, teacher performance assessments emerged as a popular approach to teacher education reform and improvement (Darling-Hammond, 2010). Intended to evaluate teacher candidates' actual classroom practice and "measure aspects of teaching related to teachers' effectiveness" (Darling-Hammond, Newton, & Wei, 2012, p. 9), performance assessments contrast with traditional measures of candidates' preparedness, including the paper-and-pencil subject-matter exams used in many states. Proponents of performance assessments regard paper-and-pencil tests not only as inauthentic, unsystematic, and unrepresentative of teacher education program quality (Pecheone & Chung, 2006), but also as "trivializ[ing]teaching rather than seriously engag[ing] teachers in the development of effective practice" (Darling-Hammond & Hyler, 2013, p. 13).

History: Assessing Teacher Performance

The late 1990s and early 2000s saw the implementation of a number of high-stakes teacher performance assessments across the United States (Chung, 2008; Darling-Hammond, 2010)—a movement inspired in part by the success and design of the standards-based National Board for Professional Teaching Standards (NBPTS) certification assessment of experienced teachers (Darling-Hammond, 2010, 2012). For example, Colorado, Kentucky, and Oregon developed performance-based assessments as part of their initial teacher licensure policies, and Connecticut implemented a performance assessment for early-career teachers (Darling-Hammond, 2010). In addition, NCATE shifted from "an input-based model of accreditation to an emphasis on the assessment of teaching performance as evidence of program effectiveness" (Wei & Pecheone, 2010, p. 99). As we show in Chapter 5, CAEP maintained this approach with the requirement that teacher education programs include multiple performance-based assessments for teacher candidates (CAEP, 2015d). Arguably, however, the most far-reaching adoption of teacher performance assessments was in California, where in 2002 a group of 12 teacher education programs launched the Performance Assessment for California Teachers (PACT) (Darling-Hammond, 2014), which grew to a consortium of more than 30 teacher preparation programs (Darling-Hammond et al., 2012). The PACT would later serve as the basis for edTPA (Sato, 2014).

The PACT was developed in response to 1998 California legislation that required all prospective teachers to pass a performance-based assessment in order to obtain teaching licensure (Chung, 2008). Dissatisfied with the structure and content of the state-commissioned performance assessment produced by the Educational Testing Service (Pecheone & Chung, 2006), members of the PACT consortium set out to "develop an integrated, authentic, and subject-specific assessment that [was] consistent with the core values of member institutions while meeting the assessment standards required by the state" (Pecheone & Chung, 2006, pp. 22–23). State-approved for use as a licensing requirement in 2007 (Darling-Hammond et al., 2012), the PACT is comprised of two key components: a common, standardized summative assessment completed during the clinical experience (known as the "Teaching Event") and a series of locally designed assessments completed throughout the course of the preparation program (known as "Embedded Signature Assessments") (PACT, n.d.). The makers of the PACT designed the assessment not only to provide evidence of a candidate's readiness to teach, but also to drive teacher preparation program improvement (Wei & Pecheone, 2010).

The PACT was well received in California (Darling-Hammond & Hyler, 2013), and interest in the assessment soon spread to other states (Darling-Hammond, 2012). By 2009, a group of teacher educators and teachers from across the United States had decided to design a national version of the assessment (Bradley, 2017; Darling-Hammond, 2012; Darling-Hammond & Hyler, 2013). With support from AACTE and SCALE (Darling-Hammond, 2012), the Teacher Performance Assessment Consortium (TPAC) was formed "to create a common initial licensing assessment that [could] be used nationwide to make preparation and licensing performance based, as well as predictive of teacher effectiveness" (Darling-Hammond, 2010, p. 11). Funded by state and private foundations (Darling-Hammond, 2010), the consortium produced the Teacher Performance Assessment (TPA), which soon evolved into what is now known simply as edTPA (AACTE, n.d.-c).

As interest in the assessment grew, the makers decided to seek "an administrative partner" (Darling-Hammond & Hyler, 2013, p. 13) and issued a request for proposals. In a move that would ultimately prove extremely controversial, the group selected Pearson, due in part to its experience managing the NBPTS assessment (Darling-Hammond & Hyler, 2013). After initial prototyping and numerous field tests (Pecheone et al., 2013), edTPA was deemed "fully operational and ready for use across the country" in the fall of 2013 (AACTE, n.d.-c). At the time of this writing, 764 teacher education programs in 40 states were participating in edTPA, with 16 states having approved it as part of policies related to program completion, licensure, and/or program accreditation (AACTE, n.d.-d).

Basics: Structure, Cost, and Scoring

Aligned with both the InTASC standards for beginning teacher licensing and the Common Core State Standards (CCSS) (Pecheone et al., 2013), edTPA is a summative assessment with specific content-area versions for 27 teaching subjects and grade levels ranging from early childhood through secondary (AACTE, n.d.-b). "Designed around job-related practices that teachers employ throughout their teaching career" (Pecheone et al., 2013, p. 9), the assessment follows a portfolio design and features a uniform structure focused on three key tasks: planning, instruction, and assessment (Pecheone et al., 2013). For the planning task, candidates describe their instructional and social contexts, provide lesson plans, and reflect on their planning. For the instruction task, candidates demonstrate "enactment" of their plans by submitting unedited video recordings of actual classroom instruction along with written commentaries analyzing that instruction. For the assessment task, candidates document "impact" by analyzing student work and providing evidence of feedback and support. Across all three tasks, candidates reflect on the various teaching decisions they made (Pecheone et al., 2013).

To complete the assessment, candidates must register online with Pearson (2017) and pay a $300 fee, which covers operational costs such as delivery, scoring, and customer support for both teacher candidates and teacher educators (AACTE, n.d.-b). Finalized portfolios are submitted via a web-based system and scored by experienced educators trained and paid by Evaluation Systems, a division of Pearson (AACTE, n.d.-b). Following scoring, detailed performance summaries and overall scores are sent to the candidates and their programs. While all submissions are scored against consistent standards, specific cut scores for passing or failing are determined by states and/or by individual preparation programs (AACTE, n.d.-b).

edTPA: AN EIGHT-DIMENSIONAL ANALYSIS

In this section, we use our eight dimensions of accountability framework to unpack edTPA as a highly visible example of accountability-based teacher education reform. Our analysis suggests that edTPA is different in many ways from the teacher education accountability initiatives discussed in Chapters 4 through 6, particularly in terms of its structure and underlying concepts. However, it shares with the other initiatives a number of key assumptions and issues related to power relationships and the purpose of education. Below we use the eight dimensions of accountability organized by clusters—foundations of accountability, the problem of teacher education, and power relationships in accountability—to examine those similarities and differences and expose the unique theory of change underlying edTPA (see Figure 7.1).

Foundations of Accountability: edTPA's Values, Purpose, and Concepts

The three dimensions of values, purpose, and concepts are related to the ideologies underlying edTPA and the initiative's relationship to broader reform agendas. In terms of the values dimension, the discourse in edTPA documents emphasizes three core values: workforce preparation for candidates and pupils, the professionalization of teaching with high standards, and the improvement of teacher education based on authentic data. With regard to workforce preparation for students and teachers, early architects of edTPA highlighted the importance of teaching the "complex skills students increasingly need to succeed in the rapidly evolving US society and economy" (Darling-Hammond, 2017, p. 1). For teacher candidates, Pecheone and Whittaker (2016) suggested that "states should be responsible for establishing performance standards that ensure that new teachers are well-prepared, competent, and ready to teach" (p. 9). In relation to professionalization and standards, key supporters point out that "edTPA is the first standards-based assessment to become nationally available" (AACTE, n.d.-c), and they compare edTPA to the licensing exams of other highly respected professional fields such as law and medicine (AACTE, n.d.-b). The stress on high standards and comparisons to other professions reflects the fundamental assumption behind edTPA that teaching should be on par with other professions. To move in that direction, performance-based credentialing assessments like edTPA are intended to elevate both teaching quality and the public's perception of teaching. Finally, edTPA materials emphasize the importance of "authentic" data, often meaning evidence of effective teaching (AACTE, n.d.-b, n.d.-c; Pecheone, Whittaker, Shear, & Klesch, 2015). SCALE also uses empirical data to support their claim that edTPA measures teacher effectiveness (Pecheone et al., 2015; Pecheone, Whittaker, & Klesch, 2016; Wilson, Hallam, Pecheone, & Moss, 2014). Price (2014) suggests that edTPA's emphasis on data, especially quantifiable data, is part of an increasingly prevalent ideology in education that he calls "the 'evidence' paradigm" (p. 220). This ideology stresses standardized evidence as a driver of educational change. It is important to note that while the focus on standardized *data* seems to link edTPA to the accountability paradigm introduced in Chapter 2 and elaborated in Chapter 8, edTPA also values *authenticity* (Pecheone et al., 2016). This combination creates tension within the underlying ideology of edTPA, and some critics have pointed to the contradictions in SCALE's depiction of edTPA as both authentic and standardized (Au, 2013).

Figure 7.1. Dimensions of Accountability: edTPA

Thematic Cluster	Dimension	edTPA
Foundations of Accountability	Values	• Preparing teacher candidates and students for the workforce • Professionalizing teaching with high standards • Improving teacher education based on authentic data
	Purpose	• Assessing uniformly candidate knowledge and readiness to teach • Improving teacher education programs and the field
	Concepts	• Effective teaching based on constructivist views of knowledge and practice • Measurement of success determined by multiple measures • Uniformity of teaching as local and nonstandard, but practice as measurable in a standardized way • Gatekeeping for high-quality assessment
The Problem of Teacher Education	Diagnostic	• Uneven teaching and teacher education quality combined with lack of professional standards results in inconsistent teaching quality and the low status of the teaching profession
	Prognostic	• Uniform and authentic (i.e., performance-based) assessment based on high standards will "fix" teacher education • Actionable data will drive program improvement
Power Relationships in Accountability	Control	• SCALE and Pearson administer the assessment adopted by states and programs • External to programs, internal to the profession (in creation)
	Content	• Programs held accountable for preparing candidates to be effective from day one of teaching • Measured by teacher candidates' performance on videos and reflections, assessed along standard, subject-specific rubrics
	Consequences	• Certification eligibility for candidates determined by edTPA standards • Existing inequities reinforced as a result of edTPA disproportionately screening out candidates of color

Regarding values, there are debates about edTPA's stance on equity. In describing edTPA, documents from both AACTE (n.d.-b) and SCALE (Pecheone et al., 2013) assert that teachers should be ready to teach "all" learners but otherwise make no mention of equity, even though, ironically, the word "equity" is actually part of SCALE's name. Along these lines, several analyses of edTPA point to the lack of clarity about equity and even to contradictions between an assessment meant to support all types of learners, on one hand, and uniform standards that pay little attention to the diversity of learners, on the other (e.g., Madeloni & Gorlewski, 2013; National Association for Multicultural Education [NAME], 2014; Sato, 2014; Tuck & Gorlewski, 2016). Sato (2014), a member of edTPA's national design team, acknowledges the limitations in how equity is incorporated into edTPA performance tasks:

> edTPA tasks represent a commitment to educational equity as defined specifically through a culturally relevant pedagogy theoretical framework; *yet the assessment depends on the preparation programs to instill in their candidates the knowledge, skills, and dispositions to enact this framework.* (p. 427, emphasis added)

The published literature about edTPA generally affirms Sato's point that teacher educators must choose whether to include or ignore equity-based approaches during edTPA preparation. Several teacher educators with first-hand experience using the assessment point out that due to time constraints, the absence of specific equity-oriented standards, and/or the time-consuming nature of the assessment, discussions of justice or equity are often left out of edTPA portfolios (An, 2016; Picower & Marshall, 2016; Tuck & Gorlewski, 2016). What this means is that while edTPA hypothetically allows opportunities for teacher candidates to demonstrate equitable practices, in reality, there is mounting evidence that edTPA constraints sometimes interfere with teacher candidates' ability to focus on equity in their portfolios.

In terms of purpose, edTPA is meant to enhance teacher effectiveness at improving student outcomes, improve the quality of teacher education, and elevate the status of teacher education as a profession. According to AACTE (n.d.-b), "[t]he education profession has recognized the need for a common, standards- and performance-based assessment of teaching effectiveness that would measure the classroom readiness of aspiring teachers and provide information for program improvement." The operating assumption here about teacher quality is that good teaching drives students' learning. In fact, edTPA supporters share a "common goal of making sure new teachers are able to teach each student effectively and improve student achievement" (AACTE, n.d.-c, para. 2). Additionally, in separate documents, Darling-Hammond (2010) and Pecheone and Whittaker (2016) each framed the introduction of performance assessments in general and edTPA in particular as a response to negative perceptions about teachers, suggesting that widespread implementation of edTPA would improve both teacher quality and the status of teaching. Frequent comparisons of edTPA to a "bar exam" for teaching further stress the goal of elevating the teaching profession (AACTE, n.d.-b.; Au, 2013; Richmond, 2014).

Finally, the concepts dimension of edTPA reveals a major difference between edTPA and other compliance-based accountability initiatives. Most importantly, edTPA draws on a constructivist approach to learning (Sato, 2014, p. 427). For example, its developers emphasize both inquiry (McKee, 2015) and the need for student-centered instruction (SCALE, n.d.-b). Furthermore, the very fact that edTPA is a performance assessment suggests that it is grounded in a conception of teaching as something that is unavoidably contextualized and that a valid assessment of good teaching cannot be separated from practice. In this sense, edTPA supporters reject the idea that teaching quality is measurable through abstract, purely academic tests. Instead, edTPA supporters emphasize authenticity as an important concept embedded into edTPA.

Analyzing these three dimensions helps to explain a rift within the teacher education community regarding edTPA's focus on measurement and standards. A key purpose of edTPA is to improve student outcomes, construed broadly (AACTE, n.d.-b). For this reason, SCALE's reports about edTPA focus on outcomes as a measure of validity (Pecheone et al., 2015, 2016). SCALE (2015b) also states that the validity of a teacher licensure exam is predicated on an assumed "relationship between the theoretical constructs that define effective teaching and the individual characteristics that define successful job performance" (p. 1). In this case, the assumed relationship is between what teachers do in the classroom—their practice, as measured by their performance on edTPA—and student outcomes. However, edTPA's critics argue that because edTPA has become a standardized process, it actually narrows the concept of teacher practice, especially when the effectiveness of teacher performance is measured by student outcomes (Au, 2013; Picower & Marshall, 2016; Price, 2014). This raises questions about whether "authentic practice" and standardized outcomes can coexist within the same accountability initiative. In other words, does edTPA align more with the dominant accountability paradigm, which we define in Chapter 8, or with progressive, constructivist approaches to teaching and teacher education? Perhaps this is a false dichotomy? We further examine these questions in our review of the recent empirical research on edTPA in a later section of this chapter.

The Problem of Teacher Education: Professionalization and Improvement

We turn now to the diagnostic and prognostic dimensions of edTPA. As Pecheone and Whittaker (2016) rightly suggest, an ongoing policy issue in education has been the widespread perception that teaching is something anyone can do, which of course ignores the many complexities within the profession:

> There is a perception that other professions are more difficult, complex, and take years of preparation. Still, some policy makers question why preparing teachers takes so much time, and they [sometimes] . . . lower standards that can ease the pathway into teaching. Such approaches can result in hiring under-prepared teachers who often serve children with the most challenging learning needs. (p. 9)

The authors suggest that no licensure test has yet been able to demonstrate novice teachers' readiness to be effective in the classroom. The authors frame universal use of edTPA, a single uniform assessment, as a response to the problem of the public's low esteem for the profession. The idea is that universal implementation of edTPA would be a dramatic improvement over the currently weak and disparate standards required for new teacher certification (Pecheone & Whittaker, 2016).

Darling-Hammond (2010) identified another problem in teacher education with her claim that traditional teacher licensure assessments do not predict the success of novice teachers. She suggests that "[p]erformance assessments that measure what teachers actually do in the classroom, and which have been found to be related to later teacher effectiveness, are a much more potent tool for evaluating teachers' competence and readiness, as well as for supporting needed changes in teacher education" (p. 5). Darling-Hammond wrote this before edTPA was created, and her point was about performance assessments in general. But this perspective is consistent with Darling-Hammond's general argument that performance assessments like edTPA can solve the problem of low teacher quality by assessing what candidates know and can do prior to the point of licensure, using uniform assessment. Again there is tension here: problem statements like those above align edTPA with an accountability paradigm that emphasizes standards and testing, at the same time that the focus on performance (i.e., what teachers actually do) sets edTPA apart from other accountability initiatives.

Identifying edTPA's explicit and implicit assumptions about the problem of teacher education helps to uncover edTPA's theory of change. The theory starts with the idea that as a valid and reliable performance assessment, edTPA can provide meaningful and systematic data about teacher candidates' practices (Pecheone et al., 2015, 2016) that should be considered alongside other measures of teacher success, including teachers' and administrators' perceptions of teacher performance (Darling-Hammond, 2014). The assumption that edTPA data should inform programmatic and organizational improvement aligns with edTPA's purpose of professionalizing teaching and teacher education. From this perspective, the idea is that edTPA will improve teacher quality, and that improvement will contribute to teacher professionalism in terms of both actual quality and public perceptions of that quality.

Power Relationships in Accountability: By Whom, For Whom?

We turn now to power relationships and edTPA. Regarding the control dimension of accountability, edTPA developers emphasize that edTPA was created "by and for" the profession (AACTE, 2014b) in that teacher educators at SCALE were responsible for its creation (AACTE, n.d.-c). However, edTPA evaluation and management are completed by Pearson employees far removed from individual programs. Given that a higher education institution (SCALE at Stanford University) and a corporate body (Pearson) actually own and administer edTPA, it seems clear that in reality, there is little to no internal control for individual teacher education programs despite edTPA's claims of ownership by the profession. In addition, in states where edTPA is required, state-level policymakers determine cut scores and the consequences for teacher candidates who do and do not make the cut. State oversight further diminishes local control and the agency of individual programs and teacher educators. Accordingly, many critiques of edTPA have to do with power and control and include questions about: Pearson's role as manager of edTPA data collection, storage, and scoring (Au, 2013; NAME, 2014); concerns over inconsistent implementation policies (Reagan, Schram, McCurdy, Chang, & Evans, 2016); and tensions related to how teacher educators can cultivate critical and culturally responsive dispositions in teacher candidates while also preparing candidates to pass edTPA (Tuck & Gorlewski, 2016).

In terms of the content dimension—or what teacher education is held accountable for and how it is measured—edTPA focuses on teacher candidates' professional judgments, practices, and reflections. According to edTPA supporters, traditional licensure testing is inauthentic insofar as it is dislocated from practice, while edTPA goes far beyond decontextualized knowledge to examine candidates' actual practice. However, to make edTPA nationally available, SCALE had to standardize performance-based indicators and the assessment of written reflection. Performance assessments in general "require teachers to document their plans and teaching for a unit of instruction, videotape and analyze lessons, and collect and evaluate evidence of student learning" (Darling-Hammond, 2014, p. 555). This means that with edTPA, the content dimension (what teacher education is accountable for) has to do with teacher candidates' classroom performance, which is not so easily standardizable.

In terms of the consequences dimension, edTPA's intended consequence is to sort out well-prepared, ready-to-teach candidates from those who are not, thus enhancing overall teacher quality and boosting the status of the profession. However, we also found that an unintended consequence was that edTPA constrained teacher educator agency in terms of curricular and instructional decision making. In addition, edTPA "intrude[s]" (Tuck & Gorlewski, 2016, p. 203) on programs by creating demands that may contradict their core values (Lit & Lotan, 2013) because the priority has to be ensuring that candidates pass the test and obtain certification. This is a hotly debated issue (Miller, Carroll, Jancic, & Markworth, 2015). States often decide the consequences for teacher candidates required to take edTPA, such as whether edTPA scores determine licensure. This means that edTPA acts as the gatekeeper into the teaching profession, preventing failing candidates from becoming certified (Ledwell & Oyler, 2016). On a related note, some critics question whether the gatekeeping function of edTPA actually reinforces existing inequities by screening out candidates of color. Some point to discrepancies between the scores of white teacher candidates and candidates of color (Goldhaber, Cowan, & Theobald, 2016), while others raise issues such as cultural disconnects and cost (Picower & Marshall, 2016). These discrepancies call into question whether a larger, unintended consequence of edTPA is to inhibit diversity in a teaching force that is already unrepresentative of American students. High-stakes, nationwide implementation of edTPA may reproduce and maintain longstanding inequities.

CLAIMS AND EVIDENCE:
AUTHENTICITY, IMPROVEMENT, AND PROFESSIONALIZATION

Within just the two-year period from 2015 to 2017, a flood of research studies, accounts of experiences, and commentary examining edTPA has emerged. Whereas previous research on performance assessments in teacher education tended to focus on measurement issues (e.g., Cowan & Goldhaber, 2014; Duckor, Castellano, Téllez, Wihardini, & Wilson, 2014), the recent literature is more varied. Some of it provides what might be considered "voices from the field" (e.g., Picower & Marshall, 2016), which include critiques of edTPA as lacking contextualized, critical approaches to assessment, as well as analyses of promising areas like rigorous standards (e.g., Miller et al., 2015). There are also accounts that explore individual teacher educators' or programs' experiences with edTPA (An, 2016, 2017; Girtz, 2014), as well as policy analyses (Reagan, Schram, et al., 2016). In short, edTPA is increasingly popular as a focus of inquiry and provocative critique, which we suspect reflects its growing use at program and state levels. In this section, we dig into this research to unpack the claims of edTPA promoters, specifically the claim that it will boost the quality of teachers and teacher education programs as well as public perceptions of these fields.

As detailed above, proponents of edTPA assert that teaching has failed to develop as a legitimate profession with uniform expectations (Darling-Hammond, 2009; Pecheone, Pigg, Chung, & Souviney, 2005). They further assert that the implementation of state licensure policies requiring standardized, high-stakes performance assessments can fix the problem of inconsistent expectations regarding teacher candidates and also enhance the legitimacy of the profession. This theory of change is based on three claims about how the widespread implementation of edTPA can presumably boost the quality of teacher education programs (and teacher quality). First, there is an *authenticity claim* that edTPA authentically measures candidate performance and predicts teachers' future success. Second, there is an *improvement claim* that meeting the requirements of edTPA positively impacts the professional learning of teacher candidates and also prompts continuous program improvement. Finally, there is a *professionalization claim* that the widespread implementation of edTPA will drive self-regulated improvement from inside teacher education and thus enhance the status of the profession.

Authenticity Claim: Positioning edTPA as a Valid Assessment

Advocates of edTPA assert that it is an authentic measurement tool that both reflects and predicts teacher candidates' success in the classroom (Darling-Hammond, 2009, 2017; Darling-Hammond et al., 2012), and ultimately improves student learning by improving teacher quality (Darling-Hammond & Hyler, 2013). This claim has been investigated from multiple perspectives by both edTPA developers and independent researchers. Some have focused on teacher candidates' performance on edTPA in relationship to teachers' effectiveness at improving student test scores, while others have looked at candidates' and administrators' perceptions of the assessment in order to assess whether and how it authentically measures teacher effectiveness.

Several papers have investigated edTPA's reliability and validity, most concluding that there is evidence that edTPA is both valid and reliable as a measurement tool. SCALE's reports provide substantial evidence of edTPA's internal consistency (Pecheone et al., 2013, 2015) and ability to predict teacher performance (Pecheone et al., 2016). In addition, we located four independent analyses related to edTPA validity. Based on value-added measures, two studies found that a candidate's performance on edTPA predicted later effectiveness (Bastian & Lys, 2016; Goldhaber et al., 2016). Another correlated edTPA scores with undergraduate GPA (Evans, Kelly, Baldwin, & Arnold, 2016). Two caveats arise in these studies. First, Goldhaber et al. (2016) stressed that their results were mixed, as edTPA only predicted limited aspects of teachers' value added to students' reading and math scores. Second, because Evans et al. (2016) used GPA as a stand-in for teachers' general quality, their findings have substantial limitations. Additionally, Lalley (2016) evaluated SCALE's reports and found that "no evidence [was] provided that links performance and the edTPA with actually teaching in the profession" (p. 66). Still, SCALE has provided substantial evidence supporting its assertion about edTPA's validity and reliability, and while Lalley (2016) rejects this claim on theoretical grounds, the empirical studies we located cautiously support it.

Several studies have also considered teacher educators' and candidates' *perceptions* of edTPA's authenticity, as opposed to its psychometric qualities. Evidence from a number of studies indicates that contextual factors, such as instructors' curricular choices, local implementation conditions, and candidates' attitudes or beliefs influence how well edTPA scores equate with teacher success as well as educators' overall evaluations of edTPA's authenticity (An, 2016, 2017; Lin, 2015; Meuwissen, Choppin, Shang-Butler, & Cloonan, 2015; Thompson, Owens, Seed, & Key, 2014; Tuck & Gorlewski, 2016). In short, users' perceptions about the capacity of edTPA to authentically measure performance vary based on *how*, *where*, and *with whom* edTPA is used. This suggests that individuals and programs that use edTPA have some agency over how it is implemented and whether it is implemented well.

Variations in teaching specialties also complicate the claim that edTPA is an authentic measurement tool. Even though there are multiple subject-specific versions of edTPA, it is not clear that a standardized assessment of teaching performance works well for all content areas. Specifically, there have been questions about edTPA's validity for assessing teaching performance in art (Parkes & Powell, 2015) and special education (Ledwell & Oyler, 2016; Pugach, 2017). Critiques highlight discrepancies between a standardized, summative assessment on the one hand, and the contextualized, complex practice it is meant to measure, on the other. In addition, edTPA does not account for variations in individual test-takers or teacher education programs. For this reason, educators in less common teaching fields sometimes question edTPA's authenticity as a measurement and learning tool.

Improvement Claim:
Fostering Candidate Learning and Program Improvement

The improvement claim underlying edTPA as an effective accountability mechanism is that it has a positive impact on the professional learning of the teacher candidates who complete it and that it prompts continuous program improvement (AACTE, n.d.-c). According to edTPA materials, "As an educative assessment of teacher performance, candidate preparation for [edTPA] is embedded in multiple learning experiences across the teacher preparation program, and the assessment provides actionable data designed to support candidate development and program renewal" (Pecheone et al., 2013, p. 6). While edTPA proponents tout its benefits for the professional learning of teacher candidates, the evidence supporting that assertion is decidedly mixed. There is some evidence that teacher candidates believe that edTPA improved their teaching practice (Barron, 2015) and prepared them for inservice teacher evaluations (Barron, 2015; Heil & Berg, 2017). In particular, some studies suggest that specific aspects of the assessment bolster professional learning, such as the videotape component (Huston, 2017), the focus on academic language (Heil & Berg, 2017), and the opportunities edTPA provides for reflection (Peterson & Bruster, 2014). However, other studies indicate that preparing for and taking the assessment has a negative impact on teacher candidates because they experience it as unfair, unclear, time-consuming, and/or stress-inducing (Meuwissen et al., 2015; Ressler, King, & Nelson, 2016). In addition, some critics have suggested that edTPA limits the professional learning of candidates in the areas of diversity, social justice, and other "realities of the field" (Picower & Marshall, 2016, p. 196). The weight of the evidence so far suggests that as a tool intended to support the development of prospective teachers, edTPA may not be as "educative" as its supporters claim.

Similar to the mixed findings concerning edTPA's influence on teacher candidates' professional learning, we also found that there were conflicting conclusions about the impact of the assessment on program improvement and renewal. Some studies conclude that edTPA has a positive institutional and curricular impact (Barron, 2015; Lys, L'Esperance, Dobson, & Bullock, 2014; Pecheone & Whittaker, 2016; Thompson et al., 2014). For example, some program participants and leaders report that edTPA affirmed their conceptual frameworks, led to beneficial revisions of key assessments, and fostered targeted program improvements (Pecheone & Whittaker, 2016). Others, however, view edTPA in a negative light. Specifically, they raise concerns about both the pedagogical and curricular adjustments needed to make time to prepare candidates for the assessment and the important content sacrificed in order to accommodate those adjustments (Picower & Marshall, 2016; Ressler et al., 2016). Ledwell and Oyler (2016) studied the reactions to program changes made in response to edTPA of teacher educators across programs at one large institution. They found that there were "a range of reactions, from pride and satisfaction to distress and regret" (p. 130). Looking across this study and the other evidence, we found that while edTPA appears to prompt changes in programs, those changes are not always regarded as improvements and may have a subtractive impact on the curriculum.

Professionalization Claim: Boosting the Status of the Profession

Finally, there is a professionalization claim underlying edTPA, which presumes that widespread implementation of edTPA will drive improvement from inside teacher education (Darling-Hammond, 2009; Pecheone et al., 2005) and that this self-regulation will boost the status of the teaching profession (Darling-Hammond & Hyler, 2013). According to AACTE (n.d.-b), and as we have noted above, edTPA is intended to "serve as the same type of career-entry assessment requirement as those for aspiring lawyers, doctors, architects and professionals in many other fields" (para. 6). The professionalization claim underlying edTPA rests on the assumption that widespread adoption of the assessment by programs and states has the power to enhance public perceptions about university-based teacher education, ultimately giving it the same kind of prestige and respect afforded a number of other professions.

As is the case with most education reform initiatives, only time will speak to the long-term impact of edTPA on teacher education quality, teacher quality, and the public's perception of teaching professionals. However, many participants within the teacher education community have expressed deep and wide-ranging concerns about edTPA that could preclude its broad acceptance and perhaps even limit its viability. Along these lines, Ledwell and Oyler's (2016) conclusion that edTPA is "an *impotent* gatekeeper" (p. 130) calls into question whether it really has the power to "define an expert profession" (Darling-Hammond & Hyler, 2013, p. 13) in the way that the high-stakes, career-entry requirements of other professions do. In addition, as we discussed in Chapter 3, the current dominant approach to education reform in the United States equates teacher effectiveness with boosting student achievement and *not* with teachers' professional judgment, which is at the heart of edTPA. Thus, it may be that those outside teaching will actually have very little interest in (or even awareness of) edTPA, and it will ultimately have little impact on the status of the profession. As Au (2013) suggests, "Reformers are focused on test scores and could care less about performance assessments like the edTPA" (para. 25).

Overall, our examination of the three claims outlined above shows that while edTPA is a valid and reliable assessment of *some* valued aspects of teaching, psychometric analyses provide only part of the story. In addition, the evidence is mixed regarding edTPA's impact on the professional learning of teacher candidates and/or on program improvement, with both positive and negative effects reported by candidates and programs. Furthermore, given that the dominant approach to education reform in the United States equates teacher effectiveness with boosting students' test scores, rather than with teacher candidates' professional judgment and reasoning, it is possible that those outside education will actually have very little interest in how programs and teacher candidates fare on edTPA. This means that even if edTPA becomes more widespread than it already is, it may have little effect on professional status.

IMPACT AND IMPLICATIONS:
EXAMINING edTPA'S INFLUENCE ON TEACHER EDUCATION

Our analysis of the evidence supporting edTPA's three claims raises questions about how and whether this performance assessment is reshaping teacher education. What impact has the assessment had on those involved in the teacher education enterprise? Is the edTPA initiative meeting its intended goals, or have unintended consequences emerged? What does edTPA mean for ongoing efforts to improve and professionalize teacher education? We address these questions and discuss ongoing issues related to the assessment below.

Implementation:
edTPA vs. State-Specific Performance Assessments

We have noted that by the end of 2017, a total of 764 teacher education programs in 40 states were participating in edTPA, with 16 states having approved it as part of policies related to program completion, licensure, and/or program accreditation (AACTE, n.d.-d). While these figures are impressive at face value, our deeper analysis indicates that edTPA's widespread implementation has been bumpy and that national adoption either through a federal requirement or through state policies is unlikely.

One factor inhibiting the widespread adoption of edTPA is that some states, while acknowledging the benefits of performance-based assessments, have elected to implement their own state-specific performance assessments rather than the nationally available edTPA. For example, although a number of teacher education programs in Massachusetts served as pilot sites for edTPA in 2014–15 and Massachusetts was on a fast track to adopt assessment, the state ultimately decided not to do so. After a state task force cited concerns including cost, time, and consequences for teacher candidates from traditionally marginalized backgrounds (Massachusetts Department of Elementary and Secondary Education, 2014), the state chose to create and implement "a state-specific instrument to meet the Commonwealth's objectives for a meaningful performance assessment" (Massachusetts Department of Elementary and Secondary Education, 2016, p. 3). Similarly, teacher education programs in New Hampshire elected to implement a state-specific teacher performance assessment, which borrowed heavily from California's PACT, but was designed to ensure local control and statewide consistency (Evans-Brown, 2014).

Even where edTPA has been adopted statewide, there are ongoing concerns about its impact, especially on teacher candidates from diverse backgrounds. In New York, for example, after its initial implementation, the state lowered the passing score cutoff for edTPA, delayed its consequential status multiple times, and incorporated a multiple measures review into the certification processes of students who failed the assessment (New York State Education Department, 2017). An expert panel recommended these adjustments after it was revealed that Black teacher candidates failed edTPA disproportionately in comparison with candidates of other racial or ethnic backgrounds (Taylor, 2017).

It is important to note that while edTPA's potential impact is certainly diminished by the fact that some states have decided not to implement it or have been compelled to make revisions after its implementation, use of the assessment continues to expand (Bradley, 2017). According to Lynn M. Gangone, the current president of AACTE, "As the field continues to gain experience with teacher performance assessments and becomes savvier about using them for program improvement, coaching and induction support, the value of edTPA also grows" (as quoted in Bradley, 2017, para. 7). On the other hand, according to Reagan, Schram, and colleagues (2016), implementation has varied so greatly across preparation programs that it raises questions about "whether the edTPA can be considered 'one assessment' when it is implemented in a variety of ways, by different stakeholders, for different purposes" (p. 18). In short, this means that although its supporters claim that edTPA in increasing in value, there is substantive variation in both the reception of edTPA by states, institutions, and programs and in predictions about the influence it might have on the field.

Reception: From Acceptance to Resistance

There has been a range of reactions to edTPA, reflected in the split between opponents and proponents in the burgeoning teacher education literature about the assessment. Many people promote edTPA as an authentic, inquiry-based measure of candidate performance that also provides useful data for program improvement (Barron, 2015; Darling-Hammond & Hyler, 2013; Girtz, 2014; Huston, 2017; Pecheone & Whittaker, 2016; Peterson & Bruster, 2014). However, as we have shown, edTPA has also been widely criticized.

Perhaps the most important critiques of edTPA have to do with its claim that it is an authentic measure of candidates' readiness to teach. In discussing the authenticity claim above, we detailed the considerable statistical evidence supporting SCALE's claim that edTPA is both valid and reliable. In addition to validation studies, however, there are multiple studies and commentaries about edTPA, based primarily on teacher educators' experiences, that evaluate the authenticity of the assessment. These studies work from various perspectives on how to define teacher quality. Some suggest that edTPA is a flexible assessment, potentially appropriate for multiple contexts, depending on implementation policies and practices (An, 2016, 2017; Sato, 2014). This flexibility means that teacher educators can use edTPA to enhance candidates' understandings of both social justice issues and inquiry-based instruction. Others claim that edTPA adds rigor to programs (Thompson et al., 2014), which contributes to the notion of edTPA as driver and predictor of candidate success.

On the other hand, multiple studies dispute edTPA's claim of authenticity and raise a number of issues, including that edTPA lacks a formative approach to teacher quality (Ledwell & Oyler, 2016; Price, 2014), decontextualizes and ignores the constraints of local school contexts (Cochran-Smith et al., 2013; Dover & Schultz, 2016; Gary, 2015; Greenblatt, 2016; Lit & Lotan, 2013; Meuwissen et al., 2015), may be inappropriate for a number of teaching specialties (Parkes & Powell, 2015; Pugach, 2017), and, most importantly, lacks (and may actually inhibit) a social justice orientation (Au, 2013; Madeloni & Gorlewski, 2013; Picower & Marshall, 2016; Tuck & Gorlewski, 2016). Looking across the work of both proponents' and critics, we found many variations in policy- and program-level implementation, including varying commitments to equity, inquiry, and critical theories, as well as multiple variations in how programs use edTPA data. In fact, the nature of implementation seems to be the key in determining whether edTPA authentically drives and predicts candidates' future success as classroom teachers. As a result, for some, edTPA leads to authentic inquiry and supports social justice orientations, but for others, it constrains those goals.

Further reflecting these apparently inconsistent perspectives on edTPA, a number of teacher educators have simultaneously critiqued and commended edTPA, describing positive outcomes that were inspired by the test but actually occurred in spite of it. An (2016, 2017) used the concept of "constructive resistance" to describe her own and other teacher educators' use of the assessment's requirements. While preparing candidates for edTPA, she made positive changes in her teacher education courses and helped her students develop a critical stance on the assessment and on Pearson's role in bringing it to scale. This kind of balancing act is described in multiple articles about edTPA, which provide detail about how teacher educators critiqued edTPA while also capitalizing on the changes or disruptions it brought in order to improve their instruction or programmatic structures (Gurl et al., 2016; Lys et al., 2014; Meuwissen et al., 2015; Price, 2014; Pugach, 2017; Tuck & Gorlewski, 2016). State-level policy choices, like cutoff scores and how quickly edTPA becomes consequential once adopted, further complicate how edTPA is implemented. So do variations in local contexts, institutional structures, student populations, and educator dispositions. All of this leads us to agree with the conclusion that edTPA is not one single, uniform, universal assessment but rather multiple tests (Reagan, Schram, et al., 2016) with multiple consequences for teacher candidates and programs.

As we noted above, a major factor contributing to the resistance of widespread implementation of edTPA has to do with the involvement of Pearson (Au, 2013; Madeloni & Gorlewski, 2013). Described as an "operational partner," the makers of edTPA assert that Pearson's involvement was necessary to bring the assessment to scale and "meet demand among a wide educational audience" (AACTE, n.d.-b). Specifically, AACTE (n.d.-b) states that Pearson is not only responsible for "the systems infrastructure" of edTPA, but also "helps recruit scorers, manages the scoring pool, monitors scoring quality, and provides a training and delivery platform for the SCALE-developed scorer training curriculum" (para. 28). Despite AACTE's explicit description of the nature of the corporation's involvement, many in the teacher education community remain suspicious. According to Carter and Lochte (2016), for example, "Pearson closely guards all aspects of the edTPA, requiring scorers, education faculty, and students to sign non-disclosure contracts that have succeeded in silencing those most knowledgeable about the inner workings of the edTPA" (p. 19). This careful monitoring, shrouded in "secrecy" (Lambert & Girtz, 2016, p. 184), raises a number of concerns about lack of transparency (Lalley, 2016; Lambert & Girtz, 2016), trust (DeMoss, 2016), and information-sharing (Lambert & Girtz, 2016).

The silencing of participants and the general wariness that results from Pearson's vigilant monitoring of edTPA has heightened concerns that Pearson's role in edTPA contributes to the corporatization and privatization of public education in the United States. Along these lines, Jordan and Hawley (2016) argue that teacher educators do not need "to outsource our goals as teacher educators to a third party corporation that employs individuals to watch twenty minutes of video clips from a stranger from a part of the country they may have never visited. We can do much better than this and should" (para. 13). Some opponents of edTPA raised concerns like these early in edTPA's implementation (Madeloni & Gorlewski, 2013; NAME, 2014). While the outsourcing of edTPA to a corporate entity has been discussed and often criticized in the published literature, there has been no empirical examination of the direct effects of Pearson's involvement. Future researchers might examine whether there are direct consequences of Pearson's involvement in edTPA and, if so, whether and how they are problematic on a practical level.

Finally, there are a number of ongoing tensions related to edTPA that go beyond the involvement of Pearson and issues related to implementation. For example, there are concerns about the basic architecture of the test. edTPA attempts to standardize the scoring of videos and written reflections. Its supporters claim that the assessment can move programs toward reflective inquiry and away from compliance (McKee, 2015; SCALE, 2015a). However, others have questioned whether critical aspects of performance, such as a video snapshot of practice or a reflection, can actually ever really be standardized (Au, 2013; NAME, 2014). In addition, some scholars have raised concerns about equity, including issues of access, cost, and uneven performance among demographic groups on edTPA (Goldhaber et al., 2016; Greenblatt, 2016; NAME, 2014; Picower & Marshall, 2016; Ratner & Kolman, 2016). Last, in terms of edTPA as policy, Pullin (2015) suggests that there are potential legal issues related to both videotaping underage students and ownership of data. Combined, these issues suggest that edTPA may not be reshaping teacher education for the better.

THE UNCERTAIN FUTURE OF edTPA

As a teacher education accountability initiative, edTPA is rife with tension and conflict. It positions teachers as valuable and capable professionals, but embraces elements of compliance-based accountability and neoliberal ideology. It grew from an assessment that valued local context and norms, but it has been transformed into a standardized assessment, scored by individuals far removed from local programs and local knowledge. It emphasizes performance and practice, but exists as a high-stakes, summative assessment. It is based on the belief that improvement should come from inside the profession, but is entwined with an external (and controversial) corporate entity. It aims to provide a quality education to all schoolchildren, but fails to address issues of inequity directly and may in fact diminish the diversity of the teaching force.

These incongruities, combined with major implementation issues in some states, make the future of edTPA uncertain. Could it continue to have a positive impact on *some* teacher candidates and *some* teacher preparation programs? Possibly. Will it prompt the widespread professionalization of teaching and produce a national workforce of educators prepared to meet the needs of each and every student? Probably not, and this is not a truly realistic expectation. Our analysis shows that edTPA has the potential to have a positive impact on professional learning for some candidates and programs if implemented gradually and with adequate support. However, in aiming for uniformity and standardization, edTPA does not adequately address the importance of local contexts and stakeholder involvement. And it gives very little attention to social justice and equity issues as critical avenues for improving teacher education quality. These inadequacies suggest that edTPA, like the three other initiatives we've detailed in this book, runs counter to the democratic project in many ways.

Part III

RECLAIMING ACCOUNTABILITY

CHAPTER 8

The Problem
with Accountability

In the preceding chapters, we took a deep dive into the four most visible and far-reaching national accountability initiatives that were proposed, debated, and, in all but one case, implemented during teacher education's era of accountability. Using hundreds of policy documents, tools, media items, and critiques as evidence, we analyzed each initiative as a case of a far-reaching but controversial effort to "fix" teacher education by holding it accountable. Now we shift to a different level of analysis that builds on the individual cases and makes an argument about what this adds up to and what it means for teacher education. It's worth asking here why we spent so much time on these four accountability initiatives, given that we disagree fundamentally with many of their principles and given that we have concluded they do not serve the larger democratic project. We do so because these accountability initiatives—all highly publicized and deeply controversial—have to a great extent hijacked the public discourse about teacher education quality and because the values and assumptions underlying these initiatives now drive many program, institutional, and professional decisions. We cannot argue for a democratic alternative to the accountability paradigm without thoroughly understanding the accountability paradigm in the first place.

Our assertion here is that despite their differences—and there are many, as Chapters 4 through 7 make clear—the major teacher education accountability policies and initiatives developed in the United States over the last 20 years to solve the teacher quality problem are characterized by core similarities and cross-cutting themes. These include underlying ideologies, rhetorical structures, operating logics about the problem of teacher education, and conceptions of equality and equity. The major argument of this chapter is that these cross-cutting themes, assumptions, and practices constitute a dominant accountability paradigm in teacher education that was shaped by, but also helped to shape, the political, policy, and professional forces that constitute the accountability era. This accountability paradigm has myriad flaws and failings, which this chapter and the preceding chapters have exposed by application of our accountability framework.

THE ACCOUNTABILITY PARADIGM IN TEACHER EDUCATION

In teacher education in the United States, there is an exceptionally clear and consistent conceptual and practical model of: determining expectations; evaluating whether and to what extent programs, institutions, and candidates comply with those expectations; and meting out rewards and punishments for compliance or noncompliance. In short, it is fair to say that there is a dominant accountability paradigm in teacher education. In a very important sense, it is surprising—and remarkable—that a coherent accountability paradigm can be identified, given the existence of multiple accountability policies and initiatives with disparate histories, founders, funders, methods, theories of change, and political agendas. In another sense, however, the existence of a dominant accountability paradigm is not so surprising. Over the last 20 years, every individual, organization, agency, and advocacy group involved in any way with education policy, practice, and reform—regardless of their own positions and perspectives—has lived in the same larger educational milieu. As we pointed out in Chapters 2 and 3, Lipman (2011) called this milieu the result of the "ideology project" for the "neoliberalization of public education" (p. 115). Mehta (2013) characterized it as a new "education policy paradigm" (p. 286) that emerged in the United States in the mid-1980s, reflecting the galvanizing impact of *A Nation at Risk* (National Commission on Excellence in Education, 1983). Lipman's ideology project and Mehta's policy paradigm are not identical, but they both highlight the central premises of the larger milieu, which we elaborated on in Chapters 2 and 3. In these chapters, we worked from the "top down" to describe the accountability era, informed by the larger ideas related to neoliberalism and human capital theory that are part of the general milieu and part of teacher education.

Chapter 8 does something different. Although our arguments in this chapter are informed by our analysis of key ideas in the educational milieu, here we work primarily from the "bottom up" to identify the specific features of the teacher education accountability paradigm. That is, we look across the major national accountability policies and initiatives we deconstructed and evaluated in the preceding chapters to identify cross-cutting themes and patterns that have explanatory power across the four initiatives. The bottom-up approach identifies the similarities of accountability initiatives in terms of broad principles and mechanisms, the claims proponents make regarding the efficacy of initiatives and their underlying theories of change, and the many controversies involved. At the same time, this approach also points to important differences. As described in detail in Chapter 3, our accountability framework's eight dimensions are thematically organized into three clusters, the "foundations of accountability," the "problem of teacher education," and "power relationships in accountability." While the eight dimensions permit a fine-grained analysis of every aspect of a single initiative or policy, working at the cluster level produces a cross-cutting view of underlying logics, ideals, and arrangements. To identify both broad similarities and important differences, this chapter is organized around the three clusters, as indicated in Figure 8.1.

THE FOUNDATIONS OF THE ACCOUNTABILITY PARADIGM

The "foundations of accountability" is a cluster of three thematically related dimensions of teacher education accountability: values, purposes, and concepts. As we have suggested in the previous chapters, this cluster assumes that no practice or policy in teacher education is neutral or value-free. Rather, all practices and policies are shaped by underlying ideologies, ideas, values, and principles related to the roles of teaching and teacher education in society, the causes of and cures for inequality, and the meanings of teacher quality and teacher education quality. Below we describe the two most salient themes in the foundations of the dominant accountability paradigm, which we refer to as "teacher quality and market ideology" and "inequality and the teacher quality gap."

Teacher Quality and Market Ideology

Across all the accountability policies and initiatives we examined, core values were remarkably consistent in language and logic. At one level, they can be summarized in three words—"teachers matter most." In the context of teacher policy, this mantra is more than two decades old. It hearkens back to Sanders's (Sanders, 1998; Sanders & Horn, 1998) Tennessee studies of the value added by teachers to students' achievement and to a series of reports by Darling-Hammond and NCTAF arguing that what teachers know and can do is the single most important influence on what students learn (Darling-Hammond, 1998; Darling-Hammond & Sykes, 1999; National Commission on Teaching & America's Future, 1996, 1997). The sentiments of these and many other U.S. reports not only resonated with each other, but also resonated with a steady stream of highly influential international reports (e.g., McKinsey and Company, 2007; OECD, 2005), which created a kind of echo chamber among policymakers and education reformers about the singular importance of teacher quality in a competitive global economy.

It is clear that the foundation of the four initiatives highlighted in this book is a belief in the singular importance of teacher quality. But is it fair and accurate to say that this reflects market ideology? Lipman (2011) offers a helpful list of the assumptions of market ideology: teacher quality is defined by testing and performance outcomes; students' learning is equated with test performance and workforce preparedness; market mechanisms can be used to increase human capital; and the cause of school failure is primarily teachers, teacher education programs, and schools. We found that with three of

Figure 8.1. The Dominant Accountability Paradigm in Teacher Education

Thematic Cluster	Cross-Cutting Themes	Description
Foundations of Accountability	Teacher Quality and Market Ideology	• Teacher quality assumed to be singularly important in the global knowledge society • International competitiveness of the workforce assumed to depend on schools/teacher quality
	Inequality and the Teacher Quality Gap	• Teacher quality gap seen as major cause of educational and social inequities • Equal distribution of teacher quality seen as primary way to redress inequalities and create equity
The Problem of Teacher Education	Lack of Public Confidence and Need for Data	• Mediocre teacher preparation as the primary cause of pervasive low-level teacher quality, threatening national economic security • No public confidence that university teacher preparation can solve the problem • University preparation programs characterized as operating blindly, uninformed by solid data based on sophisticated data systems • Rigorous accountability systems with uniform measures assumed to have the capacity to solve the problem by prompting good programs to thrive and bad programs to close
Power Relationships in Accountability	Top-Down, External Sources of Expectations and Authority	• Programs held accountable for program impact and teacher effectiveness in classrooms • Power and source of expectations regarding accountability held by regulators and agencies outside teacher education programs and institutions • Teacher effectiveness measured primarily by standardized assessments of students' achievement

the four initiatives we highlighted in the previous chapters, Lipman's list was broadly applicable, and with the fourth initiative it applied partially.

As we recounted in Chapter 2, under the Obama administration, the USDOE boldly defined teacher effectiveness in terms of students' test scores and required states competing for funds and applying for NCLB waivers to establish databases linking student achievement to teacher education program evaluation. This approach, aligned with market ideology, was at the heart of the Title II regulations proposed in 2014 and approved in 2016. In something of a contrast, CAEP's standards require programs seeking national accreditation to document their teacher candidates' knowledge and skill *in addition to* their programs' and graduates' impact on students' achievement. These knowledge and skill requirements notwithstanding, CAEP's approach is closely aligned with the approach underlying the Title II regulations, and CAEP makes no bones about what counts the most: "Surmounting all other [efforts], [CAEP should] insist that preparation be judged by outcomes and impact on P-12 student learning and development—results matter" (CAEP Commission on Standards and Performance Reporting, 2013, p. 9). This suggests that like the Title II regulations, the CAEP accreditation process is also aligned with market ideology.

Although NCTQ's teacher preparation reviews focus on course syllabi and program documents rather than outcomes, they wholeheartedly embrace the idea that market mechanisms can be used to increase teacher quality (and thus human capital), and their discourse is consistent with the market-oriented idea that "effective teaching must be rooted in academic results for students. Whatever else they accomplish in the classroom, effective teachers must improve student achievement" (Doherty & Jacobs, 2013, p. i). In terms of its foundational values, edTPA is a little different. On one hand, the language and rhetoric of its advocates coincide closely with the idea that teacher quality is paramount to securing the nation's economic success in a global society, a perspective aligned with the neoliberal project (Darling-Hammond & Rothman, 2015; Tucker, 2011). At the same time, however, edTPA's creators and supporters regard teachers as professional decision makers and eschew narrow definitions of teacher effectiveness tied to test scores (Darling-Hammond, 2015a). These two sets of values are in tension with each other in edTPA.

Although there are some differences across the four major accountability policies and initiatives we reviewed, we found that the market ideology behind the "teachers matter most" mantra was clear. All four reflect the ideas popularized in Thomas Friedman's (2005) best-selling *The World Is Flat: A Brief History of the Twenty-First Century*. Friedman argued that we live in a "flat world" of global competition wherein knowledge is the critical commodity, and previous geographic and historical divisions are less relevant. Darling-Hammond and others applied this perspective to education, arguing that in the flat world, a country's international competitiveness depends on the ability of its teachers to teach all students 21st-century knowledge and skills and recommending that the United States emulate the approaches of top-performing countries (Darling-Hammond, 2015b; Darling-Hammond & Rothman, 2015; Tucker, 2011). We say more about this below.

Inequality and the Teacher Quality Gap

The second major idea that is part of the foundations of teacher education's dominant accountability paradigm is a commitment to equity. Of course, very few reformers would say they were not in favor of equity. However, beneath the surface of the equity rhetoric, the accountability paradigm is animated more by the notion of *thin equity* (i.e., the assumption that equity will result from individuals' equal access to good teachers) than *strong equity* (i.e., the assumption that in addition to equal access to good teachers and schools, getting to equity requires multiple social policies, not just education policies, that challenge the structures and systems that produce and reproduce inequity in the first place). Embedded in the accountability paradigm are two interrelated assumptions. One is that the "teacher quality gap" (Education Trust, 2008; Peske & Haycock, 2006) is a major cause of educational (and social) inequity. And the second is that increasing the supply and equalizing the distribution of teacher quality will achieve equity without necessarily addressing larger social problems, including health care, employment, transportation, housing, and early childhood services, and without recognizing the intersecting systems of inequality that reproduce inequity.

With the 2016 Title II reporting regulations, for example, the claim is simply that the new requirements and the new data collected from institutions and states will create a "feedback loop" leading to higher-quality teachers, "especially for students in high-need schools" (Office of the *Federal Register*, 2014, p. 71821). In short, closing the teacher quality gap is assumed to be the cure for educational and social inequity.

CAEP materials give relatively more attention to equity issues than the 2016 Title II requirements did. Although CAEP requires that diversity be a "pervasive characteristic" of the programs it accredits (CAEP Commission on Standards and Performance Reporting, 2013), equity is not mentioned in its original mission statement (CAEP, 2010). Further, it was not until 2017 that CAEP established an "Equity Committee" to define equity and ensure that it is part of accreditation decisions (CAEP, 2017c; Dantley, 2016). In addition, CAEP's controversial selectivity standards regarding teacher candidates' GPAs and scores on nationally normed ability/achievement assessments are in tension with its requirement that programs document their progress toward creating a diverse teaching force. Despite CAEP's stated commitments to diversity, there is nothing in its documents that acknowledges that high-stakes testing has historically disadvantaged minoritized racial groups (Au, 2016). And there is nothing acknowledging that neither test scores nor GPAs are intended to predict the effectiveness of teachers or their impact on students' achievement (Cochran-Smith, Baker, et al., 2017; Meyer, 2017). In addition, CAEP standards do not require programs to show evidence that their teacher candidates are prepared to identify and work with others to challenge the structural and systemic aspects of inequity.

NCTQ has little to say about equity. In fact, NCTQ bluntly asserts that despite the challenges faced by "socioeconomically disadvantaged" students, nothing is more important "in determining their achievement gains than their teachers" (United States House of Representatives, 2011, pp. 1–2). In short, implicit in NCTQ materials is the assumption that holding programs accountable to NCTQ's standards will fix the equity problem because consumers will choose effective programs and employers will choose effective teachers. There is no acknowledgment of the history and structural conditions that have shaped who actually has educational choices and opportunities or which groups actually are and are not able to take advantage of access and choice to make gains. In particular, there is no mention of the long history of lack of access for minoritized and disadvantaged groups.

Like edTPA's stance on market ideology, its position on equity is blurrier than the positions of the others. A major goal of edTPA is to ensure that all students have access to teachers who respond to their academic needs and strengths, and as we note above, edTPA developers reject test scores as the major indicator of achievement and teacher quality. As we showed in Chapter 7, however, although edTPA documents say that teaching should be "driven by a stance of equity" (Sato, 2014, p. 6), there is nothing in the assessment that requires this. Presumably individual programs are expected to instill in teacher candidates the knowledge, skills, and dispositions to enact "culturally relevant" frameworks (Sato, 2014, p. 6). However, as we showed in the last chapter, numerous critiques have charged that edTPA's requirements and strict space limits actually may discourage candidates from including social justice, equity, or culturally responsive perspectives in their portfolios (Au, 2013; Picower & Marshall, 2016; Tuck & Gorlewski, 2016).

Our conclusion is that a thin equity perspective underlies and helps to define the dominant accountability paradigm in teacher education. We want to be very clear here about what we are and are not saying. We are *not* saying that teachers don't matter. Nor are we saying that all the proponents of teacher education's major accountability initiatives fail to understand that poverty, income inequality, and lack of social policies have a harmful impact on school outcomes. For example, Darling-Hammond, one of the chief creators and advocates of edTPA, thoughtfully chronicles the impact of poverty on school achievement and lauds international education systems that fund schools equitably in order to counteract families' income inequalities (Darling-Hammond & Rothman, 2015; Darling-Hammond et al., 2017). What we *are* saying, however, is that underlying the accountability paradigm is a belief in the capacity of teaching and teacher education to address unequal opportunity and mitigate the impact of poverty, a belief that is consistent with the larger belief underlying U.S. social policy since the 1960s that "inequality and poverty are susceptible to educational corrections" (Kantor & Lowe, 2016, p. 38).

The Problem with the Foundations of the Accountability Paradigm

In sum, the dominant accountability paradigm in U.S. teacher education is animated by a key idea derived from market ideology (Engel, 2000; Stone, 2011): The quality of the country's education system—defined by the quality of its teachers and measured primarily by students' test scores—is the sine qua non of the nation's ability to compete in the global knowledge economy. This is presumed to be essential for the nation (and individuals) to survive and thrive in the 21st century. Specifically, the assumption is that strong teacher quality can ensure economic security for the nation and achieve equity across groups.

There are multiple problems with the market ideology underlying the accountability paradigm, as others have argued in detail—it consolidates global economic power for the benefit of a few (Perkins, 2004; Sleeter, 2009), and it masks the systemic and structural aspects of inequality that reproduce inequities for marginalized groups (Au, 2016). In addition, the discourse of democracy is a silenced discourse in the dominant accountability paradigm. That is, in the policy documents and tools representing the four major accountability initiatives highlighted in this book, there is virtually no mention of democracy, democratic education, democratic goals, or teaching and learning in democratic societies. This is no accident. The premises of market ideology are fundamentally inconsistent with the premises of a strong democracy (Barber, 1984; Engel, 2000). In a strong democracy, the work of teachers and teacher educators is assumed to be a public enterprise for the common good rather than a market enterprise based on individual competition for private goods. In Chapter 9, we say more about the problem with the dominant accountability paradigm and develop the idea of democratic accountability in teacher education in partial response to this critique.

THE PROBLEM OF TEACHER EDUCATION
IN THE ACCOUNTABILITY PARADIGM

The "problem of teacher education" is the label we use for the second cluster of thematically related dimensions of teacher education accountability—the diagnostic and the prognostic dimensions. We developed this cluster to highlight the language and rhetoric used by the advocates of particular teacher education accountability initiatives to frame and promote particular viewpoints about who or what "caused" the problem of teacher quality/teacher education in the United States, what kind of problem it actually is, and what strategies, treatments, tools, or approaches are most likely to solve the problem. Below we show that the dominant accountability paradigm consistently frames "the problem of teacher education" as teacher education's failure to earn public confidence and its failure to produce and utilize meaningful data for continuous improvement. We also show that, accordingly, the dominant accountability paradigm frames the solution to the problem as the development of national data systems, assessments, and data analytics that provide a feedback loop for continuous improvement. Following the ideas of policy analyst Deborah Stone (2011), who suggests that policy problems are often constructed as narratives, we characterize the problem of teacher education in the dominant accountability paradigm as what Stone would call a story of "helplessness and control."

A Story of Helplessness and Control

All the teacher education accountability initiatives and policies we've considered in this book were designed to address the problem of presumed threats to the nation's economic health and security, which depends on the quality of the nation's education system, particularly teachers. Beneath the surface of the economic issues, however, the dominant accountability paradigm frames the problem of teacher education as its lack of public confidence and its failure to collect and utilize meaningful effectiveness data. Although the four initiatives frame these problems somewhat differently, the implication is that until these deficiencies are remedied, the nation's security—economic and otherwise—cannot be ensured. Given this common framing of the problem, it's not surprising that the favored solution of the four accountability initiatives is the creation of either a national data system that systematically rates, ranks, and evaluates preparation programs *or* a nationally available uniform performance assessment tool that rates and evaluates teacher candidates and—indirectly—the teacher educators and programs that prepare them. As we have shown, there is scant evidence to support this solution as a way to improve teacher education quality.

From the perspective of the dominant accountability paradigm, teacher education's lack of public confidence stems in part from data system deficiencies, a problem that is wrapped up in what Stone (2011) calls a "story of helplessness and control" (p. 138). Stone emphasizes that policy problems are not found or fixed and that preferred policy solutions are not the straightforward result of rational choices among alternatives. Building on the idea that policy problems are constructed, not fixed, Stone suggests that definitions of policy problems usually have narrative structures (e.g., beginnings, middles, and ends) and engaging characters (e.g., heroes, villains, and victims), and they often pit the forces of evil against the forces of good. Compelling policy stories persuade people about both how to understand a problem and what to do about it. Stone proposes that there are two story lines that repeatedly recur in the policy discourse, what she calls "stories of decline" and "stories of helplessness and control." Stone says that with stories of decline, the narrative is that during a prior time period, things were good, but now they are bad, and something must be done to avoid further decline or avert a crisis. On the other hand, with stories of helplessness and control, the narrative is that things are bad, and we had thought the situation was out of our control, but now we have a way to fix things.

With the dominant accountability paradigm in teacher education, the problem of teacher education is framed in terms of the second story line—a story of helplessness and control. The story goes like this: The pervasive low level of teacher quality in the United States, which threatens our national economic security, is the fault primarily of mediocre teacher preparation. Even worse, the story goes, politicians, policymakers, and the public have no confidence that university preparation programs are able or willing to rise to the occasion and do a better job of training teachers. In fact, the public and policymakers thoroughly mistrust the motives, knowledge, methods, and will of teacher educators and their institutions. The story line continues: One very good reason to mistrust preparation programs is that they operate blindly, uninformed by solid data about program impact and graduates' performance and without benefit of a system of continuous improvement based on methodical collection and analysis of data. Without reliable performance data that can be used to hold teacher education accountable by publicly rating, ranking, and evaluating preparation programs and candidates, the story continues, the situation is hopeless. The denouement of this story line is that there can be a happy ending because the technology now exists to control the problem in the form of rigorous accountability systems using uniform indicators, cutting-edge assessment tools, and sophisticated data analytics. With these accountability mechanisms in place, the story line concludes, good programs (and candidates) will rise to the top while bad ones can be remediated (or excluded).

Variations on a Narrative Theme

Across the four accountability initiatives that we have interrogated in this book, there are several variations on the narrative outlined above. The major story line, however, is remarkably consistent.

The story behind the 2016 Title II reporting requirements was that colleges and universities do not produce effective teachers, and the federal government has no confidence that programs or state regulators are trying to be more effective. The victims in this story were portrayed as the nation's schoolchildren and the American public. The villains were both preparation programs that don't use meaningful evaluation data to improve *and* states that don't fulfill their legal obligations to identify, improve, and eliminate low-performing programs (Office of the *Federal Register*, 2016). The hero in the Title II story was the USDOE itself, which mandated the establishment of data systems in every state with the intention to wield the carrot/stick of extending or denying the authority to distribute TEACH grants. The assumption was that new data systems would deliver a happy ending—more effective preparation programs, more transparent public information, and more students with teachers who knew how to prepare them for the workforce. As we showed in Chapter 4, however, there is almost no evidence to support these assumptions.

With CAEP's story line, the problem and victims are similar to those above. But the villain in the CAEP story is more complex, and, according to this story, the major villains are particularly sinister. Villains include the new education reformers who threaten the field's "professionalization and its stature" by aiming to dismantle licensure and bypass the institution of accreditation (Cibulka, 2015) as well as the university teacher education community, which has failed to develop the culture of evidence and innovation that is well-known by other professions and the business world to promote continuous improvement (CAEP, 2015a). Interestingly, unlike the Title II story, where the hero was federal regulators who would surveil and monitor programs and states, the hero in the CAEP story is the CAEP organization itself. According to the CAEP-promoted story, the organization has taken on the Herculean task of demanding that programs meet high impact standards using proven measures, cutting-edge technology, and sophisticated methods of data analysis. The presumed happy ending to this story is that the profession, embodied in CAEP, polices itself and thus reassures the public that the attainment of CAEP accreditation guarantees that a preparation program is fulfilling its ethical and professional responsibilities to produce effective teachers (APA Task Force Report, 2014). Unfortunately, the lack of evidence that CAEP accreditation actually improves teacher education quality or teacher quality makes this story more a fairytale than anything else.

The plot of the NCTQ story starts with the familiar problem of a workforce unable to compete. This problem is laid squarely at the feet of the story's villains—colleges and universities that prepare teachers. According to the NCTQ story line, universities have utterly failed to "train" teachers and have not selected academically strong candidates in the first place (NCTQ, 2015). In addition to the American public in general, the victims in this story are consumers—prospective teachers and employers who don't have solid information about program quality and therefore can't make informed choices (Greenberg et al., 2013). According to the NCTQ story line, the solution to this problem is NCTQ's "exhaustive and unprecedented examination" (Greenberg et al., 2013, p. 1) of teacher education programs nationwide and its massive dissemination network, which makes everything transparent and gets the word out about winners and losers. The hero in the NCTQ story is the market itself and, of course, NCTQ, which unleashes market forces that are "far more powerful than a myriad of policy attempts" (Greenberg et al., 2013, p. 7). With the NCTQ story line, the happy ending occurs when consumers vote with their feet, thus causing highly rated programs to thrive and poor programs to wither. Again, it is important to note that there is virtually no evidence to support this story line: NCTQ ratings do not provide information that programs can actually use to improve, nor do they predict the effectiveness of graduates or correlate with other measures of quality.

The edTPA story line begins with a similar take on the larger problem of inadequate teacher quality, but it also emphasizes that the victims are marginalized students without the benefit of good teachers. Like the CAEP story, the edTPA narrative characterizes these problems in part as teacher education's failure to develop as a legitimate professional community (like medicine or law) with uniform expectations and profession-wide impartial assessments (Darling-Hammond, 2010; Pecheone & Whittaker, 2016). This construction of the problem leads directly to the conclusion that the way to fix the problem is implementation of policies requiring profession-wide uniform standards and assessments (like edTPA) that authentically represent the work of teaching. The villains and the heroes in the edTPA story are not drawn as sharply as in the other stories. But edTPA advocates make it clear that it is the profession that has the responsibility to solve the problem by universally using edTPA and adjusting standards, curriculum, and program experiences to ensure that teacher candidates are prepared to pass the assessment (Darling-Hammond, 2010; Pecheone et al., 2015). This story line implies that teacher educators who reject uniform standards and universal measures are part of the problem, not the solution. However, as we discussed in Chapter 7, there is a burgeoning body of research related to edTPA implementation at program and state levels that suggests that the edTPA story is unlikely to have a happy ending.

The Problem with "The Problem of Teacher Education" in the Accountability Paradigm

In sum, the story line that weaves throughout major teacher education accountability policies and initiatives in the United States is Stone's (2011) story of helplessness and control: Teacher quality and teacher education quality are poor, which has exacerbated the achievement gap and weakened the nation's ability to compete in the global economy. The public and policymakers have no confidence in the teacher education community, and—the story goes—the victims include the entire nation, especially schoolchildren. With this story, the cause of the problem is to a great extent teacher education programs' own failure to collect and utilize reliable data about program impact and graduates' effectiveness, and the solution is the flip side of the problem—putting rigorous national data systems into place based on uniform standards and evidence-based measures that hold teacher education programs accountable and force them to improve or shut down.

There are multiple problems with "the problem" of teacher education as constructed by the dominant accountability paradigm. The Title II and CAEP story lines tend to reify test scores as the decisive measure of teacher and program effectiveness and marginalize other outcomes. In addition, the Title II, CAEP, and NCTQ story lines work from a simplistic view of the problem of teacher education, assuming that there is a more or less linear causal link from teacher preparation to teacher quality to student achievement, despite the fact that there is no evidence to support this. The NCTQ story zeroes in on the power of the market to fix the problem of teacher education, assuming that prospective teachers, employers, and teacher educators all work from self-interested individualistic motives when making choices, without concerns about the common good or about larger educational and social inequities. The edTPA story line focuses on the profession's failure to develop uniform, standardized, universal assessments that would put it on par with other professions. But this ignores the fact that a trusted profession is not built out of compliance and control with universal expectations that ignore the importance of local communities. Finally, all four of the initiatives suffer from problematic underlying theories of change and from lack of evidence about their efficacy as accountability mechanisms that actually have the capacity to improve the quality of teacher education programs. We return to problems with the dominant accountability paradigm in the next chapter.

POWER RELATIONSHIPS IN THE ACCOUNTABILITY PARADIGM

"Power relationships" is the phrase we use to refer to the third and final thematic cluster in our teacher education accountability framework, which includes the control dimension, the content dimension, and the consequences dimension. As we said in Chapter 3, this cluster is based on the assumption that no aspect of teacher education policy or practice is apolitical. This means that unpacking and critiquing the power dimensions of accountability is not a matter of politicizing teacher education, as some critics argue, but is rather a matter of recognizing that it is already and always politicized (Bruner, 1996). Below we capture the power relationships in the dominant accountability paradigm by focusing on control and jurisdiction and then considering the politics of accountability across the four initiatives.

Control and Jurisdiction

Control is the key to this cluster. This has to do with authority and jurisdiction—specifically, which institutions, professional organizations, regulatory agencies, or advocacy groups have (or should have) the authority to oversee teacher education and determine the consequences. But this also has to do with how the entities in control define what teacher education must be accountable for, what they stipulate about the terms of the evidentiary warrant for accountability, and what other parties they invite to the table to negotiate these issues.

In teacher education accountability, power issues are complex and multilayered. As we noted in Chapter 3, Romzek (2000) characterized the issue of control in public-sector accountability by focusing on sources of expectations and authority. She suggested that these sources ranged along a continuum from internal to external to the occupational groups being held accountable. With teacher education, however, as we show in Chapters 5 and 7, there are tricky issues about whether internality and externality are defined relative to the preparation programs and institutions being held accountable or relative to "the profession" in a collective sense. In addition, control involves matters of voice and choice, including whether and to what extent the groups being held accountable have any power to contribute to the development of standards and to mechanisms and tools of evaluation and whether they have any opportunity to decide whether to join in or opt out of particular accountability schemes.

The Politics of Accountability

As we have shown throughout this book, there are multiple overlapping accountability initiatives in U.S. teacher education, and thus it is reasonable to expect that there would be substantial variation in issues related to internality/externality and voice/choice. Below, however, we show that although the politics of the four accountability policies and initiatives we have highlighted in this book vary somewhat in terms of internality/externality, voice/choice, and content, the major contours of power are similar.

The 2016 Title II regulations, proposed by the USDOE in 2014, finalized in 2016, and rescinded in 2017, were external in the extreme. That is, the source of accountability expectations was external to the teacher education programs and institutions they focused on, external to the teacher education profession, and external to state regulators. The regulations were very explicit about power and control: "The final regulations establish necessary definitions and requirements for IHEs [institutions of higher education] and states related to the quality of teacher preparation programs and require states to develop measures for assessing teacher preparation programs" (Office of the *Federal Register*, 2016, p. 75495). In short, the Title II regulations used the legal and fiscal power of the USDOE to demand compliance from states and programs, and there was no choice about participation. Even though there was no funding for the Title II mandate, every state and every teacher education program would have been required to comply or face significant consequences. The only opportunity for a voice in the development of expectations was the relatively slim window of time for public comments on the proposed regulations, which many professional organizations, individuals, and institutions submitted. Despite some modifications, however, the final version of the Title II regulations demanded that programs prove their effectiveness in terms of student learning gains, employer satisfaction, and teacher evaluation measures and that states rate programs accordingly. These expectations were entirely consistent with the definition of teacher quality spelled out in RTTT funding guidelines under Obama in 2009 and reflected in Obama's first plan to improve teacher preparation in 2011.

With CAEP accreditation, the content of accountability is very similar to the content of accountability in Title II regulations. Although CAEP requires programs to produce evidence about teacher candidates' knowledge and skill, their documents make it crystal clear, as we emphasized above, that impact on students' learning "surmount[s] all other" expectations (CAEP Commission on Standards and Performance Reporting, 2013, p. 9). The difference between the Title II and CAEP requirements has little to do with content and everything to do with power and jurisdiction. Unlike the completely external source of expectations in the Title II regulations, the source of CAEP accountability expectations is external to preparation programs and institutions but internal to the profession, at least insofar as CAEP defines the profession and understands its own position relative to the institutions it accredits. As we detailed in Chapter 5, to establish its standards, CAEP convened diverse stakeholders in a "non-adversarial" environment (CAEP Commission on Standards and Performance Reporting, 2013, p. 6.). CAEP's plan was to lock down its authority and credibility as the sole national accreditor of educator preparation, demonstrate that it was on board with the larger accountability agenda of USDOE and many education reformers, and unify the entire field. None of this came to fruition. Instead, CAEP has been fraught with leadership issues, a no-confidence vote from AACTE membership, and resistance from programs. In addition, even though CAEP has lobbied for mandatory national accreditation, it continues to be voluntary in most states, and some elite universities and many small colleges simply opt not to participate. In addition, a rival teacher education accreditor has now emerged, to which we return in Chapter 9, and some former USDOE officials have called for school districts and charter organizations to serve as accreditors. In short, with national accreditation, there is an abundance of choice—and a fair amount of chaos—about accountability. The result has been a serious diminution of CAEP's power and authority.

NCTQ is a private advocacy organization with a historically anti-university teacher education agenda. Like the Title II reporting regulations, NCTQ standards and methods were developed external to the programs they rate and rank. Unlike the federal regulations, however, and unlike CAEP's accountability expectations, NCTQ has no legal, fiscal, or professional authority in teacher education. So what is the source of NCTQ's considerable power in teacher education? As we detailed in Chapter 6, part of it is that for many public institutions in the United States, there has been little choice about "participation" in NCTQ reviews. Rather, at many public universities, programs have been instructed by leaders at the highest levels to deliver to NCTQ the materials requested in keeping with universities' perceived responsibility as public institutions. In the early years, NCTQ followed up on some institutions' failure to deliver materials with Freedom of Information Act petitions; NCTQ also paid for syllabi from students and in at least one case filed a lawsuit demanding materials (Cochran-Smith et al., 2013). More recently, NCTQ has relied heavily on website materials and rated aspects of some programs solely on publicly available documents (NCTQ, n.d.-g). NCTQ's claim to have constructed a comprehensive national database about preparation programs lends credibility to its reviews (Greenberg et al., 2013). Another part of NCTQ's power is its remarkably effective and far-flung publicity and dissemination network, which delivers slickly packaged materials directly to policymakers, university presidents, the media, and the larger education reform network of which NCTQ is part.

edTPA contrasts with the dominant accountability paradigm in terms of content, given its focus on teaching practice and teacher judgments and the explicit rejection of students' test scores as the best way to assess teacher candidates' capacity. In terms of power relationships, however, edTPA has a contentious history. Advocates describe it as an assessment created "by the profession, for the profession" (AACTE, 2014b; Pecheone et al., 2016), while some critics claim it was created "by the academic elite and now functions to oppress vulnerable preservice teachers" (Jordan & Hawley, 2016, para. 3). It is worth noting that the PACT, the California forerunner of edTPA, was indeed created by representatives of the teacher education programs and institutions that were to be held accountable and was intended to be consistent with local program norms and values (Cochran-Smith et al., 2013). As we pointed out in Chapter 7, however, 40 states are now participating in edTPA, with 16 states having approved it as part of policies related to program completion, licensure, and/or program completion. Pearson now manages the scoring and storage of teacher candidates' portfolios. As a uniform and standardized assessment that is judged by scorers far removed from local contexts, there is no longer any opportunity for program or candidate voice in the determination of content, and in states where edTPA is required, there is no choice for programs or candidates. A major part of the controversy about edTPA involves power and control, particularly who represents or speaks for the profession. The growing number of critiques of edTPA suggests that it is increasingly experienced by teacher candidates and teacher educators as an externally imposed assessment not respectful of or consistent with the values and norms of local work (e.g., Lys et al., 2014; Picower & Marshall, 2016; Tuck & Gorlewski, 2016).

The Problem with Power Relationships in the Accountability Paradigm

In sum, the power in teacher education's dominant accountability paradigm is held by regulators and agencies outside of teacher education programs and institutions. Specifically, and with variations from state to state, the source of accountability expectations is external to the programs and institutions that are held accountable, with very few opportunities for participants to have a voice in determining accountability content and measurement tools or to have the choice of joining in or opting out. This reflects deep mistrust of programs and the profession. The content of accountability—that is, what programs and institutions are actually held accountable for—varies somewhat across major initiatives from effectiveness defined in terms of programs' and graduates' impact on students' learning, to program and course characteristics presumed to produce effectiveness, to teachers' performance presumed to predict effectiveness.

There are multiple problems with the power arrangements of the accountability paradigm. Even with accountability systems or tools that were supposedly created "by the profession, for the profession," implementation and management arrangements have transformed these into external requirements with little to no room for the viewpoints and perspectives of multiple stakeholders. These power relations are not consistent with democratic means of evaluation. Just as problematic, democratic education and preparing students to live and work in a deeply divided but avowedly democratic society have no part in what teacher education programs and teacher candidates are held accountable for. In fact, none of the standards and expectations across major accountability policies and initiatives speak to these goals, a failing we elaborate on in Chapter 9.

REJECTING THE ACCOUNTABILITY PARADIGM, PRESERVING ACCOUNTABILITY

There are many complex problems with the concepts, values, and assessments that are part of the dominant accountability paradigm in teacher education in the United States. Failings include narrow definitions of teaching and the purposes of schooling, reification of test scores as the quintessential measure of learning, and pushing out of the teacher education curriculum purposes other than those directly related to boosting teacher quality. In addition, the accountability paradigm relies primarily on top-down external control of programs and institutions, with little regard for local commitments and goals, local knowledge, and local relationships with communities.

Even if we accepted the accountability paradigm on its own terms, however, there is very little evidence to suggest that its mechanisms and underlying theories of change actually have the capacity to produce the desired change. Although proponents of the various initiatives claim that the summative evaluations these policies and initiatives produce will improve programs and boost teacher quality, these claims are not evidence-based. Indeed, summative evaluations intended to influence policy decisions generally do not provide information that is actually useful for program improvement, a conclusion that even proponents of these initiatives draw (Cochran-Smith, Stern, et al., 2016). Further, underlying these initiatives is the assumption that there is a more or less direct relationship between the implementation of public summative evaluations, such as ratings and rankings of teacher education programs or candidates, and the improvement of teacher preparation program quality and ultimately teacher quality, defined in terms of enhanced student achievement. The irony here is that while the accountability policies and initiatives we have highlighted in this book call for teacher education programs and institutions to make decisions based on evidence, the policies themselves are not evidence-based. Thus, there is good reason to question their validity as policy instruments that have the capacity to boost teacher quality by boosting teacher education quality.

As we said in the very first chapter of this book, despite the many problems with the current accountability paradigm, we are not here to reject accountability in teacher education. Rather, we want to preserve teacher education accountability by rescuing and reclaiming it for the democratic project. This requires reconceptualizing the values and purposes of accountability, reconstructing the problem of teacher education, and reconfiguring power relationships in keeping with the ideals and principles of strong democracy. In the final chapter of this book, we take a major step toward rescuing and reclaiming by proposing a new approach—*democratic accountability in teacher education*. We consider what it would mean to establish democratic accountability in teacher education and then what it would take to actually implement it in teacher education programs, in accreditation standards and procedures, in assessments of teacher performance, and in public information for prospective teachers and prospective employers.

Democratic Accountability in Teacher Education

Teacher education accountability is mired in market ideology, thin equity, externally controlled monitoring schemes, and narrow definitions of effectiveness. Based on deep mistrust of the profession and theories of change that are not supported by strong evidence, the teacher education accountability paradigm has constricted the curriculum, reduced the spaces for critical discussion, and diminished the possibilities for teachers and teacher educators to work with others as agents of school and social change. The dominant accountability paradigm has also reified test scores as the most important measure of students' learning and venerated international comparisons as the key indicator not only of a nation's place in the global economy but also of its educational values.

Despite these issues and the fact that the accountability paradigm has not been effective at bringing about real change, we do not conclude this book by rejecting accountability or by arguing that teacher education should be radically local, with each program operating completely independently and responsible only to itself. To the contrary, we believe that both local and larger goals are critical in a democratic society and that education professionals ought to be responsible for something beyond their own commitments and the priorities of their own communities. Instead of rejecting accountability in teacher education, then, we want to rescue it from the market quagmire and reclaim it for the democratic project. This is an exceedingly difficult task. To forward a democratic approach to accountability, we must find ways to define accountability's purposes and goals in terms of the common good, change the narrative about the problem of teacher education, and radically disrupt existing power relationships. All of this must happen in the context of an acutely polarized society wherein individualism and private goods have been valorized, and there are vast divides in people's deepest beliefs about the purposes of education, the challenges posed by diversity, and the meanings of equity, effectiveness, and national progress.

The major purpose of this chapter is to conceptualize democratic accountability in teacher education according to the major thematic clusters of the accountability framework we have used throughout this book.

In addition, woven throughout our discussion are three ideas that make democratic accountability in teacher education generally "democratic." First, democratic accountability is based on the assumption that in order to survive, 21st-century democratic societies need deliberative and critical democratic education that teaches all students how to analyze multiple perspectives and engage in deliberative dialogue. This means that teacher education programs ought to be accountable for democratic education itself. Second, democratic accountability is founded on the assumption that in democratic societies, teaching and teacher education are enterprises for the public good, rather than market-oriented enterprises based on individual competition for private goods. From this perspective, the goal of teacher education is to prepare teachers who understand that part of the job is recognizing inequities in schools and society and working with others to challenge the structures that reproduce inequities. Third, democratic accountability in teacher education is based on dialogue and participation of all stakeholders, including external agents, those at the institutions and programs that are being held accountable, and the families and communities with whom they work. In this sense, democratic accountability is consistent with ideas about democratic evaluation based on dialogue and inclusion.

The second purpose of this chapter is to explore a number of intriguing and instructive projects and initiatives in teacher education that are relevant to the idea of reclaiming accountability for the democratic project. We consider the lessons that can be drawn from selected projects, programs, networks, and policies that are in sync in certain ways with the larger democratic project and with notions of strong equity. We intentionally selected these promising practices because they are different from one another. They operate at different levels of educational systems, and they represent different ideas about what it means to be accountable. These promising practices are examples of ways that teacher educators can enact democratic accountability in teacher education.

THE FOUNDATIONS OF DEMOCRATIC ACCOUNTABILITY IN TEACHER EDUCATION

In Chapter 8, we unpacked and critiqued the dominant accountability paradigm in teacher education in terms of the three thematic clusters in our accountability framework: the foundations of accountability, the problem of teacher education, and power relationships in accountability. As we've shown, the foundations cluster has to do with underlying values, ideologies, and principles related to the nature of society, the roles and purposes of teaching/teacher education in society, and the causes and cures of inequality. Below we use this same framework to structure our conceptualization of democratic accountability, as indicated in Figure 9.1. As we elaborate

Figure 9.1. Democratic Accountability in Teacher Education

Thematic Cluster	Themes	Description
Foundations of Accountability	Strong Democracy	• Deliberation and participation essential to new understandings of democracy • Mutual interdependence of democracy, democratic education, democratic teacher education, and democratic accountability for teacher education
	Strong Equity	• Redistribution of teachers prepared to enact deliberative democratic education • Respect and recognition of the knowledge and experiential frameworks of minoritized students, families, and communities • Recognition of and challenges to the structures/processes that produce and reproduce inequities seen as central to teaching and teacher education • Reframing common assumptions about power of education to redress poverty
The Problem of Teacher Education	The Dominance of the Accountability Paradigm	• Promotes uniformity and compliance • Narrows the spaces for discussions/actions regarding equity, social justice, and democratic education • Lacks evidence to support the effectiveness of the dominant accountability paradigm in teacher education
	Democratic Accountability as an Alternative	• Democratic accountability as an alternative and additive framework that embraces democracy • Intended to create a more just and democratic society • Values judgments and commitments of local programs
Power Relationships in Accountability	Intelligent Professional Responsibility	• Grounded in trust of the profession: builds on professionals' knowledge and collective commitments • Balance and equity of power across stakeholders who jointly determine accountability mechanisms • Involves a generative and reciprocal relationship between internal and external accountability
	Deliberative and Critical Democratic Education	• Rejects uniformity and compliance with a single norm or universal assessment that presumably signals effectiveness • Prepares teachers who have the capacity and commitment to enact deliberative and critical democratic education

below, the bedrock values and concepts that animate democratic accountability in teacher education are strong democracy and strong equity.

Strong Democracy

In his discussion of market ideology versus democratic values in public education, Engel (2000) suggests that any challenge to the dominant direction of American educational policy involves, by necessity, a challenge to market ideology along with description of a democratic alternative in both theory and practice. But Engel also asserts that proposing a democratic alternative—in the case of this book, a democratic alternative to teacher education accountability—also requires a political justification, which is particularly tricky in today's context. As Engel points out, there is broad consensus in today's political context that democracy is already triumphant in the United States (and has been ever since the fall of communism). From this perspective, market-based policies, on the one hand, and democratic principles, on the other, are often seen as mutually reinforcing of one another and are understood by many people as one and the same. Engel thus concludes that "it makes little sense to argue that educating for democracy is somehow antithetical to market ideology—*unless the concept of democracy is understood differently*" (p. 44, emphasis added).

What does this mean for our efforts to reconceptualize accountability in teacher education? First and foremost, it means that the concept of democratic accountability in teacher education depends entirely on what kind of democracy we're talking about. Are we talking about the kind of democracy that is more or less equated with market ideology—that is, democracy that protects individual interests and property and that values the freedom of the market above all other freedoms? Or do we mean "democracy understood differently" (p. 44), in Engel's words—that is, democracy that involves something well beyond participants voting in elections and organizing special-interest groups to lobby for their own viewpoints and advantages? We start with Barber's (1984) phrase, "strong democracy," and his now classic distinction between thin and strong democracy, which was the inspiration for our parallel distinction between "thin and strong equity" (Cochran-Smith, Stern, et al., 2016). We elaborate upon each of these ideas below.

We use "strong democracy" to signal that at the very base of a democratic alternative to accountability in teacher education is a notion of "democracy understood differently." Barber's (1984) strong democracy is consistent—although not synonymous—with related concepts, including Hudson's (1995) "participatory democracy," Engel's (2000) "popular democracy," Dewey's (1916) ideas about democracy as "a model of associated living," and Gutmann's (1999) and Young's (2000) different takes on "deliberative democracy." Barber rejects liberal democracy as a "thin" theory of democracy that focuses on individualistic ends, private property, and market capitalism while at the same time lacking a viable theory of citizenship, participation, public goods, and civic virtue (p. 4). Barber asserts that thin democracy is "concerned more to promote individual liberty than to secure public justice, to advance interests rather than to discover goods, and to keep men [sic] safely apart rather than to bring them fruitfully together" (p. 4). In contrast, Barber offers the concept of strong participatory democracy, which depends on the idea of a "self-governing community" united not so much by the same interests as by civic education and participatory institutions. From this perspective, politics is a way in which people with different interests can live together communally "not only to their mutual advantage but also to the advantage of their mutuality" (p. 118). With strong democracy, Barber conceptualizes a political community that is capable of "transforming dependent, private individuals into free citizens, and partial and private interests into public goods" (p. 132).

Clearly, people are not born knowing how to participate in a self-governing community, resolve conflict through (sometimes very difficult) participatory processes, engage in moral reciprocity, or build and take advantage of their mutuality with others. To the contrary, participants in a strong democratic society have to learn these and other critical habits of mind and learn how to enact and participate in democratic practices in the crucible of social and political life. This means that inherent in the notion of strong democracy is a critical role for "*education* understood differently*," to tweak Engel's phrase—that is, education understood as the basis of strong democracy rather than education for global competition.

Democratic education alone is not sufficient to challenge the dominance of market ideology or to create a strong democratic society, but it is abundantly clear that sustaining a strong democratic society is impossible without democratic education. In short, strong democracy depends on strong democratic education, which Dewey (1916) famously conceptualized and others have both critiqued and elaborated (Apple & Beane, 2007; Ayres, Sandford, & Coombes, 2017; Gutmann, 1999; Gutmann & Thompson, 1996; Young, 2000). Dewey (1916) suggested that democracy was much more than a form of government. He said it was a way of living that provided for the participation of all its members on equal terms: "Such a society must have a type of education which gives individuals a personal interest in social relationships and control, and the habits of mind which secure social changes without introducing disorder" (p. 56). Our argument here is that just as a strong democratic society depends on democratic education, democratic education depends on democratic teacher education and on democratic accountability in teacher education.

The purpose of democratic accountability in teacher education is threefold: to assess the extent to which teacher education programs and institutions ensure that their teacher candidates are prepared to enact deliberative and critical democratic education and prepare their students to participate in democratic society; to evaluate the extent to which the power and knowledge relationships involved in the accountability process are democratized; and to provide feedback that enhances program improvement and the learning of teacher educators and teacher candidates in keeping with the democratic project. We say more about democratic education below in our discussion of the content and power relationships of democratic accountability—that is, what teacher education is actually held accountable for, what counts as evidence of this, and who decides.

Strong Equity

The second building block in the foundations or values of democratic accountability in teacher education is strong equity. We introduced the idea of strong equity and contrasted it with thin equity (Cochran-Smith, Stern, et al., 2016) in Chapter 2, drawing on Barber's (1984) ideas and language related to strong and thin democracy. In this chapter, we elaborate on strong equity as a cornerstone of democratic accountability in teacher education.

All the major teacher education accountability initiatives in the United States include promoting equity as one of their goals, but underlying most initiatives is a notion of thin rather than strong equity. From the perspective of thin equity, the operating assumption is that assimilation into "shared goals" is a fundamental purpose of the education of minoritized students and that providing equal (that is, "the same") access to teachers, curriculum, and schools will bring about equity. Thin equity is in some ways consistent with notions of distributive justice and is related to a strand of political philosophy that prioritizes a politics of redistribution above a politics of recognition (Cochran-Smith, 2010; Fraser & Honneth, 2003; Gewirtz & Cribb, 2002; North, 2006). The distributive view of justice grew out of liberal democratic theory, particularly its focus on equality of individuals and a common political commitment to all citizens' autonomy (Rawls, 1971). From the distributive perspective, *in*justice—and *in*equity—are defined in terms of inequalities rooted primarily in the socioeconomic structure of society. Thus the remedy is redistribution of material and other goods, including access to "good" teachers, "good" curriculum, and "good" schools, with the goal of establishing a society based on fairness and equality.

In contrast, from the perspective of strong equity, the operating assumption is that there are highly complex and intersecting historical, economic, and social systems that create and maintain unequal access to teachers, curriculum, and schools. This means that teachers, teacher educators, and schools alone—no matter how good—cannot bring about equity. From the perspective of strong equity, it is assumed that genuine change requires identifying and working with others to undo the racialized, structural, and systemic aspects of schools and society that maintain inequity, including interrogating and unlearning deep-seated ideas about meritocracy and individualism as well as learning to recognize and build on the knowledge and values of historically marginalized groups.

These ideas about strong equity are, in many ways, consistent with the recognition view of social justice. From the perspective of recognition, the argument is that justice and equity are not reducible to distribution. Along these lines, Young (1990, 2000) admits that redistribution is important but rejects the idea that justice and equity can be reduced to distribution. Instead she calls for a liberatory "politics of difference" (Young, 1990) that affirms group differences and requires a reconception of equality and equity (Honneth, 2003). Our notion of strong equity is consistent with the perspective that differences are valuable assets, not deficits. Along these lines, Young (1990) rejects the efforts of institutions (like schools) to "melt away differences" and instead calls for "institutions that promote . . . respect for group differences without oppression" (p. 47). From this perspective, the argument is that efforts to achieve equity by providing equal or "the same" material goods and access may actually work to deny difference and reinforce the oppression of social groups.

To qualify the discussion above, it is important to note that in contemporary political philosophy, the question is not whether to theorize justice and equity as matters of *either* distribution *or* of recognition. Rather, the question is how to conceptualize distributive justice in relation to the politics of identity and difference (Fraser, 2003; Gewirtz & Cribb, 2002; Honneth, 2003; Young, 1990).

What do theories of equity and justice, derived primarily from political philosophy, have to do with our efforts to make the case for an alternative approach to accountability in teacher education? Drawing on the above work in political philosophy and on Cochran-Smith's (2010) theory of social justice teacher education, our notion of strong equity as a cornerstone of democratic accountability in teacher education has four core ideas: *redistribution, recognition, reframing,* and *resolving tensions.*

First, strong equity assumes that there must be wide *redistribution* to all schools of teachers who are committed to working with others for social change and who know how to prepare students to engage in democratic deliberation. The second core idea of strong equity is that there must be wide redistribution to all schools of teachers who *recognize* and challenge the school and societal structures and systems that produce and reproduce inequities, including the historical oppression and lack of representation of the values and knowledge traditions of minoritized students, families, and communities (King, 2008; Young, 1999). The assumption here, as King (2006) rightly reminds us, is that equal access to a faulty curriculum or a faulty set of "shared goals" is not justice. The coupling of the first two core ideas in our concept of strong equity links redistribution with recognition, but does not assume that they are "mutually irreducible" (Fraser, 2003). Rather, our coupling of these two emphasizes that with strong equity, although redistribution is important, recognition is a central moral aspect (Honneth, 2003).

The third core idea in our notion of strong equity is *reframing* of common assumptions and prevalent frames related to equity, equality, and justice. Educational frames are tools of power that are used to achieve political ends in that they position people in relation to dominant ideologies and influence activities in classrooms, schools, and the larger policy context (Hand, Penuel, & Gutiérrez, 2012). Two of the most powerful educational frames that shape the ways we think about equity are color blindness and meritocracy (Nasir, Scott, Trujillo, & Hernández, 2016). With strong equity, there is an emphasis on unpacking, interrogating, and unlearning these and other powerful frames that assume objectivity and thus mask the structural and racialized nature of inequality within a discourse of individualism and equal access (Au, 2016).

Finally, the fourth core idea in strong equity is *resolving* tensions. This has to do with acknowledgment of the inherent tensions and contradictions among valid but competing ideas about the nature of equity and managing these in teacher education programs in knowingly imperfect but concrete ways. This is not so easy to do. Gewirtz and Cribb (2002) have argued that most contemporary theorizing about justice and equity in education has glossed over the inherent tensions at an "a priori level or at a high level of abstraction" (p. 506), rather than understanding and managing them concretely. With democratic accountability, the idea is that teacher educators would struggle collectively and deliberately at the level of local practice to resolve the tensions that emerge, even while knowing that resolutions are temporary.

Accountability grounded in the notions of strong democracy and strong equity, as we conceptualize them above, is disruptive. It frames the problem of teacher education differently from the way it is usually framed, as we show below, and thus calls for different accountability solutions. We explore these in the final section of this chapter.

THE PROBLEM OF TEACHER EDUCATION
FROM THE PERSPECTIVE OF DEMOCRATIC ACCOUNTABILITY

The "problem of teacher education" is the label we use for the second cluster of thematically related dimensions in our accountability framework. Initially we developed this cluster to draw attention to the language and frames used by the advocates of particular accountability initiatives to forward their own conclusions about who or what "caused" the problem of teacher quality/teacher education, along with their favored approaches for "solving" the problem. In this chapter we use the problem cluster to ask a slightly different question: If strong democracy is our objective, what is the problem with teacher education? And what would solve it?

The Dominance of the Accountability Paradigm

Before we answer this question, we return briefly to the problem of teacher education as constructed by the dominant accountability paradigm. As we argued extensively in Chapter 8, the problem has consistently been framed from a market perspective that alleges that university-sponsored teacher education has failed to produce a competitive workforce. Thus the market perspective pinpoints the cause of this problem as the generally low quality of teacher education programs and their failure to engage in data-driven improvement. There is a lot that is wrong with this framing of the problem, but it also gets some things right, and it is important to note that our call for democratic accountability is *not* an uncritical defense of the teacher education status quo. To the contrary, we recognize that there are many legitimate problems with university teacher education. These include the marked unevenness of program quality across institutions, difficulty attracting a diverse pool of teacher candidates, insularity and lack of recognition that teacher education itself reproduces inequities and does not adequately recognize the racialized nature of schooling , and reinforcing (unintentionally or otherwise) the idea that there is a gap between theory, which lives at universities, and practice, which lives in schools.

These and other issues represent genuine and serious problems in teacher education, and we do not deny them. However, if strong democracy is our objective, then one major obstacle is the dominance of the accountability paradigm itself and its negative effect on teaching and teacher education. Along these lines, Apple (2014) suggests that there has been a "conservative restoration" in education policy and practice—an ideological movement "away from social democratic principles and an acceptance of more right-wing positions in social and educational policy" (p. 21). Apple argues that the restoration happened because dominant groups framed educational problems and solutions to appeal to people's "common sense" and resonate with their experiences and felt needs. Apple suggests that one outcome of conservative restoration is a "divided and amoral political community" (p. 3). Another outcome is that people's views about good schools, good teachers, and appropriate educational goals, means, and ends have shifted in keeping with the dominant paradigm's emphasis on producing the workforce needed for global competition.

In teacher education specifically, there have been similar negative outcomes as a result of the dominance of the accountability paradigm, which is animated by the ideology of the market coupled with thin equity and driven by tests and international comparisons. To capture the general impact of the accountability paradigm on teacher education, we use the word "subtractive," a phrase developed by Valenzuela (1999) to refer to the structural qualities of schools that "culturally subtracted" from—or dismissed—the resources Mexican American youth brought to school with them and thus relegated them to academic failure. We showed in Chapters 4 through 7 that the dominant accountability paradigm in teacher education has prompted uniformity and compliance, redefined how teacher educators understand their roles, emphasized narrow outcomes, and subtracted from the spaces in the teacher education curriculum for discussion and action related to equity, social justice, and democratic education. The dominant accountability paradigm has also prompted a somewhat technical view of teaching and learning and a linear understanding of the relationships among teacher education, teacher quality, students' achievement, and economic prosperity. Jenlink (2016) does a good job of synthesizing these impacts, pointing out that under the influence of the audit culture, teacher education has become "distanced from its public purpose of educating citizens for a democratic society as the culture of accountability imposes new forms of central control" (p. 164).

A second major problem with the accountability paradigm in teacher education is that it has dominated the field despite the fact that there is very little evidence to suggest that it is effective as a way to improve the quality of teacher education programs. As noted, we reached this conclusion in a policy brief based on careful analysis of the claims and the weight of the available evidence regarding major United States accountability initiatives:

> There is *thin evidence* to support the claims proponents make about how the assumed policy mechanisms will actually operate to improve programs. . . . Summative evaluations intended to influence policy decisions generally do not provide usable information for program improvement. The irony here is that while these policies call for teacher education programs and institutions to make decisions based on evidence, the policies themselves are not evidence-based. Further, there is good reason to question their validity as policy instruments that will have a positive impact on teacher education quality. (Cochran-Smith, Stern, et al., 2016, p. 3)

If the major accountability initiatives in U.S. teacher education are not organized to provide well-founded, effective, and actionable feedback that guides decision making, then what is their purpose? At the end of the day, we believe that the dominant accountability paradigm is largely about accountability for accountability's sake—that is, accountability initiatives that rate, rank, and monitor programs and candidates are put into place primarily for the sake of rating, ranking, and monitoring rather than for program improvement, because these activities appear on the surface to signal that somebody is "finally" holding teacher education accountable.

An Alternative to the Dominant Accountability Paradigm

If strong democracy is our objective and a major problem with teacher education is the subtractive impact of the dominant accountability paradigm, then the solution, or at least part of the solution, is a democratic—and additive—approach to accountability. This entire chapter is about that alternative. First and foremost, democratic accountability challenges and rejects the assumption that the primary goal of teacher education is preparing teachers who can boost test scores and thus, presumably, enhance the nation's ability to compete in the global economy. Rather, from the perspective of democratic accountability, the goal of teacher education is preparing teachers who know how to create democratic learning environments that enhance students' academic, social, and emotional learning and also prepare them to participate in a complex, diverse, and divided democratic society. Westheimer's (2015) commentary on citizenship education is instructive here:

> If things are going to improve, parents, administrators, and politicians alike will have to acknowledge that educators in a democratic society have a responsibility to create learning environments that teach students how to think, how to critically analyze multiple perspectives, and how to develop the passion for participation in the kind of dialogue on which a healthy democracy relies. But only those teachers who are free to work as professionals, exploiting their own interests and passions, have any chance of achieving these goals. (p. 33)

Clearly, there is no way to flip a switch that instantly transforms teacher education accountability from its basis in the ideology of the market and thin equity to a basis in the ideology of strong democracy and strong equity. Nor is there any easy way to transform teacher education accountability from a system that demands compliance and uniformity to a system that cultivates the development of passionate professionals working for the democratic project. But we believe there are possibilities for movement. As Apple (2014) reminds us, "The widespread recognition that there were, are, and can be more equal modes of economic, political, and cultural life can only be accomplished by organized efforts to teach and expand this sense of difference. Clearly there is educational work to be done" (p. 194). We offer democratic accountability as a central part of that work in teacher education.

Accountability should serve democracy. This premise is very different from accountability for its own sake, and it's also very different from the idea that accountability is objective, neutral, or value-free—simply a collection of data and "brute facts" that can be used to make disinterested decisions. With the notion of democratic accountability, we work from the premise that accountability, like all educational policies and practice, is value-laden. Along these lines, House and Howe (1999) argue persuasively that evaluation for deliberative democratic purposes rejects the notion of objectivity that "depends on stripping away all conceptual and value aspects and getting down to the bedrock of pristine facts" (p. 9). As we have shown, the dominant accountability paradigm in teacher education is decidedly *not* disinterested. Although it is touted by many as objective and data-based, it is actually highly interested in ensuring the place of the United States in the global economy, which benefits primarily the elite, by standardizing teaching and teacher education.

Democratic accountability in teacher education is not disinterested either. It is passionately interested in creating a more just and democratic society, and it is interested in holding teacher education programs and institutions accountable for their efforts to do so. House and Howe's (1999) seminal concept of "deliberative democratic evaluation" is very helpful here. Their approach to evaluation is not simply "democratic" in the sense that all those affected by an evaluation are included in dialogue and deliberation. This requirement is important, but just as important is that democratic evaluation is based on the fundamental premise that "citizens in democracies are [not] responsible only to the fulfillment of their own preferences" (p. 132). Rather, their own preferences "must be tied to democratic principles argued, debated, and accepted by the evaluation community" (House & Howe, 2000, p. 4). What makes these principles acceptable is deliberation within which the principles of argument are honored and participants maintain a healthy skepticism about each other's viewpoints.

We readily admit that democratic accountability in teacher education is based on lofty goals. In order to get any work done along these lines, we need to change the terms of the debate about teacher education accountability. Ayers, Kumashiro, Meiners, Quinn, and Stovall (2016) conclude their book about teaching toward democracy in K–12 classrooms and schools with a chapter entitled "Improving Educational Policy: Reframing the Debate, Reclaiming Public Voice" (p. 153). The chapter—and the larger book—revolve around the idea that educational frames have an enormous, although often invisible, impact on: students' learning experiences in school, how society thinks about teachers and their work, and the policies that manage and evaluate teachers, students, and schools. Ayres and colleagues identify the dominant frames in the U.S. educational system as standards, accountability, sanctions, and choice. They assert that "setting the frame turns out to be a particularly powerful piece of work—who names the world and who frames the issues matters" (p. 156). Our concept of democratic accountability in teacher education is a call to action in U.S. teacher education—to rename the world and reframe the issues. This is a necessity. It is not a pie-in-the-sky aspiration or a romanticized point of view. Given the increasing polarization of our society and people's growing inability and unwillingness to engage in deliberative disagreement, we must take a new approach.

POWER RELATIONSHIPS IN THE DEMOCRATIC APPROACH TO TEACHER EDUCATION ACCOUNTABILITY

Accountability is always value-based rather than neutral, and it always has to do with power relationships and control. We have argued throughout this book that with the dominant accountability paradigm, the source of accountability expectations is external to programs and institutions, with few opportunities for participants to help determine what they are actually held accountable for. The content of accountability is primarily teacher effectiveness and program impact, narrowly defined. Democratic accountability turns this approach on its head by replacing external control and internal compliance with intelligent professional responsibility and replacing narrow definitions of effectiveness with complex ideas about deliberative and critical democratic education.

Intelligent Professional Responsibility

In terms of issues of control and jurisdiction, we propose that a central part of democratic accountability in teacher education is what we are calling *intelligent professional responsibility*. This notion braids together three ideas—intelligent accountability, democratic evaluation based on dialogue and deliberation, and professional accountability.

O'Neill (2002) introduced the term "intelligent accountability" in a series of lectures about the audit culture that had emerged in the United Kingdom and elsewhere because the public had lost trust in policymakers and professionals. She argued, however, that the audit culture's intense monitoring and surveillance had not improved the quality of work in the public sector and the professions. To the contrary, it "distort[ed] the proper aims of professional practice and damage[d] professional pride and integrity" (p. 14). O'Neill called instead for intelligent accountability that begins with trust, presuming that the people who do the work in a given profession or policy sector have knowledge about that work and generally want to be better at it. Extending O'Neill's ideas to K–12 education in New Zealand, Crooks (2003) suggested six criteria for intelligent accountability: preserving trust among the participants in the accountability process, including participants in the process, encouraging deep rather than superficial responses, acknowledging the limitations of educational performance indicators, providing feedback that supports thoughtful decisions about practice, and enhancing participants' enthusiasm and motivation regarding their work. Applied to teacher education, the most important things we take from this concept are: intelligent accountability is grounded in *trust* rather than *mistrust* of teacher education programs and institutions; it involves the active participation of the professionals who are being held accountable; and, it is deliberately organized to yield information that can actually be used for thoughtful program improvement. These characteristics of control in intelligent accountability are dramatically different from the features of control in the dominant accountability paradigm.

We add to the above ideas about intelligent accountability, the major principles of deliberative democratic evaluation. House and Howe (1999) suggest there are three key features: inclusion, dialogue, and deliberation. Along these lines, they argue that all of those with "legitimate, relevant interests" (House & Howe, 2000, p. 5) in an evaluation should be included in decisions that affect those interests and that there should be a "rough balance and equality of power" (p. 6) so that dialogue and deliberation can happen. The dialogue and deliberation House and Howe favor involves rationally examining the values and interests of all stakeholders and making choices based on collective consideration of common goods. To conceptualize our idea of intelligent professional responsibility, we are applying House and Howe's ideas about deliberative democratic evaluation to teacher education and integrating them with ideas borrowed from intelligent accountability. This means that with democratic accountability in teacher education, accountability mechanisms, processes, and content are jointly determined by relevant professional organizations, participants in teacher education programs and institutions, and members of the local communities, schools, and families with whom teacher education programs work. This also means that the content of accountability can not be completely predetermined but instead integrates the local commitments and goals of programs. Along similar lines, school leaders and community members function as co-equal teacher educators, not simply as the co-occupants of the spaces used to prepare teachers.

Finally, in our conceptualization of intelligent professional responsibility as a key aspect of democratic accountability in teacher education, we draw from Fullan, Rincon-Gallardo, and Hargreaves' (2015) argument about accountability in K–12 schools. They argue that in order to support K–12 teacher and student learning, external accountability (or "back-end" accountability) should be replaced by internal professional accountability. In other words, Fullan and colleagues suggest that in K–12 education, the priority for policymakers should not be mandating external accountability policies that entice and/or coerce schools to comply by using carrots and sticks. Rather, they suggest that the priority should be creating the conditions for strong professional accountability, defined as "individuals and groups willingly taking on personal, professional, and collective responsibility for continuous improvement and success for all students" (p. 4). Professional responsibility emphasizes capacity-building and stakeholders collaborating within and across institutions. We take two key ideas from this work for our conception of intelligent professional responsibility in democratic accountability. First is the distinction between accountability and responsibility. In today's teacher education climate, the term *accountability* connotes obligation and coercion, while the term *responsibility* suggests professional willingness and commitment. Second is the relationship between internal and external accountability. Fullan and colleagues suggest that there will always be some sort of external accountability in K–12 education, and we believe this is true—and appropriate—in teacher education as well. But there is an enormous difference between external accountability that is primarily about monitoring compliance, on one hand, and external accountability intended to build the capacity for strong internal accountability based on local and larger goals and commitments, on the other hand. Our notion of intelligent professional responsibility as a key aspect of democratic accountability in teacher education includes the latter idea that external accountability mechanisms and processes should aim to strengthen the internal accountability of local programs and institutions.

To sum up, we use the phrase *intelligent professional responsibility* as a key part of our larger proposal for reclaiming accountability in teacher education. We intend *intelligent professional responsibility* to be an umbrella term signaling that democratic accountability in teacher education is grounded in trust of the profession, builds on professionals' knowledge and collective commitments to local and larger goals, and yields useful and usable information concerning program improvement. To do so, there is balance and equality of power across stakeholders, who jointly determine accountability mechanisms, processes, and content through rational consideration of individual and common interests. All of this is based on development of a generative and reciprocal relationship between internal and external accountability.

Deliberative and Critical Democratic Education

As we have shown throughout this book, the power relationships cluster involves not only *who* determines accountability expectations, but also *what* expectations are stipulated and *how* these are demonstrated. The what and how comprise the *content* of accountability. Our argument here is that with a democratic approach to accountability, the *what* of accountability is the preparation of teachers who have the capacity and commitment to enact deliberative and critical democratic education, and the *how* involves multiple measures, tailored to local contexts.

To explain what we mean when we say that teacher preparation programs should be accountable for democratic education, we unite ideas about deliberative democratic education with ideas related to the politics of difference. Gutmann (1987, 1990; Gutmann & Thompson, 1996) argues that moral disagreements are inevitable in democratic societies that respect human beings as autonomous agents. Deliberative democratic education, which develops young people's capacity to deliberate about decisions that are mutually binding, is essential to democratic societies and is the primary concern of public education (Gutmann, 1987). Gutmann argues that deliberation is a complex skill:

> Why should deliberation be considered primary even for public education when the opportunity for most [participants] to live a good life today requires many more basic skills and virtues, such as numeracy, literacy, and nonviolence? Deliberation is not a single skill or virtue. It calls upon skills of literacy,

numeracy, and critical thinking, as well as contextual knowledge, understanding, and appreciation of other people's perspectives. The virtues that deliberation encompasses include veracity, nonviolence, practical judgment, civic integrity, and magnanimity. By cultivating these and other deliberative skills and virtues, a democratic society helps secure both the basic opportunity of individuals and its collective capacity to pursue justice.

The willingness to deliberate about mutually binding matters distinguishes democratic [participants] from self-interested [participants], who argue merely to advance their own interests, and deferential [participants], who turn themselves into passive subjects by failing to argue, out of deference to political authority. (p. xiii)*

What this quotation suggests is that democratic deliberation is simultaneously the most basic and the most complex of skills. It is the sine qua non of a strong democracy because it ensures that participants individually can pursue meaningful lives and collectively can pursue common goods. As we are conceptualizing it here as the content of accountability in teacher education, democratic deliberation depends on complex skills in literacy and numeracy, understanding of cultures and contexts, empathic perspective-taking, the ability to make judgments based on evidence and argument, and genuine respect for the rights of individuals and groups to embrace values different from one's own.

It should be clear, then, that holding teacher education accountable for democratic education is *not* a matter of preparation programs making choices about whether to emphasize "the usual" knowledge and skills for teacher candidates—that is, content and pedagogical knowledge, classroom management and organizational skills, knowledge of learners and learning—*or instead* emphasizing the knowledge and skill required to enact deliberative democratic education. This is a false choice. The capacity to enact deliberative and critical democratic education unconditionally requires content and pedagogical knowledge as well as knowing how to construct and maintain positive learning environments. Enacting deliberative democratic education also unconditionally requires a deep and complex understanding of the fact that we live in a diverse, contentious, and heterogeneous society.

Arguing in the mode of critical theory, Young (1990, 1996, 2000) offers a positive vision of diversity, as we noted above—the "politics of difference" (Young, 1990). This positive vision is essential to our ideas about what teacher education must be accountable for from the perspective of democratic accountability in teacher education. She calls for moving "beyond deliberative democracy" and recognizing group differences as relational,

---

*In this excerpt, we substitute "participants" for Gutmann's "citizens" to emphasize that not all the stakeholders in public education have the privilege of citizenship, but all should have the right of participation

shifting, and positive, which explodes the implicit definition of "difference as deviance in relation to a norm, which freezes some groups into a self-enclosed nature" (p. 171). Young (2000) further argues that moving beyond deliberative democratic education requires critical consciousness about the structures that produce domination and oppression of minoritized groups. These ideas are essential to our proposal for democratic accountability in teacher education.

With democratic accountability in teacher education, as we are proposing it here, the goal is not uniformity or compliance with a single norm or universal assessment. Democratic accountability does not assume that all teacher education programs would meet exactly the same goals or use the same assessments, but it does assume that all teacher education programs would be responsible for preparing teachers to identify and challenge inequities in schools and society and prepare their students to live and work in a democratic society. This does not mean that there are no common measures that would be widely appropriate across programs. For example, the Institute for Democratic Education in America (IDEA) (2012) at the University of California, Los Angeles (UCLA) has developed a number of assessments related to democratic education. Along these lines, one IDEA instrument assesses the degree to which the learning environment of a school is democratic, which provides a counterpoint to test-based evaluations of schools. A similar tool could be developed to assess the degree to which teacher education programs and/or institutions are democratic and/or whether and how they teach candidates to incorporate democratic deliberation in the curriculum.

Over the last decade, some scholars and practitioners whose work is in or closely related to teacher education have explored some of the ideas we consider above, including problems with the dominant approach to accountability, the skills necessary to promote democratic education, teacher education outcomes that are consistent with democratic education, and analysis of individual programs or assignments that support a democratic approach (e.g., Au, 2016; Ayres et al., 2017; Cochran-Smith, 2005, 2010; Jenlink, 2016; Krise, 2016; Michelli & Keiser, 2005; Stitzlein, 2010). This is important work, but it is important to note that it is largely on the margins of teacher education and almost entirely on the margins of teacher education accountability. In fact, the discourse of democratic education, democratic accountability, and democratic evaluation is almost entirely absent from mainstream discussions about accountability in U.S. teacher education. Even at universities where there are strong graduate programs in areas related to democratic education, these are not teacher education programs (Stitzlein, 2010).

To conclude this discussion of the features of democratic accountability in teacher education, we focus specifically on its features in contrast to those of the dominant accountability paradigm. Figure 9.2 outlines the major differences between the dominant accountability paradigm in teacher education and democratic accountability.

Figure 9.2. Dominant Accountability Paradigm vs. Democratic Accountability in Teacher Education

Thematic Cluster	Dominant Accountability Paradigm	Democratic Accountability in Teacher Education
Foundations of Accountability	• Market ideology • Thin equity • Absence of democratic discourse • Education as a private enterprise for individual goods	• Ideology of strong democracy • Strong equity • Emphasis on democratic discourse • Education as a public enterprise for the common good
The Problem of Teacher Education	• Problem is teacher education's failure to produce a work force for the competitive global knowledge society • Caused by teacher education's failure to earn public confidence and use rigorous data systems for improvement • Problem of teacher education framed simplistically through a managerial/human capital lens • Based on a problematic theory of change that lacks evidence	• Problem is teacher education's failure to prepare teachers and students to engage in deliberative democratic education • Caused by negative effects of the dominant accountability paradigm, which is subtractive and reproduces inequity • Problem of teacher education framed in a complex way through a critical democratic lens • Based on a democratic theory of evaluation and change that builds on promising practices
Power Relationships in Accountability	• External control that demands internal compliance by programs and institutions • Based on and fosters mistrust of the profession • Excludes relevant local stakeholders from participation in accountability decision making • External accountability mechanisms require compliance, uniformity, and standardization internally • Programs accountable for preparing teachers to pass standard performance measures and enhance students' test scores • Standard, universal, external measures and accountability tools	• Generative and reciprocal relationship between internal and external accountability • Based on and fosters trust of the profession • Includes active participation and joint decision making among relevant local stakeholders • Builds capacity for internal accountability mechanisms that focus on intelligent professional responsibility • Programs accountable for preparing teachers to enact deliberative and critical democratic education so students can engage in democratic deliberation • Multiple complex local and external measures and accountability tools

TOWARD DEMOCRATIC ACCOUNTABILITY IN TEACHER EDUCATION: PROMISING PRACTICES

At the beginning of this chapter we agreed with Engel's (2000) assertion that any challenge to the dominant direction of U.S. education policy would necessarily require both a challenge to market ideology and a description of a democratic alternative *in both theory and practice*. The chapter so far has described a democratic alternative to teacher education accountability *in theory*. The last section of this chapter takes a very different turn by exploring several innovative projects, programs, networks, organizations, and policies that suggest promising directions for democratic accountability *in practice*. We selected these particular projects and programs, which we refer to from here on simply as *practices* or *promising practices*, for several reasons. First, each of these practices is relevant in certain ways to our argument that we need to reclaim accountability in teacher education by rethinking goals, reframing the narrative, and reconstituting power relationships. Second, these practices are in sync with one or more of the dimensions of democratic accountability, such as strong equity or intelligent professional responsibility, as we have elaborated on them in this chapter. Exploring these practices thus gives us a chance to consider how these ideas play out in practice. Third, these practices are different from one another and are drawn from different levels of practice, including local teacher education programs, a teacher performance assessment developed by a statewide network of programs, a national educator preparation accreditor, a national advocacy organization of education school deans, and the teacher education accountability policies and policy tools of a country. Finally, some of these practices are analogous to the major accountability policies and initiatives we analyzed and critiqued in earlier chapters of this book, which allows us to make salient comparisons. Our point in the following section is that we can learn something from each of these examples about what particular aspects of democratic teacher education accountability might look like in practice.

Before we turn to these promising practices, we want to highlight how our approach is different from some other proposals for improving teacher education by "learning from examples." For example, inspired by Friedman's (2005) treatise on "the flat world," there have been multiple proposals for the improvement of U.S. teacher education (and education more broadly) based on the identification and implementation of the policy approaches of high-performing countries. The rationale for this approach is stunningly explicit in the title of Tucker's (2011) agenda for rebuilding American education—*Surpassing Shanghai*—which he elaborates on with the book's first lines.

> This book answers a simple question: How would we redesign the American education system if the aim were to take advantage of everything that has been

learned by the countries with the best education systems in order to build a system better than any that now exists anywhere? That question is important because a growing number of countries are out-performing the United States on the most respected comparisons of student achievement. . . . (p. 1)

The book follows up with chapters about Finland, Singapore, Canada, Japan, and, of course, Shanghai, all places with superior student performance on the Programme for International Student Assessment (PISA) tests.

Our point here is that Tucker's selection of these examples is rooted in market ideology, including the assumption that the point of teaching and teacher education is to produce a workforce that can compete successfully in the global economy. Even countries like Finland and the province of Ontario, Canada, which have teacher education policies and practices that are in sync with some of our ideas about democratic accountability, are exemplars for Tucker first and foremost because of their students' superior test performance. No one envied Finland's teacher education system before the country emerged from relative obscurity to wide acclaim as a top PISA performer.

Our approach to selecting promising practices in this chapter is very different. We work from the assumption that a major purpose of education is to prepare young people to participate in democratic deliberation and that a major purpose of teacher education is to prepare teachers who enact deliberative and critical democratic education. Democratic deliberation is a complex skill that depends on literacy and numeracy skills but is not equated with them. Thus, we chose practices that have promise for a strong democracy, not for establishing U.S. superiority in global society. It is important to note that we are not suggesting that any one of the nine promising practices described below reflects all the features of democratic accountability in teacher education as we have outlined the approach in this chapter. To the contrary, each example draws attention to a particular aspect of democratic accountability but may not reflect other aspects. This is why we call them promising practices rather than exemplars or models.

Democratizing Teacher Education: Four Local Programs

In the United States, accountability expectations are determined almost exclusively by agencies and organizations that are external to local teacher education programs, which are then regularly monitored for compliance with teacher effectiveness standards and goals. Despite the dominance of this approach, there are some individual teacher education programs wherein educators have worked to democratize knowledge and content. There are also some programs that have made democratic education the centerpiece of the curriculum and the standard of evaluation. Below we briefly describe four individual programs.

The "Schools Within the Context of Community" program (Ball State University [BSU], 2017; Zygmunt & Clark, 2015) at Ball State University is an immersive, 18-credit semester program that emphasizes that knowledge about the communities in which children live and learn is an essential ingredient to being a good teacher (BSU, 2017). In this program, community mentors help candidates examine "funds of community knowledge in children's lives both in and outside formal schooling" (BSU, 2017). Program leaders suggest that "the intentional engagement of community wisdom and expertise in the training of teachers is a missing piece in preparing future educators [but] . . . this work can be accomplished in partnership with universities, schools, and the communities in which children live and learn" (Zygmunt & Clark, 2015, p. 6). A second example is teacher education programs at the University of Washington, where there is an emphasis on community expertise across all four quarters of the program's duration (Kretchmar & Zeichner, 2016; Zeichner, Payne, & Brayko, 2015). This includes field placements in community-based organizations, community-based educators with co-equal status as teacher educators, and a community-family-politics strand in the program. One goal of program leaders is to create "new hybrid spaces in university teacher education where academic, school-based, and community based knowledge come together in less hierarchical and haphazard ways to support teacher learning" (Zeichner et al., 2015, p. 3).

These two programs assume that a problem with teacher education is the disconnect between teacher candidates and the communities they serve, including a lack of local community knowledge. However, these programs do not simply instruct teacher candidates about structural inequities or require them to spend time in local communities. Rather, as Kretchmar and Zeichner (2016) note, "Programs must offer more than just critiques of structural inequities; they must actually shift power and knowledge to value community and family members" (p. 428). These two programs have structures in place that shift power relationships by incorporating the knowledge of community members and families and by working with communities as co-teacher educators. These programs are in sync with the principles of inclusion, dialogue, and deliberation that are part of our conception of intelligent professional responsibility, which is central to our framework of democratic accountability.

Two other programs serve as promising practices for "democratizing teacher education" in a different sense—making democratic content integral to programs and using principles of democracy as yardsticks against which teacher candidates' skills are evaluated. One example is the teacher education program at Lesley University that prepares educators to teach autistic students* by focusing on the three tenets of self-advocacy, social justice, and democratic education. From these perspectives, teacher candidates are prepared to teach autistic students in ways that position them as equals in the community and ensure that their voices are heard. Teacher candidates complete observations and assignments in both school and community organizations and complete a final self-evaluation on which they are asked to document how they met particular competencies, including, "know[ing] and articulat[ing] philosophies of democratic education," and "factor[ing] student voice into placement, program and service decisions to align with the goals of democratic education" (Keefe, 2015, 2016). A second example is the teacher education program that is part of the larger Center X community of practice at UCLA, which has been in existence for more than 15 years. The center's description makes the point clearly: "We believe that transformative work must tackle head on the deep social inequalities manifest in schools as gaps in educational opportunities and achievement . . . we remain committed to public schooling as one of the best democratic spaces for working to become a better, more just society" (UCLA Center X, n.d.). The Center X program expects teachers to be activists and evaluates teachers in part on the basis of their "demonstrating their mastery of activist skills" in working with immigrant families and other minoritized students, families, and communities (Quartz, 2003).

These two programs work from the assumption that teacher candidates and teacher education programs ought to be assessed in part on the basis of how they help teacher candidates and teachers create and maintain schools as democratic spaces wherein all players are considered equal participants. The content and curriculum of these two programs are consistent with our ideas that teacher education ought to be accountable for preparing teachers who enact democratic education.

Preparing Teacher Candidates for Strong Equity: A Local Program Scales Up

Although most teacher education reforms include equity as one of their purposes, we have argued that many are consistent with thin equity. That is, they define equity in terms of equal access for students, including those from minoritized groups, but without complementary emphasis on the structures and systems that reproduce inequities and without inclusion of the values and knowledge sources of minoritized communities in the development of so-called "shared" educational goals. From our perspective of democratic accountability, however, teacher candidates need to have a strong equity perspective. This means that they need to have not only the knowledge and

---

*Identity-first language is used here in keeping with the preference of self-advocate colleagues and the recommendation of the Autistic Self Advocacy Network [ASAN] (ASAN, n.d.). This language is explicitly intended to be a disruption of typical language used in the field.

skills to teach well, but also critical consciousness about the structures and processes that produce and reproduce inequities and about powerful educational frames such as color blindness and meritocracy that mask the structural and racialized nature of inequality. Below we describe one teacher program that explicitly prepares teacher candidates for strong equity in theory and in practice. We consider this program separately from the local programs above for two reasons: it is located in Australia rather than the United States, and it has "scaled up" to include multiple sites.

The National Exceptional Teaching for Disadvantaged Schools program (NETDS), which began at Queensland University of Technology, is a university-based teacher education program that recruits top-performing students from university education programs and is committed to the goal of teacher candidates (and the beginning teachers they become) working long-term alongside teachers and families in historically marginalized, high-poverty communities in rural and urban Australia (Burnett & Lampert, 2016; Lampert & Burnett, 2015; Lampert, Burnett, Comber, Ferguson, & Barnes, 2017). Now in its 8th year, the program has "scaled up" to seven universities, supported by funding from the Queensland Government Education Department and private foundations. This support was forthcoming because of demonstrated evidence that the program increased the number of high-achieving teacher candidates who chose to teach in high-poverty and lower-performing schools. We include NETDS in our discussion of promising practice not only because it features strong relationships with communities, but also because it explicitly focuses on preparing teachers who operate from the perspective of strong equity. Prior to placements in high-poverty communities, NETDS teacher candidates have extensive coursework that helps them understand poverty from a perspective that includes redefined notions of "redistribution, recognition, and representation" (Scholes et al., 2017). This view explicitly rejects individualistic and universalistic definitions of equity and instead helps teacher candidates understand the conditions that produce and sustain inequity.

The NETDS program is a promising practice related to democratic accountability in teacher education. In Australia as in many countries, Teach for Australia, which is part of the larger Teach for All organization, recruits top-performing college graduates to teach in high-needs schools for short terms and with little preparation. NETDS is a response to and a rejection of the growing number of neoliberal educational reforms like Teach for Australia and the general Teach for All network, which grew out of Teach for America in the United States. NETDS recruits top-performing teacher education program students to work in high-poverty schools and thus is intended to increase the access minoritized students have to teacher quality. However, it also fosters teachers' long-term commitments to working in these communities and explicitly prepares teacher candidates to understand the conditions and causes of poverty prior to work in those schools and communities.

Taking Back Control: A State-Level Consortium

As we have shown, accountability expectations in the United States are determined almost exclusively by agencies and organizations external to local teacher education programs, which are then monitored for compliance. Granted, there are some accountability initiatives that were purportedly created "by and for the profession," with the stated intention of fostering local program improvement and enhancing the learning of teacher educators and candidates. However, these initiatives have multiple agendas, including bringing teacher education on par with other professions through standardization of expectations and universal assessments. The latter agendas almost always trump the former, and the complex management and implementation demands of national-level assessments almost always override local needs. The result is that even accountability initiatives by and for the profession are transformed into and experienced by teacher education programs as primarily top-down demands for compliance. Despite the dominance of this approach, there are some efforts to take back control. Below we describe a state-level consortium that has established a bottom-up, low-stakes assessment of teacher candidate performance consistent with both local values and professional standards.

The New Hampshire Institutions of Higher Education (NH IHE) Network, which is a consortium including all 13 educator preparation programs in the state of New Hampshire, was created in 2011 and endorsed by the NH Commissioner and DOE in 2013. This teacher educator-founded and voluntary initiative was explicitly intended to put aside competition, build trust, and get to know one another's programs while "working collegially to influence policy makers and engage practitioners" (NH IHE Network, n.d.-a, para. 1). One of the consortium's key accomplishments is the development and statewide use of the New Hampshire Teacher Candidate Assessment of Performance (NH TCAP) (NH IHE Network, n.d.-b). Although the TCAP is an adaptation of the PACT, which was created by California teacher educators and is the forerunner of edTPA, the NH consortium explicitly rejected a single-measure, high-stakes, top-town, externally controlled state policy such as those in place in states that require edTPA for teacher certification. They concluded that high-stakes mandated performance assessments, which are grounded in competition rather than collaboration, undermine the formative benefits of performance assessment and position teacher educators as reactive rather than proactive (Reagan, Terrell, et al., 2016). Although the consortium explicitly embraces accountability as an opportunity for learning and improvement, it insists that accountability should be grounded in trust and professional expertise, with the goal of joint professional responsibility for the learning and performance of New Hampshire teacher candidates (Reagan, Schram, et al., 2016).

The NH TCAP and the work of the NH IHE network are promising practices for democratic accountability in teacher education. The content, scoring rubrics, and passing standards for the assessment were negotiated and agreed upon by all of the network's institutions. As a result of extensive deliberation, the NH TCAP is used primarily for formative assessment in keeping with the group's joint commitment that it should be "*for* learning as well as *of* learning" (Terrell, McCurdy, Birch, Schram, & Tompkins, 2018). This means that teacher candidates' TCAP scores remain at the candidates' home institution, and the consequences vary from institution to institution, although each uses the scores as part of a multifaceted assessment of candidates' readiness to teach. The TCAP assessment and the mode of operation of the NH IHE network are closely consistent with our notion of intelligent professional responsibility that is a core idea of democratic accountability in teacher education, particularly the network's grounding in professional trust, shared responsibility, and joint deliberation about local values.

Advocating for Justice and Democracy: A Deans' Organization

The current accountability era and the larger education reform movement in the United States have attracted many new players to the teacher education enterprise, including a variety of education reform advocacy groups and new professional organizations designed to influence local, state, and national policies regarding the preparation and licensure of teachers. Many new players work from similar values and assumptions about teacher quality, which are largely in keeping with the market-based ideology of the dominant accountability paradigm, and some even share the same funders. But there are a few new advocacy organizations that have explicitly rejected the dominant narrative and are working to change the frames of the debate about education and democracy. Below we describe one such group.

Founded in 2016, the Education Deans for Justice and Equity (EDJE) is a nationwide alliance of U.S. deans/former deans of education schools. The goal of the alliance is to advance "equity and justice in education by speaking and acting collectively and in solidarity with communities regarding policies, reform proposals, and public debates" (EDJE, 2017a, para. 3). The group builds on members' previous experiences working in networks and social movements aimed at reframing policy debates about education using media and wide circulation of public documents. The group's first official act—a *New York Times* letter that sharply criticized a *Times* editorial for praising the 2016 Title II teacher education reporting regulations when they were proposed—is illustrative of the group's strategy. The EDJE letter asserted that the *Times* editorial had been based on rhetoric rather than research: "The editorial presumes that teacher education programs are mediocre and underperforming. The evidence comes from [NCTQ], whose research methods have raised enough concerns that the vast majority of the more than 1,100 institutions contacted [by NCTQ] declined to voluntarily or fully participate" (Kumashiro, 2016, p. 1). Since then, EDJE has also published principles that offer guidelines for the role of the federal government in education (EDJE, 2017b) and reflect the group's vision for education in a democratic society (EDJE, 2017c). These statements were signed by more than 200 education deans and by other civil rights, multicultural, and fair-testing advocacy groups in the United States.

We highlight EDJE as a promising practice in support of democratic accountability in teacher education because of its explicit intention to challenge the common sense of the "conservative restoration" (Apple, 2014) in American education. As the work of EDJE shows, it is pointless simply to talk about the need to change the terms of the teacher quality/teacher education debate. To make a difference, somebody actually has to change them. EDJE intends to bring to public consciousness the threats to our democratic society that are implicit in much of the rhetoric and reality of education policy and public discourse. As stated in EDJE's public letter about the role of the federal government in education, their goal is to "uphold the role of public schools as a central institution in the strengthening of our democracy . . . Students are not merely commodities or consumers, and when we treat education as a competitive marketplace fueled by privatization we set up a system that ensures that some win while many others lose. We urge you to invest in education as a public good . . ." (EDJE, 2017b, p. 2). EDJE's public plea is entirely consistent with our ideas about democratic accountability in teacher education.

Autonomy and Innovation: A National Accreditor

As we have argued throughout this book, a hallmark of the dominant accountability paradigm is its focus on uniformity and compliance. We have also argued that this push for compliance subtracts from the professional autonomy of teacher education programs and decreases the ability of programs to respond to the needs of the diverse communities they serve. Our framework for democratic accountability in teacher education calls for pushing back against external control and uniformity. The NH IHE network is one example of an effort to take back control of teacher education accountability at the state level. At the national level, the Association for Advancing Quality in Educator Preparation (AAQEP) is also an effort by certain segments of the teacher education profession to take back control by crafting a new approach to program accreditation.

Launched in July 2017, AAQEP is a national accreditor of educator preparation programs. We believe that AAQEP has promise as an initiative consistent with some aspects of democratic accountability. However, its accreditation standards have not been finalized, and no programs have yet participated in its accreditation process. As this book went to press, AAQEP had been recognized as a national accreditor by Hawaii, one of a limited number of U.S. states that require all preparation programs to obtain national accreditation, and the organization expected institutions from up to three more states to seek accreditation once standards were finalized (M. Lacelle-Peterson, personal communication, November 2017). In addition, the Higher Education Committee of the New York State Regents had voted to consider additional alternative accreditation options for educator preparation programs in New York (New York State Education Department, 2017).

AAQEP plans to seek recognition from both the Council for Higher Education Accreditation, which is the national organization that recognizes 60+ higher education accrediting organizations, and the USDOE in 2019 (Goatley & Lacelle-Peterson, 2017). Most of AAQEP's draft standards for teacher education programs focus on preparing teachers with knowledge and skills that are consistent with other frameworks for professional teaching standards, and indeed AAQEP asserts that there is little debate in the field about the things all teachers need to know (AAQEP, 2017a), a premise that is arguable, in our view. However, AAQEP emphasizes diversity and equity in their procedures, suggesting that standard solutions to local challenges will not suffice. It is apparent that AAQEP is designed to be conspicuously different from their now rival, CAEP, in terms of the very things about which CAEP has been most harshly critiqued, including transparency and consistency of processes; local control and autonomy rather than compliance with universal expectations; emphasis on teacher candidates' classroom performance rather than their impact on the tested achievement of eventual students; and support of innovations and variations in keeping with diverse local contexts and communities (AAQEP, 2017a). AAQEP is currently seeking feedback on its standards and overall accreditation framework from a wide range of constituencies.

Time will tell whether AAQEP has the will or the capacity to transform teacher education accreditation into an educative experience consistent with the values of democratic accountability. However, we believe it is possible, considering AAQEP's commitment to creating an "accreditation process that respects institutional diversity and autonomy" (AAQEP, 2017b). Given our understanding of AAQEP's intentions, we believe that it may work as an internal-to-the-profession accountability agency to support individual institutions' efforts to build the capacity for strong local internal accountability based on both local and larger professional goals. Supporting a generative and reciprocal relationship between external and internal accountability is consistent with our conceptualization of democratic accountability.

Justice, Equity and Democratic Practice: One Nation's Commitment

With the goal of boosting the quality of teacher education programs in order to boost teacher quality, the approach of the federal government in the United States for the last two decades has been to stipulate accountability expectations, which are external to the teacher education programs and institutions they focus on, external to the teacher education profession, and external to state regulators. There has been little opportunity for professional, state, or local participation in determining these expectations, and there certainly has been no attention or mention of democratic principles and goals. This is not the approach in all developed countries, even though all of them exist within the larger milieu of the global reform movement and the growing consensus that the health of a nation's economy depends on its education system, which depends on the quality of its teachers. Below we offer one promising practice for democratic accountability in teacher education at the country level.

Scotland has always had an independent education system and is somewhat of an outlier in relation to many other countries, including the countries of the United Kingdom and Ireland, with which it shares a geopolitical space (Beauchamp, Clarke, Hulme, & Murray, 2015). Although Scotland has certainly been subject to the influences of the global reform movement, historically the country has had a belief in the power of education as a force for social change and in the power of teachers and teacher educators in that process. Teacher professionalism is at the heart of the teacher education policy agenda in Scotland, as reflected in the General Teaching Council for Scotland (GTCS), which is the world's first independent, self-regulating professional body of teaching with independent status from the government. The standards of the GTCS reflect the central themes of values, sustainability, and leadership, coupled with social justice, integrity, trust, and respect. These are reflected in the mandate that teacher education be delivered through partnerships among schools, local authorities, and universities. "The partnership agenda is big . . . in terms of the negotiations, decision-making and sharing of resources—both human and financial. This reflects the broader direction of public policy-making in Scotland, and in part can be seen as a positive, social-democratic approach to policy" (Hulme & Kennedy, 2015, p. 105). A recent OECD (2014) report on Scottish education described Scotland's high regard for teachers and its commitment to the centrality of teachers' professional judgment as "an admirable counterbalance to the trends in many Western countries which have seen the status of teachers and teaching decline in past decades" (p. 125), although the report also said these standards were harder to put into practice than they were to create.

We highlight Scotland and particularly the work of the GTCS because it is a good example of country-level work that strikes the external/internal balance that is central to our framework of democratic accountability in teacher education. That is, in Scotland, the external accreditor of programs is the GTCS, which is an independent organization that represents the profession. But GTCS's goal is to increase the capacity of local programs and institutions to hold themselves accountable. In addition to more democratic control, Scotland's approach to teacher education reform reflects a larger frame of social democracy much more so than many other countries, including other countries in the United Kingdom (Hulme & Kennedy, 2015), and also beyond that geographic region.

Learning from Promising Practices

We want to repeat our point that the nine promising practices above are just that—promising practices. They are not exemplars or models of democratic accountability in teacher education, since the latter terms would suggest full-blown and thoroughly worked-out accountability systems. Rather, each of these nine promising practices reflects one or more aspects of accountability that is consistent with our proposed approach, even though the practice may *not* reflect other aspects that are part of our approach. The most encouraging take-away from these promising practices is that people at various levels of teacher education—local programs, cross-local initiatives, state-level networks, national organizations, and even whole countries—have realized the importance of pursuing more democratic means and ends in teacher education. They have worked collaboratively to democratize knowledge and power relationships across communities as they pursue new approaches to teacher education accountability. This is why we should learn from them.

NOW MORE THAN EVER

In concluding this chapter and this book, we return to the idea captured in the book's main title—*Reclaiming Accountability in Teacher Education*. It's important to reiterate that the proposals in this book are not intended to reject accountability in teacher education, but to rescue it from market ideology and individualism and to reclaim it for the democratic project. That is, we want accountability to serve democracy, not market capitalism or individual private interests. We believe that this task, which we readily admit is extremely difficult to do, is needed *now more than ever*.

In the United States we are experiencing an extraordinary moment in terms of education generally and teacher education specifically. President Trump strongly favors the privatization of education and a market-based voucher system wherein families and students are encouraged to choose among schooling options, many of which are nonpublic and some of which are for-profit. Secretary of Education DeVos believes that public education is a dead end. As we noted in Chapter 1, during Trump's first year in office, education was not a priority, and few education initiatives were developed beyond repealing Obama-era accountability policies without replacing them with anything.

But there have been many developments over the last year that make it clear that the Trump administration favors neither strong democracy nor strong equity. Rather, the Trump administration is presiding over multiple actions in a variety of areas that, taken together, may well constitute a new era of diminished protection of minoritized student groups and a new low in terms of equity agendas: DeVos appointed Candice Jackson as acting head of DOE's Office for Civil Rights despite the fact that Jackson openly opposes affirmative action (Noguera, 2017); DeVos appointed former DeVry University Dean Julian Schmoke to serve as head of the group investigating fraudulent education loans, even though he was fined more than $100 million dollars in 2011 for granting questionable loans himself (Noguera, 2017); the Trump administration backed away from protection of the rights of transgender students (Office of Special Education and Rehabilitative Services [OSERS], 2017); DeVos plans to replace the current campus sexual assault enforcement system with a system that seems to prioritize the rights of abusers over the rights of victims (Dupuy, 2017); the Trump administration rescinded regulatory guidelines that outline the rights of students with disabilities (OSERS, 2017); members of the Senate Education Committee have charged that USDOE has approved state plans to meet ESSA accountability rules even though they are not in keeping with requirements regarding support for low-performing subgroups, such as English language learners and students of color (Education and the Workforce Committee Democrats, 2017). And the list keeps growing.

Many Trump critics have claimed that the biggest day-to-day problem for educators is not the slow but mounting accumulation of multiple small-to-medium-sized policy changes that diminish protections for minoritized groups, but the daily statements and actions of the President himself. The Southern Poverty Law Center (SPLC) has tracked hate events and hate crimes since before the presidential election (Potok, 2017). They documented a dramatic increase in hate violence, harassment, and intimidation immediately after the election, with a similar increase in the nation's K–12 schools and universities in nearly every state. The greatest number of incidents were anti-immigrant or anti-Muslim, but there were also incidents that SPLC described as anti-black, anti-Semitic, anti-LGBT, anti-women, and pro-white nationalist. SPLC's surveys since the election have indicated that the vast majority of respondents report that the climate of their schools has changed for the worse since the election, with student anxiety more intense and incidents involving bullying, racial slurs, and other derogatory language mounting (Potok, 2017).

But this is not simply an American problem or a Trump problem, and the underlying issues certainly were not invented or introduced by Trump. They reflect much deeper trends and fault lines that are also present in many other developed countries, including growing income inequality and serious "gaps" between historically privileged and disadvantaged groups in terms of educational opportunities and outcomes, although some countries have much wider disparities than others. There has also been the emergence of a strong conservative nationalism that has emerged in many places and caused some to wonder if the era of internationalism is over. Across many countries, the polarization of people has increased, as has intolerance—and hatred—of viewpoints different from one's own. We see democratic accountability in teacher education *not* as a way to solve these much larger problems, but as a way to push back against an accountability paradigm in teacher education that does not serve democracy and does not bode well for the next generation.

We conclude with a call to action. Now more than ever, we need deliberative democratic education. Now more than ever, we need to rally with others to assert that democratic teaching and teacher education are indispensable to the future of our democracy. Now more than ever, we need to be accountable for fostering strong democracy and strong equity.

References

Abell Foundation. (2001a). Teacher certification reconsidered: Stumbling for quality. Retrieved from abell.org/sites/default/files/publications/ed_cert_1101.pdf

Abell Foundation. (2001b). Teacher certification reconsidered: Stumbling for quality—A rejoinder. Retrieved from abell.org/sites/default/files/publications/ed_cert_rejoinder_1101.pdf

Allington, R. (2002). *Big brother and the national reading curriculum: How ideology trumped evidence*. Portsmouth, NH: Heinemann.

Ambrosio, J. (2013). Changing the subject: Neoliberalism and accountability in public education. *Educational Studies, 49*(4), 316–333.

American Association of Colleges for Teacher Education. (n.d.-a). Teacher prep accrediting groups to merge. Retrieved from aacte.org/news-room/aacte-in-the-news/282-teacher-prep-accrediting-groups-to-merge

American Association of Colleges for Teacher Education. (n.d.-b). FAQ. Retrieved from edtpa.aacte.org/faq

American Association of Colleges for Teacher Education. (n.d.-c). About edTPA. Retrieved from edtpa.aacte.org/about-edtpa

American Association of Colleges for Teacher Education. (n.d.-d). Participation map. Retrieved from edtpa.aacte.org/state-policy

American Association of Colleges for Teacher Education. (1999). *Comparison of NCATE and TEAC processes for accreditation of teacher education*. Washington, DC: Author.

American Association of Colleges for Teacher Education. (2013a). Comments on CAEP draft standards. Retrieved from secure.aacte.org/apps/rl/res_get.php?fid=176

American Association of Colleges for Teacher Education. (2013b, July 22). Setting the record straight: AACTE's engagement on the National Council on Teacher Quality Teacher Prep Review. Retrieved from aacte.org/news-room/press-releases-statements/152-setting-the-record-straight-aactes-engagement-on-the-national-council-on-teacher-quality-teacher-prep-review

American Association of Colleges for Teacher Education. (2014a, June 18). Statement on NCTQ teacher prep review from Sharon P. Robinson, Ed.D., AACTE president and CEO. Retrieved from aacte.org/news-room/press-releases-statements/462-statement-on-nctq-teacher-prep-review-from

American Association of Colleges for Teacher Education. (2014b). edTPA provides support by the profession, for the profession. Retrieved from brockport.edu/support/institutional_assessment/tk20/edTPA%20provides%20support.pdf

American Association of Colleges for Teacher Education. (2015). AACTE board resolution on CAEP. Retrieved from aacte.org/news-room/press-releases-statements/488-aacte-board-resolution-on-caep

American Association of Colleges for Teacher Education. (2017). Federal regulations for teacher preparation programs. Retrieved from aacte.org/resources/regulations

American Association of Colleges for Teacher Education. (2018). January 2018 federal update. Retrieved from secure.aacte.org/apps/rl/resource.php?resid=593&ref=rl

American Board for Certification of Teacher Excellence. (n.d.). Our story. Retrieved from americanboard.org/our-story/

American Council on Education. (2016, October 17). Education department releases final teacher preparation regulations [Blog post]. Retrieved from acenet.edu/news-room/Pages/Education-Department-Releases-Final-Teacher-Preparation-Regulations.aspx

American Educational Research Association. (2015). AERA statement on use of value-added models (VAM) for the evaluation of educators and educator preparation programs. *Educational Researcher, 44*(8), 448–452.

American Federation of Teachers. (2013, June 18). Review of teacher preparation programs needs improvement. Retrieved from aft.org/news/review-teacher-preparation-programs-needs-improvement

American Federation of Teachers. (2016, October 12). AFT's Weingarten on teacher preparation programs regulations [Press release]. Retrieved from aft.org/press-release/afts-weingarten-teacher-preparation-programs-regulations

American Psychological Association. (2014). Assessing and evaluating teacher education programs: APA task force report. Retrieved from apa.org/ed/schools/cpse/teacher-preparation-programs.pdf

Amrein-Beardsley, A., Barnett, J., & Ganesh, T. (2013). Seven legitimate apprehensions about evaluating teacher education programs and seven "beyond excuses" imperatives. *Teachers College Record, 115*(12), 1–34.

An, S. (2016). Teaching elementary school social studies methods under edTPA. *The Social Studies, 107*(1), 19–27.

An, S. (2017). Preparing elementary school teachers for social studies instruction in the context of edTPA. *Journal of Social Studies Research, 41*(1), 25–35.

Anderson, J. A. (2005). Accountability in education. The International Institute for Educational Planning/The International Academy of Education. Retrieved from unesdoc.unesco.org/images/0014/001409/140986e.pdf

Anyon, J. (2005). *Radical possibilities: Public policy, urban education, and a new social movement.* New York, NY: Routledge.

Apple, M. W. (2006). *Educating the "right" way: Marke s, standards, God, and inequality* (2nd ed.). New York, NY: Taylor & Francis.

Apple, M. W. (2014). *Official knowledge: Democratic education in a conservative age.* London, England: Routledge.

Apple, M. W., & Beane, J. A. (2007). Schooling for democracy. *Principal Leadership, 8*(2), 34–38.

Arizona State University. (2016, December 14). ASU's undergraduate teacher-prep program recognized as one of nation's best: Independent assessment places Mary Lou Fulton Teachers College in top 1 percent. Retrieved from asunow.asu.edu/20161214-asu%E2%80%99s-undergraduate-teacher-prep-program-recognized-one-nation%E2%80%99s-best

Association for Advancing Quality in Educator Preparation. (2017a). Draft accreditation framework: Expectations, process, consistency. Retrieved from aaqep.org/uploads/1/0/9/3/109302791/aaqep_expectations_for_feedback_nov.2.2017.pdf

Association for Advancing Quality in Educator Preparation. (2017b). Innovation and accountability: Polar opposites, or perfect pairing? Retrieved from aaqep.org/uploads/1/0/9/3/109302791/aaqep_tecscu_10_8_17.pdf

Au, W. (2013). What's a nice test like you doing in a place like this? *Rethinking Schools, 27*(4). Retrieved from rethinkingschools.org/articles/what-s-a-nice-test-like-you-doing-in-a-place-like-this-edtpa-and-corporate-education-reform

Au, W. (2016). Meritocracy 2.0: High-stakes, standardized testing as a racial project of neoliberal multiculturalism. *Educational Policy, 30*(1), 39–62.

Autistic Self Advocacy Network. (n.d.). Identity first language. Retrieved from autisticadvocacy.org/about asan/identity-first-language/

Ayers, W., Kumashiro, K., Meiners, E., Quinn, T., & Stovall, D. (2016). *Teaching toward democracy: Educators as agents of change.* London, England: Routledge.

Ayres, S., Sandford, M., & Coombes, T. (2017). Policy-making "front" and "back"stage: Assessing the implications for effectiveness and democracy. *The British Journal of Politics and International Relations, 19*(4), 861–876.

Baker, P. (2017, June 23). Can Trump destroy Obama's legacy? *The New York Times.* Retrieved from nytimes.com/2017/06/23/sunday-review/donald-trump-barack-obama.html

Bales, B. L. (2006). Teacher education policies in the United States: The accountability shift since 1980. *Teaching and Teacher Education, 22*(4), 395–407.

Ball State University. (2017). Schools within the context of community. Retrieved from cms.bsu.edu/academics/collegesanddepartments/teachers/departments/elementaryed/academics/immersive-learning/scc

Ballou, D., & Podgursky, M. (1997). Reforming teacher training and recruitment: A critical appraisal of the recommendations of the National Commission on Teaching and America's Future. *Government Union Review, 17*(4), 1–53.

Ballou, D., & Podgursky, M. (1999). Teacher training and licensure: A layman's guide. In M. Kanstoroom & C. Finn (Eds.), *Better teachers, better schools.* Washington, DC: Thomas B. Fordham Foundation.

Ballou, D., & Podgursky, M. (2001). Reforming teacher preparation and licensing: What is the evidence? *Teachers College Record, 102*(1), 5–27.

Barber, B. R. (1984). *Strong democracy: Participatory politics for a new age.* Berkeley, CA: University of California Press.

Barron, L. (2015). Preparing preservice teachers for performance assessments. *Journal of Interdisciplinary Studies in Education, 3*(2), 70–76.

Bastian, K. C., & Lys, D. (2016). *Initial findings from edTPA implementation in North Carolina.* Chapel Hill, NC: Education Policy Initiative at Carolina.

Beauchamp, G., Clarke, L., Hulme, M., & Murray, J. (2015). Teacher education in the United Kingdom post devolution: Convergences and divergences. *Oxford Review of Education, 41*(2), 154–170.

Boyd, D., Grossman, P., Lankford, H., Loeb, S., & Wyckoff, J. (2009). Teacher preparation and student achievement. *Educational Evaluation and Policy Analysis, 31*(4), 416–440.

Boyd, D., Lankford, H., Loeb, S., Rockoff, J., & Wyckoff, J. (2008). *The narrowing gap in New York City teacher qualifications and its implications for student achievement in high-poverty schools* (Working Paper No. w14021). Cambridge, MA: National Bureau of Economic Research.

Brabeck, M. (2015). Open letter to AACTE [Press release]. Retrieved from caepnet. org/about/news-room/statements-press-releases/open-letter-to-aacte

Brabeck, M., & Koch, C. (2013). Why the new teacher ed. standards matter. *Education Week, 33*(4), 26–27.

Bradley, A. (2017). Annual administrative report on edTPA data shows continued growth and support for the first nationally available assessment of teacher candidates [Press release]. Retrieved from edtpa.aacte.org/news-area/ annual-administrative-report-on-edtpa-data-shows-continued-growth-and-support-for-the-first-nationally-available-assessment-of-teacher-candidates.html

Broader, Bolder Approach to Education. (2008). *Expert task force charges school reform school alone will fail in closing achievement gap.* Retrieved from bold-approach.org/

Brown, E. (2016, November 10). What a Trump presidency means for America's public schools. *The Washington Post.* Retrieved from washingtonpost.com/ news/education/wp/2016/11/10/what-a-trump-presidency-means-for-americas-public-schools/?utm_term=.3c2467283029

Brown, E. (2017, March 27). Trump signs bill overturning Obama-era education regulations. *The Washington Post.* Retrieved from washingtonpost.com/news/ education/wp/2017/03/27/trump-signs-bills-overturning-obama-era-education-regulations/?utm_term=.3aa029805e69

Bruner, J. (1996). *The culture of education.* Cambridge, MA: Harvard University Press.

Bryk, A. S., Yeager, D. S., Hausman, H., Muhich, J., Dolle, J. R., Grunow, A., . . . Gomez, L. (2013). Improvement research carried out through networked communities: Accelerating learning about practices that support more productive student mindsets. Retrieved from archive.carnegiefoundation.org/pdfs/elibrary/ improvement_research_NICs_bryk-yeager.pdf

Burnett, B., & Lampert, J. (2016). Re-thinking teacher quality in high-poverty schools in Australia. In G. W. Noblit & W. T. Pink (Eds.), *Education, equity, economy: Crafting a new intersection* (pp. 51–72). New York, NY: Springer International Publishing.

Carnoy, M., Elmore, R., & Siskin, L. (Eds.). (2003). *The new accountability: High schools and high-stakes testing.* New York, NY: Routledge.

Carter, J. H., & Lochte, H. A. (2016). Teacher blame and corporate gain: edTPA and the takeover of teacher education. In J. H. Carter & H. A. Lochte (Eds.), *Teacher performance assessment and accountability reforms: The impacts of edTPA on teaching and schools* (pp. 7–23). New York, NY: Palgrave Macmillan.

Castells, M. (2010). *The rise of the network society: The information age: Economy, society and culture.* Sussex, England: Blackwell Publishers.

Chatterjee, A., Bergeron, B., & Bordelon, D. (n.d.). Illinois educator preparation groups respond to new ratings report. Retrieved from wiu.edu/coehs/ilEducator. php

Cheng, Y., & Liu, N. C. (2008). Examining major rankings according to the Berlin Principles. *Higher Education in Europe, 33*(2-3), 201–208.

Chiang, Y., Cole, C., Delandshere, G., Kunzman, R., Guarino, C., Rutkowski, D., . . . Zhou, Y. (2011). *Using value added models to evaluate teacher preparation programs* [White paper]. Bloomington, IN: Indiana University.

Chung, R. R. (2008). Beyond assessment: Performance assessments in teacher education. *Teacher Education Quarterly, 35*(1), 7–28.

Cibulka, J. G. (2015). Dear CAEP stakeholders. Retrieved from cms.caepnet.org/~/media/Files/caep/newsroom/jim-cibulka-statement-31015.pdf

Cibulka, J., Gollnick, D., & Cohen, S. (n.d.). The proposed consolidation of NCATE and TEAC. Retrieved from ncate.org/LinkClick.aspx?fileticket=pvdlCh%2FFwtA%3D&tabid=695

Cochran-Smith, M. (2001). Constructing outcomes in teacher education policy, practice, and pitfalls. *Educational Policy Analysis Archives, 9*(11). Retrieved from epaa.asu.edu/ojs/article/view/340/466

Cochran-Smith, M. (2002). Reporting on teacher quality: The politics of politics. *The Journal of Teacher Education, 53*(5), 379–382.

Cochran-Smith, M. (2004). The problem of teacher education. *Journal of Teacher Education, 55*(4), 295–300.

Cochran-Smith, M. (2005). The new teacher education: For better or for worse? *Educational Researcher, 34*(7), 3–17.

Cochran-Smith, M. (2010). Toward a theory of teacher education for social justice. In A. Hargreaves, A. Lieberman, M. Fullan, & D. Hopkins (Eds.), *Second international handbook of educational change* (pp. 445–467). New York, NY: Springer Science & Business Media.

Cochran-Smith, M. (2015). Keeping teaching complex: Policy, research and practice. *Venue: Educational Sciences, 4*, 1–11.

Cochran-Smith, M., Baker, M., Burton, S., Carney, M. C., Chang, W-C., Fernández, M. B., . . . Stern, R. (2017). Teacher quality and teacher education policy: The U.S. case and its implications. In M. Akiba & G. LeTendre (Eds.), *The Routledge international handbook of teacher quality and policy* (pp.445–462). New York, NY: Routledge.

Cochran-Smith, M., Baker, M., Chang, W-C., Fernández, M. B., & Keefe, E. S. (2017). *Review of "Within our grasp: Achieving higher admissions standards in teacher prep."* Boulder, CO: National Education Policy Center.

Cochran-Smith, M., Burton, S., Carney, M. C., Sánchez, J. G., & Miller, A. F. (2017). *Review of "A new agenda: Research to build a better teacher preparation program."* Boulder, CO: National Education Policy Center.

Cochran-Smith, M., Carney, M. C., & Miller, A. (2016, November). Relocating teacher preparation: New graduate schools of education and their implications. Paper presented at the Lynch School of Education 10th Anniversary Endowed Chairs Colloquium Series, Chestnut Hill, MA.

Cochran-Smith, M., Carney, M. C., Miller, A. & Sánchez, J. G. (2017, April). Teacher preparation at new graduate schools of education: Studying a controversial innovation. Paper presented at the annual meeting of the New England Education Research Organization, Portsmouth, NH.

Cochran-Smith, M., & Demers, K. (2007). Teacher education as bridge? Unpacking curriculum controversies in teacher education. In M. Connelly (Ed.), *Handbook of curriculum research* (2nd ed., pp. 261–281). Mahwah, NJ: Lawrence Erlbaum.

Cochran-Smith, M., & Fries, K. (2001). Sticks, stones, and ideology: The discourse of reform in teacher education. *Educational Research, 30*(8), 3–15.

Cochran-Smith, M., & Fries, K. (2011a). Teacher education policy and social justice. In P. Earley, D. Imig, & N. Michelli (Eds.), *Teacher education policy in the United States: Issues and tensions in an era of evolving expectations* (pp. 182–207). New York, NY: Routledge.

Cochran-Smith, M., & Fries, K. (2011b). Teacher quality, teacher education and diversity: Policy and politics. In A. Ball & C. Tyson (Eds.), *Studying diversity in teacher education* (pp. 337–359). New York, NY: Roman and Littlefield.

Cochran-Smith, M., & Lytle, S. (2009). *Inquiry as stance: Practitioner research for the next generation.* New York, NY: Teachers College Press.

Cochran-Smith, M., Piazza, P., & Power, C. (2013). The politics of accountability: Assessing teacher education in the United States. *The Educational Forum,* 77(1), 6–27.

Cochran-Smith, M., Stern, R., Sánchez, J. G., Miller, A., Keefe, E. S., Fernández, B., . . . Baker, M. (2016). *Holding teacher education accountable: A review of claims and evidence.* Boulder, CO: National Education Policy Center.

Cochran-Smith, M., & Villegas, A. M. (with Abrams, L. W., Chávez-Moreno, L. C., Mills, T., & Stern, R.). (2016). Research on teacher preparation: "Charting the landscape of a sprawling field." In D. Gitomer & C. Bell (Eds.), *Handbook of research on teaching* (5th ed., pp. 439–547). Washington, DC: American Educational Research Association.

Coggshall, J. G., Bivona, L., & Reschly, D. J. (2012). *Evaluating the effectiveness of teacher preparation programs for support and accountability.* Washington, DC: National Comprehensive Center for Teacher Quality.

Cohen-Vogel, L. (2005). Federal role in teacher quality: "Redefinition" or policy alignment? *Educational Policy,* 19(1), 18–43.

College of William and Mary. (n.d.). W&M joins universities nationally to oppose a NCTQ study. Retrieved from wm.edu/about/search/index.php?q=nctq

Council for the Accreditation of Educator Preparation. (n.d.). The CAEP standards. Retrieved from caepnet.org/standards/introduction.

Council for the Accreditation of Educator Preparation. (2010). NCATE and TEAC form new accrediting body: The Council for the Accreditation of Educator Preparation (CAEP). [Press release]. Retrieved from caepnet.org/about/newsroom/statements-press-releases/ncate-teac-form-accrediting-body

Council for the Accreditation of Educator Preparation. (2012). National commission to raise bar [Press release]. Retrieved from caepnet.files.wordpress.com/2014/09/national-commission-to-raise-the-bar.pdf

Council for the Accreditation of Educator Preparation. (2013a). CAEP accreditation standards. Retrieved from caepnet.org/~/media/Files/caep/standards/caep-2013-accreditation-standards.pdf

Council for the Accreditation of Educator Preparation. (2013b). New accreditation standards adopted to ensure quality in educator preparation [Press release]. Retrieved from caepnet.files.wordpress.com/2013/08/130829-release-caep-finalized-standards-final.pdf

Council for the Accreditation of Educator Preparation. (2015a). CAEP accreditation handbook. Retrieved from caepnet.org/~/media/Files/caep/knowledge-center/caep-accreditation-manual.pdf?la=en

Council for the Accreditation of Educator Preparation. (2015b). CAEP evidence guide: January 2015, version 2.0. Retrieved from caepnet.org/~/media/Files/caep/knowledge-center/caep-evidence-guide.pdf?la=en.

Council for the Accreditation of Educator Preparation. (2015c). *Dear CAEP board members.* Retrieved from insidehighered.com/sites/default/server_files/files/Letter%20of%20Confidencepdf.

Council for the Accreditation of Educator Preparation. (2015d). Standard 2: Clinical practice. Retrieved fromcaepnet.org/standards/standard-2

Council for the Accreditation of Educator Preparation. (2016a). CAEP accreditation handbook (version 3, March 2016). Retrieved from caepnet.org/~/media/CAEP%20Accreditation%20Handbook_March%202016.pdf?la=en

Council for the Accreditation of Educator Preparation. (2016b). CAEP observations on holding teacher preparation accountable. Retrieved from caepnet.org/about/news-room/caep-observations-on-holding-teacher-pre

Council for the Accreditation of Educator Preparation. (2016c). 2013 CAEP standards. Retrieved from caepnet.org/~/media/Files/caep/standards/caep-standards-one-pager-061716.pdf?la=en

Council for the Accreditation of Educator Preparation. (2017a). Branding guide for accredited EPPs. Retrieved from caepnet.org/~/media/Files/caep/accreditation-resources/branding-guide-for-caep-accredited-eppsv.pdf?la=en

Council for the Accreditation of Educator Preparation. (2017b). CAEP answers your questions on recognition status, moving toward uniform accreditation process. Retrieved from caepnet.org/about/news-room/statements-press-releases/caep-answers-your-questions-on-recogniti

Council for the Accreditation of Educator Preparation. (2017c). Governance. Retrieved from caepnet.org/about/governance

Council for the Accreditation of Educator Preparation. (2017d). Accreditation decision outcomes. Retrieved from caepnet.org/accreditation/caep-accreditation/accreditation-decisions

Council for the Accreditation of Educator Preparation Commission on Standards and Performance Reporting (2013). CAEP accreditation standards and evidence: Aspirations for educator preparation. Retrieved from caepnet.org/~/media/Files/caep/standards/commrpt.pdf?la=en

Coupland, D. B. (2011). The cost of accreditation: Hillsdale ends its teacher certification program. *Academic Questions, 24*(2), 209–221.

Cowan, J., & Goldhaber, D. (2014). *Assessing the relationship between teacher performance on Washington State's ProTeach Portfolio and student test performance* (CEDR Working Paper No. 2014-2). Seattle, WA: Center for Education Data & Research.

Crooks, T. J. (2003, April). *Some criteria for intelligent accountability applied to accountability in New Zealand.* Paper presented at the annual conference of the American Educational Research Association, Chicago, IL.

Crowe, E. (2010). *Measuring what matters: A stronger accountability model for teacher education.* Washington, DC: Center for American Progress.

Crowe, E. (2011). *Race to the Top and teacher preparation.* Washington, DC: Center for American Progress.

Cuban, L. (2004). Looking through the rearview mirror at school accountability. In K. Sirotnik (Ed.), *Holding accountability accountable: What ought to matter in public education* (pp. 18–34). New York, NY: Teachers College Press.

Dantley, S. (2016 Examining social justice in teacher education from an accreditor's perspective. Presented at the 2016 National Education Association National

Leadership Summit. Retrieved from nea.org/assets/docs/ORG1439_Examining_
Social_Justice_in_Teacher_Education_from_an_Accreditor%27s_Perspective_
Scott_Dantley.pdf

Darling-Hammond, L. (1997). *Doing what matters most: Investing in quality teaching.* Kutztown, PA: National Commission on Teaching & America's Future.

Darling-Hammond, L. (1998). Teachers and teaching: Testing policy hypotheses from a national commission report. *Educational Researcher, 27*(1), 5–15.

Darling-Hammond, L. (2000a). Teacher quality and student achievement: A review of state policy evidence. *Education Policy Analysis Archives, 8*(1). Retrieved from epaa.asu.edu/ojs/article/view/392

Darling-Hammond, L. (2000b). Teaching for America's future: National commissions and vested interests in an almost profession. *Educational Policy, 14*(1), 162–183.

Darling-Hammond, L. (2004). Standards, accountability, and school reform. *Teachers College Record, 106*(6), 1047–85.

Darling-Hammond, L. (2009). Teaching and the change wars: The professionalism hypothesis. In A. Hargreaves & M. Fullan (Eds.), *Change wars* (pp. 45–68). Bloomington, IN: Solution Tree.

Darling-Hammond, L. (2010). *Evaluating teacher effectiveness: How teacher performance assessments can measure and improve teaching.* Washington, DC: Center for American Progress.

Darling-Hammond, L. (2012). The right start: Creating a strong foundation for the teaching career. *Phi Delta Kappan, 94*(3), 8–13.

Darling-Hammond, L. (2014). Strengthening clinical preparation: The holy grail of teacher education. *Peabody Journal of Education, 89*(4), 547–561.

Darling-Hammond, L. (2015a). Can value-added add value to teacher evaluation? *Educational Researcher, 44*(2), 132–137.

Darling-Hammond, L. (2015b). *The flat world and education: How America's commitment to equity will determine our future.* New York, NY: Teachers College Press.

Darling-Hammond, L. (2017). *Developing and measuring higher order skills: Models for state performance assessment systems.* Palo Alto, CA: Learning Policy Institute and Council of Chief State School Officers.

Darling-Hammond, L., & Bransford, J. (2005). *Preparing teachers for a changing world: What teachers should learn and be able to do.* San Francisco, CA: Jossey-Bass.

Darling-Hammond, L., Burns, D., Campbell, C., Goodwin, L., Hammerness, K., Low, E., . . . Zeichner, K. (2017). *Empowered educators: How high-performing systems shape teaching quality around the world.* Marblehead, MA: Wiley & Sons.

Darling-Hammond, L., & Hyler, M. (2013). The role of performance assessment in developing teaching as profession. *Rethinking Schools, 27*(4), 1–5.

Darling-Hammond, L., Newton, S. P., & Wei, R. C. (2012). *Developing and assessing beginning teacher effectiveness: The potential of performance assessments.* Stanford, CA: Stanford Center for Opportunity Policy in Education.

Darling-Hammond, L., & Rothman, R. (2015). *Teaching in the flat world: Learning from high-performing systems.* New York, NY: Teachers College Press.

Darling-Hammond, L., & Sykes, G. (Eds.). (1999). *Teaching as the learning profession: Handbook of policy and practice.* San Francisco, CA: Jossey Bass.

Datnow, A., & Park, V. (2009). Conceptualizing policy implementation: Large-scale reform in an era of complexity. In G. Sykes, B. Schneider, D. N. Plank, & T. J. Ford (Eds.), *Handbook of education policy research* (pp. 348–361). New York, NY: Routledge.

Deans for Impact. (2015). Comments on the Department of Education's proposed regulation under Title II of the Higher Education Act. Retrieved from deansforimpact.org/wp-content/uploads/2016/12/Deans_for_Impact_Letter.pdf

Deans for Impact. (2017). From chaos to coherence: A policy agenda for accessing and using outcomes data in educator preparation. Retrieved from www.deansforimpact.org/wpcontent/uploads/2016/11/From_Chaos_to_Coherence.pdf

DeMoss, K. (2016). New York's edTPA: The perfect solution to a wrongly identified problem. In J. H. Carter & H. A. Lochte (Eds.), *Teacher performance assessment and accountability reforms: The impacts of edTPA on teaching and schools* (pp. 25–46). New York, NY: Palgrave Macmillan.

Dewey, J. (1916). *Democracy and education: An introduction to the philosophy of education*. New York, NY: Macmillan.

Dill, W. R. (1998). Specialized accreditation: An idea whose time has come? Or gone? *Change: The Magazine of Higher Learning, 30*(4), 18–25.

Doherty, K., & Jacobs, S. (2013). *State of the states 2013 connect the dots: Using evaluations of teacher effectiveness to inform policy and practice*. Washington, DC: National Council on Teacher Quality.

Dover, A., & Schultz, B. (2016). Troubling the edTPA: Illusions of objectivity and rigor. *The Educational Forum, 80*(1), 95–106.

Duckor, B., Castellano, K. E., Téllez, K., Wihardini, D., & Wilson, M. (2014). Examining the internal structure evidence for the performance assessment for California teachers: A validation study of the elementary literacy teaching event for tier I teacher licensure. *Journal of Teacher Education, 65*(5), 402–420.

Dudley-Marling. (2013, September 1). Re: Teacher prep gets failing grade: Study faults education schools, but the schools say the study is badly flawed [Article comment]. Retrieved fromcommonwealthmagazine.org/education/003-teacher-prep-gets-failing-grade/

Dudley-Marling, C. (2015). *Preparing the nation's teachers to teach reading: A manifesto in defense of "teacher educators like me"*. New York, NY: Garn Press.

Duncan, A. (2009, October 22). Teacher preparation: Reforming the uncertain profession. Remarks presented at Teachers College, Columbia University. Retrieved from ed.gov/news/pressreleases/2009/10/10222009a.html

Dupuy, B. (2017, September 25). Is Betsy DeVos protecting rapists? College victims think so. *Newsweek*. Retrieved from newsweek.com/22-year-old-sexual-assault-advocate-says-new-guidelines-protect-rapists-670804

Earley, P. (2000). Finding the culprit: Federal policy and teacher education. *Educational Policy, 14*(1), 25–39.

Earley, P. (2002). Title II of the Higher Education Act revisited and reconsidered: An analysis of the Secretary of Education's 2002 report on teacher quality. Retrieved from gse.gmu.edu/assets/docs/cep/title_ii.pdf

Earley, P. (2004). Title II reauthorization, challenges and opportunities: White paper for the American Association of Colleges for Teacher Education (Unpublished manuscript). George Mason University, Fairfax, Virginia.

ED Lines. (2014, October). Why we said no-thanks to NCTQ. Retrieved from uvacurryschoolofeducation.cmail1.com/t/ViewEmail/t/285AC5F310573866/E2573460E5C239589A8E73400EDACAB4

Education Deans for Justice and Equity. (2017a). Home page. Retrieved from educationdeans.org/

Education Deans for Justice and Equity. (2017b). Public education, democracy, and the role of the federal government: A declaration of principles. Retrieved from nepc.colorado.edu/publication/deans-declaration-of-principles

Education Deans for Justice and Equity (2017c). Our children deserve better: A call to resist Washington's dangerous vision for U.S. education. Retrieved from nepc.colorado.edu/publication/children-deserve-better

Education Trust. (2008). *Core problems: Out-of-field teaching persists in key academic courses and high-poverty schools.* Washington, DC: Education Trust.

Education and the Workforce Committee Democrats. (2017). As Secretary DeVos invites states to test boundaries of education law, Scott, Murray urge her to follow the law [Press release]. Retrieved from democrats-edworkforce.house.gov/media/press-releases/as-secretary-devos-invites-states-to-test-boundaries-of-education-law-scott-murray-urge-her-to-follow-the-law

Eduventures. (2013). A review and critique of the National Council on Teacher Quality (NCTQ) methodology to rate schools of education. Retrieved from eduventures.com/2013/06/a-review-and-critique-of-the-national-council-on-teacher-quality-nctq-methodology-to-rate-schools-of-education/

Ehrenberg, R. G. (2002). Reaching for the brass ring: U.S. News & World Report rankings and competition. *Review of Higher Education, 26*(2), 145–162.

Elmore, R. (2002). The testing trap. *Harvard Magazine, 105*(1), 35.

Elmore, R. F., & McLaughlin, M. W. (1988). *Steady work: Policy, practice, and the reform of American education.* Santa Monica, CA: The RAND Corporation.

Engel, M. (2000). *The struggle for control of public education: Market ideology vs. democratic values.* Philadelphia, PA: Temple University Press.

Entman, R. M. (1993). Framing: Toward clarification of a fractured paradigm. *Journal of Communication, 43*(4), 51–58.

Ericsson, P. F. (2005). Raising the standards for standards: A call for definitions. *English Education, 37*(3), 223–243.

Evans, L. A., Kelly, M. K., Baldwin, J. L., & Arnold, J. M. (2016). Candidate success and edTPA: Looking at the data. *Mid-Western Educational Researcher, 28*(2), 148–160.

Evans-Brown, S. (2014, September 24). After pilot, "bar exam for teachers" set to launch state-wide. New Hampshire Public Radio. Retrieved from nhpr.org/post/after-pilot-bar-exam-teachers-set-launch-state-wide#stream/0

Ewell, P. (2013). Report of the data task force to the CAEP Commission on Standards and Performance Reporting. Retrieved from caepnet.org/standards/commission-on-standards

Farkas, S., Johnson, J., & Duffett, A. (1997). *Different drummers: How teachers of teachers view public education.* New York, NY: Public Agenda.

Feuer, M. J., Floden, R. E., Chudowsky, N., & Ahn, J. (2013). *Evaluation of teacher preparation programs: Purposes, methods, and policy options.* Washington, DC: National Academy of Education.

Fraser, N. (2003). Social justice in an age of identity politics: Redistribution, recognition and participation. In N. Fraser & A. Honneth (Eds.), *Redistribution or recognition: A political-philosophical debate* (pp. 7–109). London, England: Verso.

Fraser, N., & Honneth, A. (2003). *Redistribution or recognition? A political-philosophical exchange.* London, England: Verso.

Freedle, R. (2010). On replicating ethnic test bias effects: The Santelices and Wilson study. *Harvard Educational Review, 80*(1), 394–404.

Friedman, T. L. (2005). *The world is flat: A brief history of the twenty-first century.* London, England: Macmillan.

Fullan, M., Rincon-Gallardo, S., & Hargreaves, A. (2015). Professional capital as accountability. *Education Policy Analysis Archives, 23*(15), 1–22.

Fuller, E. J. (2015). Shaky methods, shaky motives: A critique of the National Council of Teacher Quality's review of teacher preparation programs. *Journal of Teacher Education, 65*(1), 63–77.

Furlong, J., Cochran-Smith, M., & Brennan, M. (Eds.). (2008). Politics and policy in teacher education: International perspectives. *Teachers and Teaching, 14* (4/5).

Furlong, J., Cochran-Smith, M., & Brennan, M. (Eds.). (2009). *Policy and politics in teacher education: International perspectives.* London, England: Routledge.

Gadsden, V. L., Artiles, A., & Davis, J. E. (Eds.). (2009). *Risk, schooling, and equity: Review of research in education* (Vol. 33). Thousand Oaks, CA: Sage.

Gamson, W. A. (1988). The 1987 distinguished lecture: A constructionist approach to mass media and public opinion. *Symbolic Interaction, 11*(2), 161–174.

Gary, D. (2015). What is a "good teacher"? Does "good" resonate with the edTPA? *Northwest Journal of Teacher Education Online.* Retrieved from nwate.com/2015/01/11/what-is-a good-teacher-does-good-resonate-with-the-edtpa/

Gee, J. (1996). *Social linguistics and literacies: Ideology in discourses.* London, England: Taylor & Francis.

Gewirtz, S., & Cribb, A. (2002). Plural conceptions of social justice: Implications for policy sociology. *Journal of Education Policy, 17*(5), 499–509.

Ginsberg, R., & Kingston, N. (2014). Caught in a vise: The challenges facing teacher preparation in an era of accountability. *Teachers College Record, 116*(1), n1.

Ginsberg, R., & Levine, A. (2013). New standards will demand a lot more of teacher education. *The Chronicle of Higher Education.* Retrieved from chronicle.com/article/Demanding-a-Lot-More-of/142275

Girtz, S. (2014). Ignatian pedagogy and its alignment with the new teacher bar exam (edTPA) and action research frameworks. *Jesuit Higher Education, 3*(1), 75–80.

Goatley, G., & Lacelle-Peterson, M. (2017). A new expectation framework: What matters in educator preparation and how do we measure it? [PowerPoint slides]. Retrieved from aaqep.org/uploads/1/0/9/3/109302791/aaqep_presentation_to_nyacte_nysate.pdf

Goldhaber, D. (2013). *What do value-added measures of teacher preparation programs tell us?* Palo Alto, CA: Carnegie Foundation for the Advancement of Teaching.

Goldhaber, D., Cowan, J., & Theobald, R. (2016). *Evaluating prospective teachers: Testing the predictive validity of the edTPA* (Working Paper No. 157). Washington, DC: National Center for Analysis of Longitudinal Data in Education Research.

Goldhaber, D., Liddle, S., & Theobald, R. (2013). The gateway to the profession: Assessing teacher preparation programs based on student achievement. *Economics of Education Review, 34,* 29–44.

Gonzalez, G. (2013, June 18). IU School of Education response to NCTQ Teacher Prep Review released June 18. Retrieved from newsinfo.iu.edu/news/page/ normal/24345.html?emailID=24345

Goodwin, L. (2015, February 3). Duncan's teacher ed proposals miss the mark [Blog post]. *Education Week.* Retrieved from blogs.edweek.org/edweek/op_education/ 2015/02/goodwin.html

Grasgreen, A. (2011, October 3). The new path for teacher ed reform. *Inside Higher Education.* Retrieved from insidehighered.com/news/2011/10/03/duncan_ plan_for_teacher_education_reform_focuses_on_outcome_based_measures

Greenberg, J., & Dugan, M. (2015). *Incoherent by design: What you should know about differences between training of undergraduate and graduate elementary teachers.* Washington DC: National Council on Teacher Quality.

Greenberg, J., McKee, A., & Walsh, K. (2013). *Teacher prep review 2013: A review of the nation's teacher preparation programs.* Washington, DC: National Council on Teacher Quality.

Greenberg, J., Putman, H., & Walsh, K. (2014). *Training our future teachers: Classroom management.* Washington, DC: National Council on Teacher Quality.

Greenberg, J., & Walsh, K. (2008). *No common denominator: The preparation of elementary teachers in mathematics by America's education schools.* Washington, DC: National Council on Teacher Quality.

Greenberg, J., & Walsh, K. (2012). *What teacher preparation programs teach about K–12 assessment: A review.* Washington, DC: National Council on Teacher Quality.

berg, J., Walsh, K., & McKee, A. (2014). *Teacher prep review 2014: A review the nation's teacher preparation programs.* Washington, DC: National Council Teacher Quality.

D. (2016). The consequences of edTPA. *Educational Leadership, 73*(8),

Grenot-Scheyer, M. (2013). College of Education Dean Marquita Grenot-Scheyer's response to NCTQ report. Retrieved from ced.csulb.edu/college-education-dean-marquita-grenot-scheyers-response-nctq-report

Gurl, T. J., Caraballo, L., Grey, L., Gunn, J. H., Gerwin, D., & Bembenutty, H. (2016). *Policy, professionalization, privatization, and performance assessment.* New York, NY: Springer International Publishing.

Gutmann, A. (1987). *Democratic education.* Princeton, NJ: Princeton University Press.

Gutmann, A. (1990). Democratic education in difficult times. *Teachers College Record, 92*(1), 7–20.

Gutmann, A. (1999*). Democratic education* (2nd ed). Princeton, NJ: Princeton University Press

Gutmann, A., & Thompson, D. (1996). *Democracy and disagreement: Why moral conflict cannot be avoided in politics, and what can be done about it.* Cambridge, MA: Harvard University Press.

Hand, V., Penuel, W., & Gutiérrez, K. (2012). (Re)framing educational possibility: Attending to power and equity on shaping access to and within learning opportunities. *Human Development, 55,* 250–268.

Hannah, S. B. (1996). The Higher Education Act of 1992: Skills, constraints, and the politics of higher education. *The Journal of Higher Education, 67*(5), 498–527.

Hanson, J., & Howe, K. (2011). The potential for deliberative democratic civic education. *Democracy and Education, 19*(2),1–9.

Hanushek, E. (2002). Teacher quality. In L. Izumi & W. Evers (Eds.), *Teacher quality* (pp. 1–12). Palo Alto, CA: Hoover Institution.

Hanushek, E., Peterson, P., & Woessmann, L. (2013). *Endangering prosperity: A global view of the American school.* Washington, DC: Brookings Institute Press

Hanushek, E., & Woessmann, L. (2015). *The knowledge capital of nations: Education and the economies of growth.* Cambridge, MA: MIT Press.

Hargreaves, A., & Fullan, M. (2012). *Professional capital: Transforming teaching in every school.* New York, NY: Teachers College Press.

Harvey, D. (2005). *A brief history of neoliberalism.* London, England: Oxford University Press.

Haycock, K. (2005). Choosing to matter more. *Journal of Teacher Education, 56*(3), 256–265.

Hazelkorn, E. (2015). *Rankings and the reshaping of higher education: The battle for world-class excellence* (2nd ed.). New York, NY: Palgrave MacMillan.

Heil, L., & Berg, M. H. (2017). Something happened on the way to completing the edTPA: A case study of teacher candidates' perceptions of the edTPA. *Contributions to Music Education, 42,* 181–198.

Heller, D. (2014, June 24). NCTQ misses the goal again [Blog post]. Retrieved from edwp.educ.msu.edu/dean/2014/nctq-misses-the-goal-again/

Heller, D., Segall, A., & Drake, C. (2013, December 10). An open letter to NCTQ on teacher prep. *Education Week.* Retrieved from edweek.org/ew/articles/2013/12/11/14heller.h33.html?tkn=SZSF1PvR4%2BkY3FD1Y4z3fulR0lwhc8x-4VkhL

Henry, G. T., & Bastian, K. C. (2015). *Measuring up: The National Council on Teacher Quality's ratings of teacher preparation programs and measures of teacher performance.* Chapel Hill, NC: Education Policy Initiative at Carolina.

Henry, G. T., Campbell, S. L., Thompson, C. L., Patriarca, L. A., Luterbach, K. J., Lys, D. B., & Covington, V. M. (2013). The predictive validity of measures of teacher candidate programs and performance toward an evidence-based approach to teacher preparation. *Journal of Teacher Education, 64*(5), 439–453.

Henry, G. T., Kershaw, D. C., Zulli, R. A., & Smith, A. A. (2012). Incorporating teacher effectiveness into teacher preparation program evaluation. *Journal of Teacher Education, 63*(5), 335–355.

Hess, F. (2001). *Tear down this wall: The case for a radical overhaul of teacher certification.* Washington, DC: Progressive Policy Institute.

Hess, F., & McShane, M. (2014). *Teacher quality 2.0.* Cambridge, MA: Harvard University Press.

Hickel, J. (2012, April 9). A short history of neoliberalism (and how we can fix it). *The New Left Project.* Retrieved from newleftproject.org/index.php/site/article_comments/a_short_history_of_neoliberalism_and_how_we_can_fix_it

Hill, D. (2007). Critical teacher education, new labour, and the global project of neoliberal capital. *Policy Futures in Education, 5*(2), 204–225.

Honawar, V. (2007) Teacher college group presses for single accrediting body. *Education Week, 26*(26), 7.

Honawar, V. (2008). Panel studying concept of solo teacher ed. accreditor. *Education Week, 27*(25), 8.

Honneth, A. (2003). Redistribution as recognition: A response to Nancy Fraser. In N. Fraser & A. Honneth (Eds.), *Redistribution or recognition: A political-philosophical exchange* (pp. 110–197). London, England: Verso

House, E., & Howe, K. R. (1999). *Values in evaluation and social research*. Thousand Oaks, CA: Sage.

House, E. R., & Howe, K. R. (2000). Deliberative democratic evaluation in practice. In D. Stufflebeam, T. Kellaghan, & G. Maddaus (Eds.), *Evaluation models: Viewpoints on educational and human services evaluation* (pp. 409–421). Dordrecht, the Netherlands: Springer.

Howe, K., & Murray, K. (2015). *Why school report cards merit a failing grade*. Boulder, CO: National Education Policy Center.

Huang, S., Yi, Y., & Haycock, K. (2002). *Interpret with caution: The first state Title II reports on the quality of teacher preparation*. Washington, DC: The Education Trust.

Hudson, W. (1995). *American democracy in peril*. Chatham, NJ: Chatham House.

Hulme, M., & Kennedy, A. (2015). Teacher education in Scotland: Consensus politics and the "Scottish policy style." In G. Beauchamp et al. (Eds.), *Teacher education in times of change* (pp. 91–108). Bristol, England: Policy Press.

Hursh, D. W. (2007). Assessing No Child Left Behind and the rise of neoliberal education. *American Educational Research Journal, 44*(3), 493–518.

Huston, T. (2017). edTPA, videotape, and occupational identity: A study of preservice teachers. *Teaching Education, 28*(2), 194–210.

Iasevoli, B. (2016). 17 teacher prep programs meet "tougher standards." *Education Week, 36*(15), 7.

Iasevoli, B. (2017, March 28). Trump signs bill scrapping teacher-prep rules [Blog post]. Retrieved from blogs.edweek.org/edweek/teacherbeat/2017/03/trump_signs_bill_scrapping_tea.html

Ingeno, L. (2013, June 18). Teacher ed takedown. *Inside Higher Ed*. Retrieved from insidehighered.com/news/2013/06/18/nctq-study-gives-teacher-prep-programs-failing-grades

Institute for Democratic Education in America. (2012). The vision, strategy, and learning of IDEA reclaiming the "public" in education asks that each of us renews our interest in and responsibility to the future of learning in our democracy. Retrieved from democraticeducation.org/downloads/2012_strategy6.pdf

Institute for Higher Education Policy. (2006). Berlin Principles on ranking of higher education institutions. Retrieved from ihep.org/sites/default/files/uploads/docs/pubs/berlinprinciplesranking.pdf

International Reading Association. (2013, July). Response to NCTQ Teacher Education Report. Retrieved from literacyworldwide.org/blog/literacy-daily/2013/07/02/response-to-the-nctq-teacher-education-report

Jenlink, P. M. (2016). Democracy distracted in an era of accountability: Teacher education against neoliberalism. *Cultural Studies • Critical Methodologies, 17*(3), 163–172.

Johnson, L. (1964). The war on poverty. *The Annals of America, 18*, 212–216.

Johnson, S., Campbell, N., Spicklemire, K., & Partelow, L. (2017, March 17). The Trunp-DeVos budget would dismantle public education, hurting vulnerable kids, working families, and teachers. *Center for American Progress*. Retrieved from americanprogress.org/issues/education/news/2017/03/17/428598/trump-devos-budget-dismantle-public-education-hurting-vulnerable-kids-working-families-teachers/

Jordan, A. W., & Hawley, T. (2016). By the elite, for the vulnerable: The edTPA, academic oppression, and the battle to define good teaching. *Teachers College Record*. Retrieved from tcrecord.org/content.asp?contentid=19461

Jost, A. (2014, August 27). UM system wins appeal in case over course syllabi. *Columbia Tribune*. Retrieved from columbiatribune.com/1d3c237a-9614-594d-a1c3-83b01f498479.html

Kamenetz, A. (2016, October 18). Teaching training as "part theater, part sport." *National Public Radio*. Retrieved from npr.org/sections/ed/2016/10/18/497516106/teacher-training-as-part-theater-part-sport

Kanstoroom, M., & Finn, C. (Eds.). (1999). *Better teachers, better schools*. Washington, DC: Thomas B. Fordham Foundation.

Kantor, H., & Lowe, R. (2013). Educationalizing the welfare state and privatizing education: The evolution of social policy since the New Deal. In P. L. Carter & K. G. Welner (Eds.), *Closing the opportunity gap: What America must do to give every child an even chance* (pp. 25–39). New York, NY: Oxford University Press.

Kantor, H., & Lowe, R. (2016). Educationalizing the welfare state and privatizing education: The evolution of social policy since the New Deal. In W. J. Matthis & T. M Trujillo (Eds.), *Learning from the federal market-based reforms* (pp. 37–60). Charlotte, NC: Information Age Publishing.

Keefe, E. S. (2015, June). *Autism Spectrum Disorder: Through a democratic lens*. Presentation at Wheelock College, Boston, MA.

Keefe, E. S. (2016). *Graduate studies in autism: Program matrix*. Cambridge, MA: Lesley University.

Kennedy, M. (1999). The problem of evidence in teacher education. In R. Roth (Ed.), *The role of the university in the preparation of teachers* (pp. 87–107). Philadelphia, PA: Falmer Press.

King, J. (2006). "If justice is our objective": Diaspora literacy, heritage knowledge, and the praxis of critical studyin' for human freedom. In A. Ball (Ed.), *With more deliberate speed: Achieving equity and excellence in education—realizing the full potential of Brown v. Board of education, 105th yearbook of the National Society for the Study of Education* (pp. 337–357). Chicago, IL: University of Chicago Press.

King, J. (2008). Critical and qualitative research in teacher education: A blues epistemology, a reason for knowing for cultural well-being. In M. Cochran-Smith, S. Feiman Nemser, & J. McIntyre (Eds.), *Handbook of research on teacher education: Enduring issues in changing contexts* (pp. 1094–1135). Mahwah, NJ: Erlbaum.

Koedel, C., Parsons, E., Podgursky, M., & Ehlert, M. (2012). *Teacher preparation programs and teacher quality: Are there real differences across programs?* Washington, DC: National Center for Analysis of Longitudinal Data in Education Research.

Kretchmar, K., & Zeichner, K. (2016). Teacher prep 3.0: A vision for teacher education to impact social transformation. *Journal of Education for Teaching, 42*(4), 417–433.

Krise, K. (2016). Preparing the standardized teacher: The effects of accountability on teacher education. *Journal of Curriculum Theorizing, 31*(2), 24–32.

Kumashiro, K. (2012). *Bad teacher: How blaming teachers distorts the bigger picture.* New York, NY: Teachers College Press.

Kumashiro, K. (2015). *Review of proposed 2015 federal teacher preparation regulations.* Boulder, CO: National Education Policy Center.

Kumashiro, K. (2016, October 22). Training for teachers. *The New York Times.* Retrieved from nytimes.com/2016/10/23/opinion/sunday/training-for-teachers.html

Labaree, D. (1997). Public goods, private goods: The American struggle over educational goals. *American Educational Research Journal, 34*(1), 39–81.

Labaree, D., Hirsch, E., & Beatty, B. (2004). The ed school's romance with progressivism. *Brookings Papers on Education Policy,* (7), 89–129.

Lagemann, E. C. (2000). *An elusive science: The troubling history of educational research.* Chicago, IL: Chicago University Press.

Lalley, J. P. (2016). Reliability and validity of edTPA. In J. H. Carter & H. A. Lochte (Eds.), *Teacher performance assessment and accountability reforms: The impacts of edTPA on teaching and schools* (pp. 47–78). New York, NY: Palgrave Macmillan.

Lambert, K. A., & Girtz, S. (2016). How do you talk to a politician about the edTPA? Advocacy through inquiry and social justice around high-stakes assessment. In J. H. Carter & H. A. Lochte (Eds.), *Teacher performance assessment and accountability reforms: The impacts of edTPA on teaching and schools* (pp. 177–187). New York, NY: Palgrave Macmillan.

Lampert, J., & Burnett, B. (Eds.). (2015). *Teacher education for high poverty schools* (Vol. 2). New York, NY: Springer.

Lampert, J., Burnett, B., Comber, B., Ferguson, A., & Barnes, N. (2017). "It's not about punitive": Exploring how early-career teachers in high-poverty schools respond to critical incidents. *Critical Studies in Education,* 1–17.

Ledwell, K., & Oyler, C. (2016). Unstandardized responses to a "standardized" test: The edTPA as gatekeeper and curriculum change agent. *Journal of Teacher Education, 67*(2), 120–134.

Levine, P., & Kawashima-Ginsberg, K. (2013). Teaching civics in a time of partisan polarization. *Social Education, 77*(4), 215–217.

Lewis, W., & Young, T. (2013). The politics of accountability: Teacher education policy. *Educational Policy, 27*(2), 190–216.

Leyva, R. (2009). No Child Left Behind: A neoliberal repackaging of social Darwinism. *Journal for Critical Education Policy Studies, 7*(1), 365–381.

Lin, S. (2015). *Learning through action: Teacher candidates and performance assessments* (Unpublished doctoral dissertation). University of Washington, Seattle, WA.

Lincove, J. A., Osborne, C., Dillon, A., & Mills, N. (2014). The politics and statistics of value-added modeling for accountability of teacher preparation programs. *Journal of Teacher Education, 65*(1), 24–38.

Lipman, P. (2011). Neoliberal education restructuring dangers and opportunities of the present crisis. *Monthly Review, 63*(3), 114–127.

Lipman, P., & Hursh, D. (2007). Renaissance 2010: The reassertion of ruling-class power through neoliberal policies in Chicago. *Policy Futures in Education, 5*(2), 160–178.

Lit, I. W., & Lotan, R. (2013). A balancing act: Dilemmas of implementing a high-stakes performance assessment. *The New Educator*, *9*(1), 54–76.

Loewus, L., & Sawchuk, S. (2017, October 12). Yet another group sets out to accredit teacher-prep programs. *Education Week*. Retrieved from edweek. org/ew/articles/2017/10/12/yet-another-group-sets-out-to-accredit.html?qs= loewus+sawchuk

Louisiana Board of Regents. (n.d.). Response to National Council on Teacher Quality improving teacher preparation in Louisiana Report. Retrieved from regents. louisiana.gov/assets/docs/2013/08/BORRESPONSE12413.pdf

Lowery-Moore, H. (2013, June 12). The Lamar University College of Education and Human Development response to NCTQ. Retrieved from education.lamar.edu/ about/nctq-lus-response.html

Luca, M., & Smith, J. (2011). Salience in quality disclosure: Evidence from the U.S. News college rankings (Working Paper No. 12-014). Boston, MA: Harvard Business School. Retrieved from people.hbs.edu/mluca/SalienceinQuality Disclosure.pdf

Lyon, R. (2002). Forum of the coalition for evidence-based policy with U.S. Secretary of Education Rod Paige [available in print and as a webcast]. Retrieved from excelgov.org/displayContent.asp?Keyword=prppcEvidence

Lys, D. B., L'Esperance, M., Dobson, E., & Bullock, A. A. (2014). Large-scale implementation of the edTPA: Reflections upon institutional change in action. *Current Issues in Education*, *17*(3), 1–11.

MacDonald, E., & Shirley, D. (2009). *The mindful teacher*. New York, NY: Teacher's College Press.

Machung, A. (1998). Playing the rankings game. *Change*, *30*(4), 12–16.

Madeloni, B., & Gorlewski, J. (2013). Wrong answer to the wrong question. *Rethinking Schools*, *27*(4), 16–21.

Maryville College. (2014, July 20). MC's teacher prep programs nationally recognized. Retrieved from maryvillecollege.edu/news/2014/2108/mc-s-teacher-prep-programs-nationally-recognized/

Mason, P. (2010). Assessing difference: Examining Florida's initial teacher preparation programs and exploring alternative specifications of value-added models (Unpublished working paper). Retrieved from mpra.ub.uni-muenchen.de/27903/

Massachusetts Department of Elementary and Secondary Education. (2014). Teacher performance assessment task force. Retrieved from doe.mass.edu/edprep/TPA-TaskForce.pdf

Massachusetts Department of Elementary and Secondary Education. (2016). Guidelines for the candidate assessment of performance. Retrieved from doe.mass.edu/ edprep/cap/guidelines.docx

Mayer, D. (2005). Reviving the "policy bargain" discussion: Professional accountability and the contribution of teacher-performance assessment. *The Clearing House: A Journal of Educational Strategies, Issues and Ideas*, *78*(4), 177–182.

McKee, L. (2015, March 26). edTPA: Going beyond compliance to inquiry. *Ed Prep Matters*. Retrieved from edprepmatters.net/2015/03/edtpa-going-beyond-compliance-to-inquiry-aacte-breakfast-was-forum-for-discussion/

McKinsey and Company. (2007, September). How the world's best performing school systems come out on top. Retrieved from mckinseyonsociety.com/ downloads/reports/Education/Worlds_School_Systems_Final.pdf

McLaughlin, V. (2013). A message regarding the NCTQ Teacher Prep Review. Retrieved from education.wm.edu/about/teacher-prep/

McMunn Dooley, C., Meyer, C., Chinwe, I., O'Byrne, I., Kletzien, S., Smith-Burke, T., . . . Dennis, D. (2013). Literacy Research Association response to National Council on Teacher Quality review of teacher education programs. Retrieved fromliteracyresearchassociation.org/index.php?option=com_content& view=article&id=44:policy-publications&catid=20:site-content

Mehta, J. (2013). How paradigms create politics: The transformation of American educational policy, 1980–2001. *American Educational Research Journal, 50*(2), 285–324.

Mercer, D. (2013, June 24). From Dean Debbie Mercer: Response to National Council for Teacher Quality report. Retrieved from kstate.edu/today/announcement. php?id=9059

Meredith, M. (2004). Why do universities compete in the ratings game? An empirical analysis of the effects of the *U.S. News & World Report* college rankings. *Research in Higher Education, 45*(5), 443–461.

Meuwissen, K., Choppin, J., Shang-Butler, H., & Cloonan, K. (2015). *Teaching candidates' perceptions of and experiences with early implementation of the edTPA licensure examination in New York and Washington States.* Rochester, NY: University of Rochester.

Meyer, H. D. (2017). The limits of measurement: Misplaced precision, phronesis, and other Aristotelian cautions for the makers of PISA, APPR, etc. *Comparative Education, 53*(1), 17–34

Meyer, R., Piyatigorsky, M., & Rice, A. (2014). *Evaluation of educators and educator preparation programs: Models and systems in theory and practice* (Working Paper No. 2014–6). Madison, WI: Wisconsin Center for Education Research.

Michelli, N. M., & Keiser, D. L. (2005). *Teacher education for democracy and social justice.* New York, NY: Routledge.

Mihaly, K., McCaffrey, D., Sass, T. R., & Lockwood, J. R. (2012). Where you come from or where you go? Distinguishing between school quality and the effectiveness of teacher preparation program graduates. *Andrew Young School of Policy Studies Research Paper Series, 12*(12), 1–43.

Miller, A. (2017). Creating jaw-droppingly effective rookie teachers: Unpacking teacher preparation at the Sposato Graduate School of Education (Match Education) (Unpublished doctoral dissertation). Boston College, Chestnut Hill, MA.

Miller, M., Carroll, D., Jancic, M., & Markworth, K. (2015). Developing a culture of learning around the edTPA: One university's journey. *The New Educator, 11*(1), 37–59.

Mintz Levin Strategies, LLC. (2017, January 13). MLS 2017 outlook: Higher Education Act reauthorization. *Lexology.* Retrieved from mlstrategies.com/articles/ MLStrategies-2017-Outlook_Higher-Education-Act-Reauthorization.pdf

Monks, J., & Ehrenberg, R. G. (1999). *U.S. News & World Report's* college rankings: Why they do matter. *Change, 31*(6), 42–51.

Murray, F. (2001). From consensus standards to evidence of claims: Assessment and accreditation in the case of teacher education. *New Directions for Higher Education, 113*(1), 49–66.

Murray, F. (2003). *On some differences between NCATE and TEAC.* Washington, DC: Teacher Education Accreditation Council.

Murray, F. (2005). On building a unified system of accreditation in teacher education. *Journal of Teacher Education, 56*(4), 307–317.

Murray, F. (2011). Findings from ten years of accrediting activity by the Teacher Education Accreditation Council (TEAC) in the United States. Paper presented at the International Council of Education for Teaching, 55th World Assembly, University of Glasgow, Glasgow, Scotland.

Murray, F. (2016). Abandoning founding principles hampers CAEP's effectiveness. *Education Week, 36*(4), 20.

Nasir, N. S., Scott, J., Trujillo, T., & Hernández, L. (2016). The sociopolitical context of teaching. In D. Gitomer & C. Bell (Eds.), *Handbook of research on teaching* (5th ed., pp. 349–390). Washington, DC: American Educational Research Association.

National Association for Equal Opportunity in Higher Education (2015). Search results for: The proposed regulations are overly broad and would result in a substantial expansion of federal authority into matters heretofore reserved to states and institutions with good reason. Retrieved from nafeonation.org/?s=The+proposed +regulations+are+overly+broad+and+would+result+in+a+substantial+expansion +of+federal+authority+into+matters+heretofore+reserved+to+states+and+ institutions+with+good+reason

National Association for Multicultural Education. (2014). NAME position statement on the edTPA. Retrieved from nameorg.org/docs/Statement-rr-edTPA-1-21-14.pdf

National Association of Scholars. (2005, November 2). Letter to Assistant Secretary for Post Secondary Education, United States Department of Education. Princeton, NJ: Author.

National Commission on Excellence in Education. (1983). *A nation at risk: The imperative for educational reform.* Washington, DC: United States Government Printing Office.

National Commission on Teaching & America's Future. (1996). *What matters most: Teaching for America's future.* New York, NY: Author.

National Commission on Teaching & America's Future. (1997). *Doing what matters most: Investing in quality teaching.* New York, NY: Author.

National Council for Accreditation of Teacher Education. (n.d.). Why should schools of education be NCATE accredited? [Press release]. Retrieved from ncate.org/ LinkClick.aspx?fileticket=69DJO%2bxykzQ%3d&tabid=392.

National Council for Accreditation of Teacher Education. (2000). *NCATE 2000: Teacher education and performance based reform.* Washington, DC: Author.

National Council for Accreditation of Teacher Education. (2010a). *Transforming teacher education through clinical practice: A national strategy to prepare effective teachers* (Report of the blue ribbon panel on clinical preparation and partnerships for improved student learning). Washington, DC: Author.

National Council for Accreditation of Teacher Education. (2010b). About NCATE. Retrieved from ncate.org/Public/AboutNCATE/tabid/179/Default.aspx

National Council of Teachers of English. (2014). NCTE response to US Department of Education's proposed regulations for teacher preparation programs. Retrieved from ncte.org/positions/statements/ela-teacher-prep-programs

National Council on Teacher Quality. (n.d.-a). Teacher prep overview. Retrieved from nctq.org/teacherPrep/2016/home.do

National Council on Teacher Quality (n.d.-b). Mission. Retrieved from nctq.org/about/

National Council on Teacher Quality (n.d.-c). Advisory board. Retrieved from nctq.org/about/advisoryBoard.jsp

National Council on Teacher Quality (n.d.-d). Current funders. Retrieved from nctq.org/about/funders.jsp

National Council on Teacher Quality. (n.d.-e). NCTQ: Teacher Prep: Standards: Methodology. Retrieved from nctq.org/teacherPrep/2016/standards/methodology.jsp

National Council on Teacher Quality. (n.d.-f). Standard 2: Early reading. Retrieved from nctq.org/dmsView/Standard_Book_2

National Council on Teacher Quality. (n.d.-g). NCTQ methodology for teacher prep review. Retrieved from nctq.org/teacherPrep/2016/standards/methodology.jsp

National Council on Teacher Quality. (2014a). NCTQ standards and indicators for teacher prep review 2014. Retrieved from nctq.org/dmsView/Standards_and_Indicators_Full

National Council on Teacher Quality. (2014b). Standard 1: Selection criteria. Retrieved from nctq.org/dmsView/Standard_Book_1

National Council on Teacher Quality. (2015). Don't judge these teacher ed journals by their titles! Retrieved fromnctq.org/commentary/article.do?id=176

National Council on Teacher Quality. (2016a). Landscapes in teacher prep: Undergraduate elementary education. Retrieved from nctq.org/dmsView/UE_2016_Landscape_653385_656245

National Council on Teacher Quality. (2016b). Within our grasp: Achieving higher admissions standards in teacher prep. Retrieved from nctq.org/dmsView/Admissions_Yearbook_Report

National Council on Teacher Quality. (2017). Landscapes in teacher prep: Undergraduate secondary education. Retrieved from nctq.org/dmsView/Landscapes_-_2017_UG_Secondary

National Research Council, Committee on the Study of Teacher Preparation Programs in the United States. (2010). *Preparing teachers: Building evidence for sound policy*. Washington, DC: The National Academies Press.

New Hampshire Institutions of Higher Education Network. (n.d.-a). IHE Network Mission. Retrieved from ihenetwork.org

New Hampshire Institutions of Higher Education Network. (n.d.-b). Brochure. Retrieved from ihenetwork.org/Websites/ihenetwork/files/Content/5850139/NHTCAP_brochure.pdf

New York State Education Department. (2017, March 13). Board of Regents act to amend State's teacher certification requirements based on recommendations of expert panel and public input [Press release]. Retrieved from nysed.gov/news/2017/board-regents-act-amend-states-teacher-certification-requirements-based-recommendations

Noguera, P. (2017, October 18). The big picture: School of Trump. *Public Books*. Retrieved from publicbooks.org/the-big-picture-school-of-trump/

North, C. (2006). More than words? Delving into the substantive meaning(s) of "social justice" in education. *Review of Educational Research, 76*(4), 507–535.

Office of the *Federal Register*. (2014, December 3). Teacher preparation issues. *Federal Register, 79*(232). Retrieved from gpo.gov/fdsys/pkg/FR-2014-12-03/pdf/2014-28218.pdf

Office of the *Federal Register*. (2016, October 31). Teacher preparation issues. *Federal Register*, *81*(210). Retrieved from gpo.gov/fdsys/pkg/FR-2016-10-31/pdf/2016-24856.pdf

Office of Special Education and Rehabilitative Services. (2017). List of guidance documents rescinded (outdated, unnecessary, or ineffective). Retrieved from eduptcwwwp01.ed.gov/policy/speced/reg/eo13777/eo13777-osers-outdated-guidance-list-20171002.pdf

O'Neill, O. (2002). A question of trust [Lecture transcript]. BBC Reith Lectures 2002. Retrieved from bbc.co.uk/radio4/reith2002/lecture1.shtml

Organisation for Economic Co-operation and Development. (2005). *Teachers matter: Attracting, developing and retaining effective teachers*. Paris, France: Author.

Organisation for Economic Co-operation and Development. (2014). *Improving schools in Wales: An OECD perspective*. Paris, France: Author.

Pallas, A. (2013, June 28). The trouble with NCTQ's ratings of teacher-prep programs [Blog post]. Retrieved from hechingerreport.org/the-trouble-with-nctqs-ratings-of-teacher-prep-programs/

Parkes, K. A., & Powell, S. R. (2015). Is the edTPA the right choice for evaluating teacher readiness? *Arts Education Policy Review*, *116*(2), 103–113.

Path to Teach. (n.d.). What Is Path to Teach? Retrieved from pathtoteach.org/what-is-pathtoteach.jsp

Pearson. (2017). Frequently asked questions for candidates. Retrieved from edtpa.com/PageView.aspx?f=HTML_FRAG/GENRB_FAQ_Candidates.html

Pecheone, R. L., & Chung, R. R. (2006). Evidence in teacher education: The performance assessment for California teachers. *Journal of Teacher Education*, *57*(1), 22–36.

Pecheone, R. L., Pigg, M. J., Chung, R. R., & Souviney, R. J. (2005). Performance assessment and electronic portfolios: Their effect on teacher learning and education. *The Clearing House: A Journal of Educational Strategies, Issues and Ideas*, *78*(4), 164.

Pecheone, R. L., Shear, B., Whittaker, A., & Darling-Hammond, L. (2013). 2013 edTPA field test: Summary report. Retrieved from secure.aacte.org/apps/rl/res_get.php?fid=827&ref=edtpa

Pecheone, R. L., & Whittaker, A. (2016). Well-prepared teachers inspire student learning. *Phi Delta Kappan*, *97*(7), 8–13.

Pecheone, R. L., Whittaker, A., & Klesch, H. (2016). Educative assessment and meaningful support: 2015 edTPA administrative report. Retrieved from secure.aacte.org/apps/rl/res_get.php?fid=3013&ref=rl

Pecheone, R. L., Whittaker, A., Shear, B., & Klesch, H. (2015). Educative assessment and meaningful support: 2014 edTPA administrative report. Retrieved from secure.aacte.org/apps/rl/res_get.php?fid=2183&ref=rl

Performance Assessment for California Teachers. (n.d.). A brief overview of the PACT assessment system. Retrieved from pacttpa.org/_main/hub.php?pageName=Home

Perkins, J. (2004). *Confessions of an economic hit man*. San Francisco, CA: Berrett Koehler Publishers.

Peske, H., & Haycock, K. (2006). *Teaching inequality: How poor and minority students are shortchanged on teacher quality: A report and recommendations by the Education Trust*. Washington, DC: Education Trust.

Peterson, B. R., & Bruster, B. G. (2014). Inquiry into the reflective practice of teacher candidates. *International Journal of Education and Social Science*, 1(3), 140–146.

Pianta, R. C. (2014, August 17). Signing off from one more teacher preparation ranking [Blog post]. Retrieved from huffingtonpost.com/robert-c-pianta/nctq-teacher-preparation-ranking_b_5501591.html

Picower, B., & Marshall, A. M. (2016). "Run like hell" to "look before you leap": Teacher educators' responses to preparing teachers for diversity and social justice in the wake of edTPA. In J. H. Carter & H. A. Lochte (Eds.), *Teacher performance assessment and accountability reforms: The impacts of edTPA on teaching and schools* (pp. 189–212). New York, NY: Palgrave Macmillan.

Plecki, M., Elfers, A. M., & Nakamura, Y. (2012). Using evidence for teacher education program improvement and accountability: An illustrative case of the role of value-added measures. *Journal of Teacher Education*, 63(5), 318–334.

Porter-Magee, K. (2015, February 11). Doug Lemov reveals his secret [Blog post]. Retrieved from edexcellence.net/articles/doug-lemov-reveals-his-secrets

Potok, M. (2017). The Trump effect. Retrieved from splcenter.org/fighting-hate/intelligence report/2017/trump-effect

Powell, G. (2000). *Elections as instruments of democracy: Majoritarian and proportional visions*. New Haven, CT: Yale University Press.

Price, T. A. (2014). *Teacher education under audit: Value-added measures, TVAAS, EdTPA and evidence-based theory*. Citizenship, Social and Economics Education, 13(3), 211–225.

Promoting Real Opportunity, Success, and Prosperity through Education Reform Act. (2015). H.R. 4508, 115th Cong.

Public Agenda (1997). Different drummers: How teachers of teachers view public education. Retrieved from publicagenda.org/files/different_drummers.pdf

Pugach, M. C. (2017). The edTPA as an occasion for structuring faculty dialogue across the divide? A "checklist manifesto" for a more inclusive teacher education. *Teacher Education and Special Education*, 40(4), 314–321.

Pullin, D. (2015). Performance measures for teachers and teacher education: Corporate education reform opens the door to new legal issues. *Education Policy Analysis Archives*, 23(81), 1–33.

Putman, H., Greenberg, J., & Walsh, K. (2014). *Easy A's and what's behind them*. Washington, DC: National Council on Teacher Quality.

Quartz, K. H. (2003). "Too angry to leave" supporting new teachers' commitment to transform urban schools. *Journal of Teacher Education*, 54(2), 99–111.

Ratner, A. R., & Kolman, J. S. (2016). Breakers, benders, and obeyers: Inquiring into teacher educators' mediation of edTPA. *Education Policy Analysis Archives*, 24(35), 1–29.

Ravitch, D. (2012, May 23). What is NCTQ? [Blog post]. Retrieved from dianeravitch.net/2012/05/23/what-is-nctq/

Ravitch, D. (2013, June 23). Richard Allington on the NCTQ report [Blog post]. Retrieved from dianeravitch.net/2013/06/23/richard-allington-on-the-nctq-report/

Ravitch, D. (2014, June 18). Professor: How NCTQ restricts my reading list [Blog post]. Retrieved from dianeravitch.net/2014/06/18/30853/

Ravitch, D. (2017, May 23). Don't Like Betsy DeVos? Blame the Democrats. The Democratic Party paved the way for the education secretary's efforts to privatize our

public schools. *New Republic*. Retrieved fromnewrepublic.com/article/142364/
dont-like-betsy-devos-blame-democrats

Rawls, J. (1971). *A theory of justice*. Cambridge, MA: Belknap Press of Harvard
University Press.

Reagan, E. M., Schram, T., McCurdy, K., Chang, T., & Evans, C. M. (2016). Politics
of policy: Assessing the implementation, impact, and evolution of the performance assessment for California teachers (PACT) and edTPA. *Education Policy
Analysis Archives, 24*(9), 27.

Reagan, E. M., Terrell, D. G., Rogers, A. P., Schram, T., Tompkins, P., Ward, C., . . .
McHale, G. (2016, April). A localized policy framework: A statewide collaboration toward a teacher candidate performance assessment. Paper presented at
the annual meeting of the American Educational Research Association, Washington, DC.

reclaim. (2017). In *Merriam-Webster.com*. Retrieved from merriam-webster.com/
dictionary/reclaim

Ressler, M. B., King, K. B., & Nelson, H. (2016). Ensuring quality teacher candidates:
Does the edTPA answer the call? In J. H. Carter & H.A. Lochte (Eds.), *Teacher
performance assessment and accountability reforms: The impacts of edTPA on
teaching and schools* (pp. 119–140). New York, NY: Palgrave Macmillan.

Richmond, E. (2014, September 16). Americans want teachers to take a bar exam.
The Atlantic. Retrieved from theatlantic.com/education/archive/2014/09/
americans-want-a-bar-exam-for-teachers/380276/

Romzek, B. (2000). Dynamics of public sector accountability in an era of reform.
International Review of Administrative Sciences, 66(1), 21–44.

Roth, R. A. (1996). Standards for certification, licensure, and accreditation. In J.
Sikula (Ed.), *Handbook of research on teacher education* (pp. 242–278). New
York, NY: Macmillan.

Sanders, W. (1998). Value-added assessment. *The School Administrator, 55*(11),
24–27.

Sanders, W. L., & Horn, S. P. (1998). Research findings from the Tennessee Value-
Added Assessment System (TVAAS) database: Implications for educational
evaluation and research. *Journal of Personnel Evaluation in Education, 12*(3),
247–256.

Santelices, M., & Wilson, M. (2010). Unfair treatment? The case of Freedle, the
SAT, and the standardization approach to differential item functioning. *Harvard Educational Review, 80*(1), 106–133.

Sato, M. (2014). What is the underlying conception of teaching of the edTPA? *Journal of Teacher Education, 65*(5), 421–434.

Sauder, M., & Lancaster, R. (2006). Do rankings matter? The effects of *U.S. News
& World Report* rankings on the admissions process of law schools. *Law &
Society Review 40*(1), 105–134.

Saul, S. (2016, November 21). Where Donald Trump stands on school choice, student debt and common core. *The New York Times*. Retrieved from nytimes.
com/2016/11/21/us/where-trump-stands-on-school-choice-student-debt-and-
common-core.html

Sawchuk, S. (2010, October 25). Teacher-prep accrediting groups to merge: Move
could lead to a more rigorous bar. *Education Week*. Retrieved from edweek.
org/ew/articles/2010/10/25/10merge.h30.html

Sawchuk, S. (2011, April 26). Ed schools refuse to volunteer for *U.S. News* review. *Education Week*. Retrieved from edweek.org/ew/articles/2011/04/27/29nctq. h30.html

Sawchuk, S. (2016, August 23). Teacher-prep accreditation group seeks to regain traction. *Education Week*. Retrieved from edweek.org/ew/articles/2016/08/24/ teacher-prep-accreditation-group-seeks-to-regain-traction.html

Schalock, D., & Imig, D. (2000). *Shulman's union of insufficiencies + 7: New dimensions of accountability for teachers and teacher educators*. Washington, DC: American Association of Colleges for Teacher Education.

Scholes, L., Lampert, J., Burnett, B., Comber, B. M., Hoff, L., & Ferguson, A. (2017). The politics of quality teacher discourses: Implications for pre-service teachers in high poverty schools. *Australian Journal of Teacher Education, 42*(4), 19–43.

Schrag, P. (1999, July/August). Who will teach the teachers? *University Business,* 29–34.

Scott, J. (2016). The politics of market based education reform. In M. Matthis & T. Trujillo (Eds.), *Learning from the federal market-based reforms* (pp. 9–37). Charlotte, NC: Information Age Publishing.

Senate Resolution 301. (2015). Calling on the Council for the Accreditation of Educator Preparation to modify accreditation standards of the Council to prevent the standards from negatively impacting Alaska native and Native American teacher candidates. Retrieved from congress.gov/crec/2015/10/30/CREC-2015-10-30-pt1-PgS7675-7.pdf

Sleeter, C. E. (Ed.). (2007). *Facing accountability in education: Democracy and equity at risk*. New York, NY: Teachers College Press.

Sleeter, C. E. (2009). Teacher education, neoliberalism, and social justice. In W. Ayers, T. Quinn, & D. Stovell (Eds.), *The handbook of social justice in education* (pp. 611–624). Philadelphia, PA: Taylor & Francis.

Snow, D. A., & Benford, R. D. (1988). Ideology, frame resonance and participant mobilization. *International Social Movement Research, 1,* 197–219.

Snyder, S. (2013, June 8). Reaction to national teacher quality report. *Philadelphia Inquirer*. Retrieved from philly.com/philly/blogs/campus_inq/Reaction-to-national-teacher-quality-report.html

Spring, J. (2011). *The politics of American education*. New York, NY: Routledge.

Stanford Center for Assessment, Learning and Equity. (n.d.-a). edTPA. Retrieved from scale.stanford.edu/teaching/edtpa

Stanford Center for Assessment, Learning and Equity. (n.d.-b). edTPA myths and facts. Retrieved from secure.aacte.org/apps/rl/res_get.php?fid=1331&ref=edtpa

Stanford Center for Assessment, Learning and Equity. (2015a). edTPA annotated bibliography. Retrieved from secure.aacte.org/apps/rl/resource.php?resid=511& ref=edtpa

Stanford Center for Assessment, Learning and Equity. (2015b). SCALE response to inquiries about predictive validity and edTPA. Retrieved from scale.stanford.edu/ sites/default/files/edTPA%20Predictive%20Validity%20response%202015.pdf

Stitzlein, S. M. (2010). Deliberative democracy in teacher education. *Journal of Public Deliberation, 6*(1), 1–18.

Stolz, I., Hendel, D. D., & Horn, A. S. (2010). Ranking of rankings: Benchmarking twenty-five higher education ranking systems in Europe. *Higher Education, 60*(5), 507–528.

Stone, D. (2011). *Policy paradox: The art of political decision making* (3rd ed.). New York, NY: Norton & Company.

Strauss, V. (2013a, June). Why the NCTQ teacher prep ratings are nonsense. *The Washington Post*. Retrieved from washingtonpost.com/news/answer-sheet/wp/2013/06/18/why-the-nctq-teacher-prep-ratings-are-nonsense/?utm_term=.6f0cdec7fbfc

Strauss, V. (2013b, August). Literacy experts say reformers reviving "reading wars." *The Washington Post*. Retrieved from washingtonpost.com/news/answer-sheet/wp/2013/08/13/are-reformers-reviving-reading-wars/

Strauss, V. (2017, May 22).What "school choice" means in the era of Trump and DeVos. *The Washington Post*. Retrieved from washingtonpost.com/news/answer-sheet/wp/2017/05/22/what-school-choice-means-in-the-era-of-trump-and-devos/?utm_term=.692a33f9a71f

Supovitz, J. (2009). Can high stakes testing leverage educational improvement? Prospects from the last decade of testing and accountability reform. *Journal of Educational Change, 10*, 211–227.

Tamir, E., & Wilson, S. (2005). Who should guard the gates: Evidentiary and professional warrants for claiming jurisdiction. *Journal of Teacher Education, 56*(4), 332–334.

Tan, E. (2014). Human capital theory: A holistic criticism. *Review of Educational Research. 84*(3), 411–445.

Tatto, M. T., Savage, C., Liao, W., Marshall, S. L., Goldblatt, P., & Contreras, L. M. (2016). The emergence of high-stakes accountability policies in teacher preparation: An examination of the U.S. Department of Education's proposed regulations. *Education Policy Analysis Archives, 24*(21), 1–54.

Taubman, P. M. (2009). *Teaching by numbers: Deconstructing the discourse of standards and accountability in education*. New York, NY: Routledge.

Taylor, K. (2017, March 13). Regents drop teacher literacy test seen as discriminatory. *The New York Times*. Retrieved from nytimes.com/2017/03/13/nyregion/ny-regents-teacher-exams-alst.html

Teacher Preparation Analytics. (2014). Building an evidence based system for teacher preparation. Retrieved from caepnet.files.wordpress.com/2014/09/building_an_evidence_based_system_for_teacher_preparation_201409151.pdf

Teaching Commission. (2004). Teaching at risk: A call to action. Retrieved from ctl.vcu.edu/media/ctl/documents/TeachingAtRisk.pdf

Terrell, D. G., McCurdy, K., Birch, M. L., Schram, T. H., & Tompkins, P. (2018). Forcing me to reflect: Preservice and novice teachers' reflective thinking in varied school contexts. In J. E. Many & R. Bhatnagar (Eds.), *Implementing and analyzing performance assessments in teacher education* (pp. 167–189). Charlotte, NC: Information Age Publishing.

Thomas B. Fordham Institute. (n.d.-a). Mission. Retrieved from edexcellence.net/fordham-mission

Thomas B. Fordham Institute. (n.d.-b). Chester E. Finn, Jr. Retrieved from edexcellence.net/about-us/fordham-staff/chester-e-finn-jr

Thomas B. Fordham Foundation. (1996, December). Farewell and hello again. Retrieved from edexcellence.net/about-us/farewell-and-hello-again.html

Thomas B. Fordham Foundation. (1999). The teachers we need and how to get more of them: Manifesto. In M. Kanstoroom & C. Finn (Eds.), *Better teachers, better schools* (pp. 1–18). Washington, DC: Author.

Thomas B. Fordham Foundation. (2002). Five-year report: 1997–2001. Retrieved from edexcellencemedia.net/publications/2002/200205_tbfffiveyear/report.pdf

Thompson, N. L., Owens, D. N., Seed, A. H., & Key, S. G. (2014). The evolution of a middle level education program: Where we have been and where we are going. *Current Issues in Middle Level Education, 19*(1), 50–57.

Torres, C. A. (2009). *Globalizations and education: Collected essays on class, race, gender, and the state.* New York, NY: Teachers College Press.

Tracz, S., Torgerson, C., & Beare, P. (2017). The NCTQ selectivity standard and principal evaluation of teacher preparation. *The Teacher Educator, 52*(1), 8–21.

Trow, M. (1996). Trust, markets and accountability in higher education: A comparative perspective. *Higher Education Policy, 9*(4), 309–324.

Tuck, E., & Gorlewski, J. (2016). Racist ordering, settler colonialism, and edTPA: A participatory policy analysis. *Educational Policy, 30*(1), 197–217.

Tucker, M. S. (Ed.). (2011). *Surpassing Shanghai: An agenda for American education built on the world's leading systems.* Cambridge, MA: Harvard Education Press.

UCLA Center X. (n.d.). About Center X. Retrieved from centerx.gseis.ucla.edu/

Underwood, J. (2013, June 18). Dean Underwood responds to review of teacher preparation programs. Retrieved from education.wisc.edu/soe/news-events/news/2013/06/18/dean-underwood-responds-to-review-of-teacher-preparation-programs

United States Department of Education. (2002). *Meeting the highly qualified teachers challenge: The Secretary's annual report on teacher quality.* Washington, DC: Author.

United States Department of Education. (2003). *Meeting the highly qualified teachers challenge: The Secretary's second annual report on teacher quality.* Washington, DC: United States Department of Education.

United States Department of Education. (2009). Race to the top program: Executive summary. Retrieved from ed.gov/programs/racetothetop/executive-summary.pdf

United States Department of Education. (2011). Our future, our teachers: The Obama administration's plan for teacher education reform and improvement. Washington, DC: Author.

United States Department of Education. (2015). U.S. Department of Education approves 16 states' plans to provide equal access to excellent educators [Press release]. Retrieved from ed.gov/news/press-releases/us-department-education-approves-16-states-plans-provide-equal-access-excellent-educators

United States Government Accountability Office. (2015). Teacher preparation programs: Education should ensure states identify low performing programs and improve information sharing. Retrieved from gao.gov/products/GAO-15-598.

United States House of Representatives. (2011, July 27). Statement of Kate Walsh, president, National Council on Teacher Quality before the committee on education and the workforce. Retrieved from edworkforce.house.gov/uploaded-files/07.27.11_walsh.pdf

United States House of Representatives Committee on Education and the Workforce. (2017). PROSPER fact sheet 2017. Retrieved from edworkforce.house.gov/uploadedfiles/fact_sheet.pdf

United States Senate Committee on Health, Education, Labor & Pensions. (2016). Alexander statement on education department's final regulation on teacher preparation programs. Retrieved from help.senate.gov/chair/newsroom/press/alexander-statement-on-education-departments-final-regulation-on-teacher-preparation-programs

University of Dayton. (2014, June 18). Quality educators, quality education. Retrieved from udayton.edu/news/articles/2014/06/university_teacher_education_ranking.php

University of Dayton. (2017, May 11). Top for teachers. Retrieved from udayton.edu/news/articles/2017/05/nctq_ranks_teacher_program.php

University of Houston. (2014, June 19). UH college of education teacher preparation programs nationally ranked. Retrieved from uh.edu/news-events/stories/2014/June/6%2019%20NCTQ%20Rankings.php

Valenzuela, A. (1999). *Subtractive schooling: US-Mexican youth and the politics of caring*. Albany, NY: SUNY Press.

Vergari, S., & Hess, F. (2002). The accreditation game: Can accreditation ensure quality teacher training? *Education Next, 2*(3), 48–57.

Walsh, K., Glaser, D., & Wilcox, D. D. (2006). *What education schools aren't teaching about reading and what elementary teachers aren't learning*. Washington, DC: National Council on Teacher Quality.

Walsh, K., & Jacobs, S. (2007). *Alternative certification isn't alternative*. Washington, DC: National Council on Teacher Quality.

Wei, R. C., & Pecheone, R. L. (2010). Assessment for learning in preservice teacher education: Performance-based assessments. In M. Kennedy (Ed.), *Teacher assessment and the quest for teacher quality: A handbook* (pp. 69–132). San Francisco, CA: John Wiley & Sons.

Western Governors University. (2014, June 17). WGU teacher education program ranked number one by NCTQ. Retrieved from wgu.edu/about_WGU/ teacher_ed_NCTQ_6-17-14

Westheimer, J. (2015). *What kind of citizen? Educating our children for the common good*. New York, NY: Teachers College Press.

Wilmington University. (2016, December 6). A teacher prep program at the head of the class. Retrieved from wilmu.edu/news/newsArticle.aspx?newsID=4484

Wilson, M., Hallam, P. J., Pecheone, R. L., & Moss, P. A. (2014). Evaluating the validity of portfolio assessments for licensure decisions. *Education Policy Analysis Archives, 22*(6), 1–30.

Wilson, S. M., & Tamir, E. (2008). The evolving field of teacher education: How understanding challenge(r)s might improve the preparation of teachers. In M. Cochran-Smith, S. Feiman-Nemser, & J. McIntyre (Eds.), *Handbook of research on teacher education: Enduring questions in changing contexts* (pp. 908–936). Washington, DC: American Association of Colleges for Teacher Education.

Wilson, S., & Youngs, P. (2005). Research on accountability processes in teacher education. In M. Cochran-Smith & K. Zeichner (Eds.), *Studying teacher education: The report of the AERA panel on research and teacher education* (pp. 591–643). Mahwah, NJ: Erlbaum.

Wise, A. (1999, October 20). Standards or no standards? Teacher quality in the 21st century. Retrieved from ncate.org/specfoc/preparation.htm

World Bank. (2010, May 4). Teacher politics around the world: Objectives, rationale, methodological approach and products. Retrieved from siteresources.worldbank.

org/EDUCATION/Resources/Vegasetal__Teacherpoliciesaroundtheworld.draft. pdf

Young, I. M. (1990). *Justice and the politics of difference*. Princeton, NJ: Princeton University Press.

Young, I. M. (1996). Communication and the other: Beyond deliberative democracy. In S. Benhabib (Ed.), *Democracy and difference: Contesting the boundaries of the political* (pp. 120–135). Princeton, NJ: Princeton University Press.

Young, I. M. (1999). Justice, inclusion, and deliberative democracy. In S. Macedo (Ed.), *Deliberative politics: Essays on democracy and disagreement* (pp. 151–158). Oxford, England: Oxford University Press.

Young, I. M. (2000). *Inclusion and democracy*. Oxford, England: Oxford University Press.

Zeichner, K. (2003). The adequacies and inadequacies of three current strategies to recruit, prepare, and retain the best teachers for all students. *Teachers College Record, 105*(3), 490–510.

Zeichner, K., Payne, K. A., & Brayko, K. (2015). Democratizing teacher education. *Journal of Teacher Education, 66*(2), 122–135.

Zeichner, K., & Pena-Sandoval, C. (2015). Venture philanthropy and teacher education policy in the US: The role of the New Schools Venture Fund. *Teachers College Record, 117*(6), 1–24.

Zygmunt, E., & Clark, P. (2015). *Transforming teacher education for social justice*. New York, NY: Teachers College Press.

Index

About the Authors

Marilyn Cochran-Smith holds the Cawthorne Chair in Teacher Education for Urban Schools at the Lynch School of Education, Boston College. Her scholarship over 35 years has focused on teacher education research, policy, and practice nationally and internationally, with special attention to diversity, social justice, and practitioner inquiry. She is a longtime contributor to Teachers College Press, an award-winning author, an elected member of the National Academy of Education, and a past president of the American Educational Research Association.

Molly Cummings Carney is a doctoral candidate in Curriculum and Instruction at Boston College studying teacher education and education policy. Her research focuses on innovation in initial teacher education, online teacher preparation, and equity and social justice in urban schools. She has taught in public schools in the U.S. and abroad.

Elizabeth Stringer Keefe is a teacher educator and researcher at the Graduate School of Education at Lesley University. Her research focuses on teacher education and teacher education policy, special education teacher preparation, and teacher preparedness to educate autistic students. She is president of the Massachusetts Council for Exceptional Children. She holds a Ph.D. in Curriculum and Instruction from Boston College.

Stephani Burton is a doctoral candidate in Curriculum and Instruction at Boston College. Her research explores the impact of education policies and initiatives on teacher education and students from nondominant backgrounds.

Wen-Chia Chang is an adjunct faculty member in the Department of Measurement, Evaluation, Statistics, and Assessment at Boston College. Her research focuses on theories and practice of evaluation, measurement of teaching practice for equity, and teacher education for social justice. She holds a Ph.D. in Educational Research, Measurement, and Evaluation.

M. Beatriz Fernández is a faculty researcher at Alberto Hurtado University in Chile, where she serves as director of a teacher preparation program. She holds a Ph.D. in Curriculum and Instruction from Boston College. Her research focuses on education policy and social justice in teacher education.

Dr. Fernández is a founding member of *Alto al Simce*, an activist group against K–12 standardization in Chile.

Andrew F. Miller is the Director of Academics for the Archdiocese of Boston Catholic Schools Office. He holds a Ph.D. in Curriculum and Instruction from Boston College. His research focuses on the intersections of teacher education, educational policy/accountability, and the educational reform movement.

Juan Gabriel Sánchez is a doctoral candidate in Curriculum and Instruction at Boston College. He studies teacher education and education reform, with a focus on institutional change at the school and classroom levels and its relationship to the reform environment. His dissertation research examines this relationship at a new graduate school of education that combines innovative structures and progressive pedagogies.

Megina Baker is a researcher with the Pedagogy of Play project at Harvard Graduate School of Education's Project Zero. She holds a Ph.D. in Curriculum and Instruction from Boston College and teaches courses on play and child development at Boston University.